Love You Still

a memoir

MARIA PRICE

Love You Still

a memoir

MARIA PRICE

woodhall press

Woodhall Press
Norwalk, CT

woodhall press

Woodhall Press, 81 Old Saugatuck Road, Norwalk, CT 06855
WoodhallPress.com

Cover design: Asha Hossain
Layout artist: Amie McCracken

Library of Congress Cataloging-in-Publication Data available

ISBN 978-1-949116-65-6 (paper: alk paper)
ISBN 978-1-949116-66-3 (electronic)

First Edition

Distributed by Independent Publishers Group
(800) 888-4741

Printed in the United States of America

For Julia

Chapter 1

"It's a girl!"

My husband Joe tightened his grasp on my hand, deep dimples punctuating the ends of his broad smile.

It was the day of our twenty-week ultrasound, and as I was officially over the age of thirty-five, we had been referred to a specialist for a level-two, more-in-depth examination.

"Everything looks perfect." The doctor smiled at us.

"Thank God," I breathed.

Joe and I stared at the miracle moving around on the monitor. *Perfect.* Years of infertility struggles before our son was born and a natural tendency toward worry had heightened my anxiety during pregnancy, but this was the news we had been waiting to hear.

"A girl," I mused.

"Baby *sister*," Joe noted, one eyebrow raised.

"First granddaughter of the family." I grinned at him.

"Congratulations." The doctor smiled warmly, then looked back to the file she was holding. "And you are here because you are over thirty-five?"

"Yes," I replied, feeling a bit deflated at the reminder. "Our doctor said it was a precaution?"

"Yes." She nodded. "And everything looks great. Our only recommendation is that you might want to consult with your regular OB about delivering at thirty-nine weeks instead of forty, as your risk of stillbirth increases with advancing maternal age."

A large lump of renewed worry instantly lodged itself in my throat. She said it casually, but I felt dizzy at the mention of that word.

"Stillbirth?" I asked in a hoarse whisper.

In our years of struggling to have a baby, I had read so many stories of all the things that could go wrong in pregnancy, from conception through delivery. Making it to this point in the pregnancy and receiving confirmation from the ultrasound that there were no visible signs of concern was supposed to be a huge relief, a milestone in the journey toward delivering a healthy baby. I had heard of stillbirth before. It was heartbreaking; and the thought that it could happen to me—that my baby might be at increased risk—brought my previously stifled anxiety rushing back up my face, stinging my eyes and reddening my cheeks.

"It's just a precaution," she explained, shaking her head. "Everything looks really great."

My eyes darted to Joe, and I thought I saw a flash of concern behind his eyes, but when he turned to me and dipped his chin to meet my gaze, I saw only encouragement there.

We asked a few more questions. The more we talked, the more I allowed myself to be reassured. We would do everything the doctors suggested; this was just one more worry that would probably amount to nothing later on.

Stillbirth. I worked to ignore the tightness settling into my chest as I whispered, "I can't even imagine."

"Should we?" I asked.

"I don't know," he admitted. "What do you think?"

It was an exciting conversation, one that we'd had several times over the course of a few weeks. It had taken five painstaking years of infertility before Joe and I were able to conceive our first child, Joey, and neither of us wanted to go through that kind of heartache again. I wasn't getting any younger, and we knew that the risk of complications grew with advancing maternal age. Should we attempt to give our miracle boy a little brother or sister? Could we even bring ourselves to try? Or should we just be satisfied with the gift that we had been given and raise our son as an only child?

We didn't know what to do, so we prayed. Having both grown up with a rich tradition of faith, it was how we always approached tough situations. We were certain we could trust God for the answer our family needed.

On Valentine's Day, just over two weeks later, we stood in the same spot, crying tears of incredulous joy and gratitude: I was pregnant.

We busied ourselves with doctors' appointments and making plans for our expanding family. After making it safely through the first trimester, on Easter Sunday, Joe and I announced to the world that our little Jellybean was on the way. Later, on a gorgeous May afternoon, we hosted a gender-reveal party in our backyard. Our family and friends waited with tense anticipation before erupting in boisterous applause as bright pink balloons soared triumphantly in the wind. We joyously announced that we would name our daughter after our late grandmothers, Julia and Rachel.

From the very beginning, Julia was our perfect little girl, the answer to our prayers—the completion of our little family. We were happier than we had ever been.

My pregnancy went without a hitch. I took my prenatal vitamins, did kick counts, attended all my appointments, and eagerly awaited the arrival of our little princess. As the weeks flew by and summer faded into fall, we were encouraged by our medical team: Julia looked fantastic. She was growing properly and was perfectly healthy.

Our last OB/GYN appointment was late in the afternoon of Monday, October 10. We eagerly listened to Julia's heartbeat with the nurse, had an exam with the doctor, an ultrasound, and a non-stress test. We were full of pride and growing anticipation as Julia aced each assessment. We had made an appointment for Thursday, October 13, for an early induction at thirty-nine weeks, per the recommendations for women over thirty-five, but my cervix was dilated, and she was in position, ready to be born soon. We all joked that we'd see each other again on Thursday, "if not before."

The next morning, I realized I was not feeling any movement. I did all the things I knew to do: I drank ice water, I put my feet up, and I tried to wake her. Still nothing.

Anxiously, I called my doctor's office. The nurse suggested I eat something, and if that didn't work, to come in and get checked out. As Joe and I packed our bags in the car and drove to the hospital, we still felt cautiously optimistic. We were confident that we would meet our daughter that day.

We went straight upstairs to Labor and Delivery and were greeted by Natalie, the same cheerful nurse we had seen for our non-stress test the afternoon before.

"Well, hi there! Back so soon?" she said.

We chuckled together as she led us into the same triage room where we had sat the day before. Joe helped me ease up onto the exam table where Natalie, for the second time in less than twenty-four hours, stretched the two heart monitors around my belly: one for me, one for Julia.

As Natalie worked, adjusting the straps and moving the devices from one side of my belly to the other, her mood changed, and small talk lessened.

I closed my eyes and raised my chin, silently praying words I feared to speak out loud.

By the time she'd called in a second nurse, tears were streaming down my face.

I looked to Joe and caught the fear in his wide eyes as they met mine. I watched as he closed his mouth and swallowed hard. He squeezed my hand and tried to nod his reassurance, but I saw his jaw working, his eyes blinking back tears.

Neither of us spoke or even breathed until the door reopened and Dr. Moshier walked into the room. I felt myself sit up straighter when I saw her. She had delivered our son, and she had my full confidence. I desperately wanted to believe that she would find the answers we needed to alleviate our fears.

When she applied the cold gel and moved the ultrasound transducer over my baby belly, I still clung to hope. When she took it away and bowed her head, my whole world instantly altered course.

The screams that came out of me were primal.

"No. No. No. No! No! *Noooooooo!* Not my baby! Not. My. *Baby!*"

I could hear myself begging. "Please. You can get her. You can save her. Take her now! You can do this. You can *do* this!" But despite the urgency, the pleading in my voice, she didn't look up.

And then I knew: Julia was gone.

The floodgates were unleashed, and a low, animalistic wail rose up from somewhere deep within me. How could this be happening? How could that beautiful, vigorous heartbeat we had all heard the afternoon before have been permanently silenced? How could the precious babe who had just been dancing on the ultrasound screen be so perfectly . . . *still?*

The doctor excused herself, silently stepped out, and gave us some time alone. Joe and I came together instantly, as if attracted by a magnetic force. Our embrace was desperate, anguished. We sobbed convulsively, gulping for air, and answers. How could this happen? How could our little girl, who was so alive and well the day before, be *dead?* How could we be in a place where there was no other option, no hope of a second chance?

In time, my screams subsided. We remained in that sterile room, drawn tightly together, weeping bitter tears into each other's shoulders. Eventually, Joe gently pulled back. I watched him as he drew in a breath, squared his jaw, and defied the tears welling up in his ocean-blue eyes, now rimmed in large red splotches. His strong, familiar hands that had held me so many times before now gripped my arms just below the shoulders, tenderly, but with unmistakable intensity. He checked the emotion rising in his throat, all passiveness banished from his tone.

"We are going to survive this," he promised, his lower lip trembling. "We are going to pray, and believe for a miracle."

I nodded, hot tears still coursing their way down my flushed cheeks. Our hands, fingers, and arms intertwined like knots in a rope, anchoring us to one another. Foreheads touching, with hearts extended toward Heaven, we prayed for a miracle.

Chapter 2

When Dr. Moshier returned, we began discussing the next steps on the impossibly difficult path ahead.

"I—I don't know . . . how this works." Anxiety and grief were tangled like a jumble of cords inside my throat. How could I ask questions that I didn't want to voice out loud, wait for words I couldn't bear to hear?

Would there be a C-section? Could a stillborn baby be birthed naturally?

When would it happen?

Would we be able to see her? Hold her? Was that even allowed?

What would she look like?

What would it be like to hold my *dead child?*

"We will induce your labor," Dr. Moshier explained gently. Her gaze held mine steadily, without being invasive. She explained the procedure for delivering a stillborn baby—everything much the same as the labor we had been expecting this week, except with a vastly different outcome. We would still be able to see Julia, hold her, only she would be *still.*

"You should think about going home," she advised gently. "The delivery will be intense and especially difficult. You might want to eat something, too. You will need all of your strength to get through it."

None of this made any sense. How could I think about eating? I wanted—*needed*—to see Julia, to hold her, to kiss her. Nothing else mattered.

We did agree to take some time to call our families and attempt to process this living nightmare. Stunned into silence, we followed Natalie to the hospital's garden gazebo. I took note of the bubbling fountain, felt the warmth of the bright sun on my skin. I watched cars in the distance pass by as though today were just any other normal day, as if the world hadn't just imploded all around us.

One by one, we called our loved ones. They answered excitedly, expectantly, waiting to hear good news. "Is she here?!"

I struggled to find the words, wanting to spare them the pain that was about to be unleashed on them.

"She's gone."

Wait, what? . . . Gone?! . . . What do you mean? . . . How?!

Their cries of disbelief and anguish brought the reality crashing in on top of me again and again. My heart broke for them, and I felt the guilt begin to seep into the dark corners of my heart.

She had lived inside of me; how could I not have known she was in distress? How could I have been unaware that my baby had *died* inside of me? Shouldn't I have been able to predict, or even somehow prevent, this tragedy? I was her mama. I should have known. I should have protected her. I'd let her down, and now I had also disappointed everyone who loved her.

My mom was the first to arrive at the hospital. Of course she was. She always came. Never in my life had there been a time when she didn't drop everything to be by my side, swooping in to save the day. Master of maternal instinct and nurturing, she was always so strong, a fixer, a "where there's a will, there's a way" kind of a person. But how could she fix this?

"Oh, baby," she cried, as she enveloped me in her arms. I could see that her eyes were already red and swollen, visible signs of heartbreak accentuated by her fair complexion. She had been the first one to glimpse the pink balloons at our gender-reveal party. Her ecstatic squeal of delight when she'd discovered we were expecting a girl rang in my ears, haunting me now.

"I'm so sorry, Mom," I whispered.

"Oh, honey, shhh," she replied, stroking my hair and rocking me in her arms.

I leaned into her, my baby belly—Julia—between us . . . yet not really between us, I realized. Not really here anymore at all. With this awareness came the snapping of yet another tether connecting Julia to me. I couldn't keep her here. I hadn't even held her in my arms, yet I was already losing her. She was already gone.

We pulled back and I watched as she hugged Joe, and I thought how much he probably wished for his own mom to be here right now. My heart hurt to consider how much he needed support, too. His parents would make the hours-long trip later, but for now, there just wasn't enough time. It wasn't fair. None of this was right.

"Maybe we should get you some water?" my mom suggested gently, stroking a few loose strands of hair away from my face.

I swallowed, feeling the dry patch in the back of my throat, still scratchy from all the screaming. I reached for the small square box of tissues that Natalie had given us as she walked us out to the gazebo, empty now, surrounded by its contents, now in dozens of small round balls.

We moved back inside to the adjacent dining area, thankfully vacant now, between lunch and dinner services. Afternoon sun streamed into the great room through the two-story windows that created shafts of light and shadows all around us. My mom and I settled into chairs around a small square table as Joe disappeared and then returned with bottles of water from the nearby vending machine.

As the water traced a cool path down my throat, I recalled my diligence in staying hydrated while pregnant. All the things I had been so careful to do—but why? They seemed so meaningless now.

Joe reached for my hand and pointed his chin toward the nearby elevator. I followed his gaze and saw the gleaming metal doors glide apart to reveal Addie, my best friend, standing inside. I watched her take a deep breath as she crossed the threshold to step into the room. She was still wearing her dress pants and blouse from her job as a sign language interpreter at the school where I taught. One of the most selfless people I know, it was just like her to come straightaway, to walk headlong into our pain. I watched as she made her way to me through the maze of unoccupied tables and chairs.

Addie was another fixer. After fierce hugs, she clapped her hands like an athlete waiting for the strategy from the coach. "What can I do? What do you need?"

I just stared at her, hearing her words but having no idea how to respond. My eyes, heavy and stinging, helplessly searched the empty room for an answer. I opened my mouth, then closed it again. What *did* I need? I didn't know. Rather, I did know, but it was something outside of human power to provide. I needed my *baby*. I needed a miracle.

I raised my shoulders, shook my head, and watched as her face pinched with sad understanding. She pulled me back into a powerful embrace.

Ultimately, we decided Addie could help by making a trip to a nearby store for bottled water, softer tissues than the ones provided at the hospital, lip balm, and any other items that might provide even a small measure of comfort in the evening ahead.

My dad arrived shortly afterward. I watched him approach and extend his arms toward me. In that moment, I became painfully aware of how much I needed his strong yet gentle presence. As I buried my head into his sturdy shoulder, I could feel the slight tremor from his sharp intake of breath. I looked up at him as he raised his chin, resisting his tears as they threatened to overtake him.

As a little girl, I had always considered him an invincible giant, capable of protecting me against any enemy. As I matured and became a parent myself, I learned that my worrying tendencies came from him. It was not that he was fearless. His bravery came from his willingness to face his fears in order to protect his family. Yet he could not protect me from this. I watched his jaw tremble and I knew that being here, knowing that Julia was already gone and seeing me in this kind of pain, was destroying him—but he came, because he loved me more than he loved himself.

My dad had been watching Joey, and came to the hospital after arranging for him to stay the evening with some family friends. When I'd been apprised of this plan, an objection stopped short, burning in my chest. I wanted desperately to hold Joey close, to kiss him, to be reassured of his love and his safety, but I knew this would be a selfish request. At twenty months old, he would only be frightened by my emotion. I knew he would not understand, and I didn't have the words to explain to him what had happened to his baby sister.

Minutes turned to hours, and even the warm October sun turned its face and began retreating toward the horizon. Finally, reluctantly, I agreed to leave the hospital for some dinner at the encouragement and almost insistence of Dr. Moshier and my family. *You will need all of your strength to get through it.*

I refused to go home to an empty house, with empty arms and empty expectations. After a brief discussion, we decided to go to a nearby fast-food restaurant. My parents would ride with Joe and me for support and Addie would go home, returning later in the evening.

As we made our way through the hospital parking lot to our vehicle, we realized that the infant car seat we had just installed to bring Julia home would need to be removed to make room for the passengers. I sobbed as the device, so carefully designed to protect my child, was taken away. It was useless to us; there was no more protecting her now. We would not be bringing her home.

We had hoped that we'd be early enough to beat the dinner crowd, but the restaurant was already filled with long lines of happy, hungry families when we arrived. I knew my face was swollen, red, and tear-stained. Joe and my parents took care of placing our order and finding a table while I made my way to the restroom.

On my way, I saw a former colleague in line. She greeted me warmly, pointing out my fully pregnant form and asking when the baby was due.

Hadn't I been sick when I'd delivered Joey, too? she asked. I realized that she'd assumed my scarlet nose and cheeks and puffy eyes were just symptoms of a bad cold. I didn't correct her. I somehow managed to get through a brief conversation without breaking down and explaining the truth.

Finally, I moved past her into the safety of the restroom. Grateful that it was surprisingly empty, I darted into the first stall where I retched all of the lies out of my mouth. I rested my flaming hot face against the cool metal stall door. I silently screamed, banged my fists, and allowed my tears the freedom to flow again.

When I moved to the sink I silently prayed no one would come in and interrupt my solitude. I let cool water run over my red, shaky hands and cupped them to bring small sips to rinse out my mouth and cool my burning cheeks.

I stared helplessly at a reflection I did not recognize. How was this happening? How could this precious baby I had been carrying for the last nine months still be inside of me, but . . . *still?* Anyone looking at me would think that I was just a normal pregnant woman. How could I go back out there and sit at a table and pretend that everything was fine when all I wanted to do was stand on a table and scream that everything was *not* fine.

My baby was dead and nothing would ever be normal again.

Back at the table we all sat together in silence, choking back our emotion. I didn't even taste the chicken sandwich; it dropped down my throat like a bowling ball into my stomach. Julia was still inside me, but I was no longer eating for two. Food was fuel, nothing more.

When we had all had enough, we stared at each other meaningfully around the table. It was time to go.

Chapter 3

When we got back to the hospital we solemnly repeated the walk up to the second floor that we'd just made hours before. It felt like a lifetime. The kind faces of the nurses and hospital staff welcomed us, compassion thinly veiling the sadness in their eyes.

I went through the motions of changing my clothes, removing my jewelry, preparing for the trauma of childbirth, knowing it would pale in comparison to the real pain that would come afterwards.

"Will you take my picture?" I asked Joe.

"Now?" he asked, looking as exhausted as I felt.

"I want one more picture. I need to remember what it was like to have her inside of me."

His face and shoulders slumped as if dragged down by an enormous weight. After a beat, he nodded and took the phone from me. I turned to the side, for a profile shot, like the dozens we had taken over the past several months as we'd waited for Julia to arrive. So much the same, yet completely different.

Just after five o'clock in the evening, my labor was induced. The doctor broke my waters and warm fluid poured out of me, and with it came another river of emotion, welling up from a reservoir hidden deep inside of me. I was flooded with memories of spontaneously broken water with Julia's older brother, the way it is portrayed in the movies, all of it a completely different experience than my reality in that moment. My hopes and dreams, the plans we had made, felt like they were all being washed away in the murky liquid, now saturating the crisp, white hospital sheets.

I experienced early contractions that were more emotionally agonizing than they were physically challenging. They brought memories of my labor with Joey. I had endured each of those contractions, knowing that all the pain would be worth it when I held him in my arms. Now, each tightening of the muscles in my uterus served as a cruel reminder that I would hold Julia, too, but only for a while, and that would be when the real agony would begin.

I welcomed the pain. Denial raged within me, and I wanted some part of this night, this experience, to be *normal*. Perhaps if I endured this suffering, I could pay some cosmic penance and *earn* my miracle.

I squeezed my eyes shut and held my breath. I knew this wasn't how it worked, wasn't how God worked. Yet, what did I really know? Would I have ever expected that He would allow something like this to happen to me before today?

I *wanted* to feel each contraction, to commit each moment of this night to my memory, however excruciating. I felt like I deserved the pain for letting this thing happen to my baby.

When labor intensified, though, my medical team was ready.

"There's no reason to make this any more difficult than it already is," they explained.

My questions about the use of powerful painkillers stuck in my throat as I realized there was no longer any danger of causing harm to my baby.

The anesthesiologist was called in to administer an epidural. I was comforted by his warmth and patience in waiting for the moments between contractions before inserting the needle. He looked to be about my dad's age. Did he have a daughter like me? Did I remind him of her? Or, did he have a daughter who, like Julia, was taken too soon?

He withdrew the needle and squeezed my hand sympathetically. "You will feel it start to work soon."

Yet again that evening, my heart was divided into conflicting desires. Half of me was impelled forward, yearning, *needing* to see my baby, to hold her. The other half of me was terrified, knowing that the completion of this process would bring me to the moment when I would watch them take her away.

"I can't do this."

"You're doing great—almost there. She's crowning now."

"My baby . . ."

"There she is—look at that hair!"

"I can't . . ."

"Push. Breathe. You are so strong. You can do this."

Finally, at 10:20 p.m., my beautiful daughter, Julia Rachel Price, silently entered the world.

"She's perfect."

I scrambled to propel my body upward to catch my first glimpse as the doctor gently held up Julia's beautiful, lifeless body. I had never before experienced such utter joy and total despair at the exact same moment.

I realized I hadn't been sure what to expect, but she was absolutely gorgeous and perfect. A head full of thick hair, dark as midnight, an angelic face with delectably round cheeks and full crimson lips, she was the most beautiful baby girl I had ever seen . . . yet, unmistakably, still.

"No. No. *No!* My *baby!*"

Dr. Moshier held her out and I violently ripped off my hospital gown, desperate to get her as close to me as possible. Hoping, believing, that somehow the warmth of my body and the skin-to-skin contact would prompt the miracle that modern medicine could not—that my heart, the deep throbbing through my chest, might, somehow, inspire hers to start again. That the tears of purest maternal love might awaken my little princess.

But it was not enough. Ours was not a fairy tale.

Deep sobs racked my chest as I fiercely clutched her body so close to my own that she was barely an extension of me. I rocked her as I studied her flawless hair and her eyes, her ears, counted her tiny fingers and toes. Wasn't she just sleeping? Hadn't I *just* felt her moving within me? How could this picture-perfect baby not be alive?

"She was just here," I reasoned. I searched pleadingly from the doctor to the nurses to my parents, silently asking the question, begging for the answer that could not be found.

Then to my husband, a new wave of emotion welling up as I saw my bewilderment mirrored in his face. "Joe, she was *just here.*"

His arms encircled us, me holding Julia, him holding both of us. Knowing him as I know myself, I felt his anguish as he embraced us fiercely, protectively. We wept as one for Julia, for each other, and for all the tomorrows we would never have together.

Nothing made sense. How could this have happened? How could we be standing here in a reality so entirely different from the one we had envisioned only twenty-four hours earlier? We expected to be in a hospital room, holding her, embracing each other, listening to the precious sounds of her newborn cries. Instead, the only crying in the room was coming from our own lips. It felt like the ground around us had crumbled and fallen away, and we were standing, huddled together, on an island of our shared grief.

I shifted slightly, allowing Joe a small space on the adjustable bed, and we both stared helplessly at our little girl.

"She looks like Joey," Joe said after several quiet minutes.

A voiceless laugh vented out of me. "She does." I smiled. "She does."

We marveled together at Julia's resemblance to her older brother—their thick dark hair, their tiny button noses—while silently acknowledging the contrast between his birth story and hers. Our beloved little boy at home would be wondering what had happened to his little sister. This changed everything.

I shook away the tornado of thoughts swirling in my mind. I needed to be present. I needed to remember each of the fleeting moments we had together.

I felt the dampness of Joe's cheek brush against my forehead. I turned to look up at him and saw the raw pain and helplessness that I felt, reflected in his face. His lower lip pressed tightly upward while the corners of his mouth pointed to the floor, making an effective umbrella against the deluge of tears falling from his cloudy eyes.

I moved to transfer Julia from my arms to his. His eyebrows lifted to ask the silent question, *Are you sure?*

I nodded and watched as his face told the story of his love for her. He gazed intently at this precious bundle in his arms. "She is perfect," he whispered. I watched him as he stared at this priceless gift, taken back even before she could be properly given.

His shoulders trembled with silent sobs. I knew he was holding back the intensity of his emotions, to be strong for me, his ultimate, selfless act of love. But his love for her, his unequivocal adoration, was undeniable. She was his little princess—Daddy's little girl.

My mind raced to all of the tomorrows that would never be: the daddy-daughter dates, their first dance at her wedding. By the look in his eyes, I knew he was seeing them, too. I had spent more than a decade loving this man, but in that moment, watching him with her, I felt a new depth of love and a new dimension of heartbreak.

We welcomed family and a few close friends to gather with us.

My brother and sister-in-law, Anthony and Car—short for Carol—had left their vacation when we had called earlier in the day. They had made the hours-long drive home to be with us, arriving only shortly after Julia was born.

As we invited those closest to us to hold her, I held my breath. Although I saw her as gorgeous and perfect, it did not escape me that she was also . . . dead. Would they want to touch her? Was it wrong to offer her to them? I was torn between wanting to both share her and shield her from the world and its judgment.

As it turned out, however, all we felt was overwhelming love and kindness. I watched my parents, Anthony, Car, and Addie as they cradled her, marveling at how *perfect* she was. They did not recoil or refuse her. Their love was heartbreakingly evident as they kissed her face and stroked her hair. Watching them together, the only visible indication that there was anything amiss were the sad smiles that replaced happy ones, tears of grief rather than those of joy.

The pastor and the chaplain from our church arrived to pray with us. I closed my eyes and turned my head away, anger boiling up inside of me.

Why should I pray now? What good will it do? Where were you, God, when I prayed before?

I looked around the room at the people who loved us, who would have done anything to take away our pain, or to prevent Julia's death from happening in the first place. But it was not within their power to do so. It *was* within God's power, yet here we were, still in the midst of the devastation. I loved Him. I had a relationship with Him, but I felt so empty, so abandoned. Had I not believed enough? Was my faith insufficient? Was I being punished?

I didn't know, but I wasn't going to spend any more of the precious few moments I had with my daughter considering it.

Throughout the evening we took comfort in the competent, compassionate care of our medical team. Dr. Moshier and our nurses, Lauren and Amy, attended to our every need. We smiled proudly as Lauren lovingly weighed and measured Julia, at seven pounds, fifteen ounces, and twenty inches long. After she had meticulously inked Julia's tiny hands and feet, preserving her prints on precious keepsakes, she gently bathed her and washed her hair.

I cried as I watched her. The tenderness and empathy she had for my baby girl was evident in each delicate, purposeful movement.

But I also cried for myself. *I* should have been the one to give Julia her first bath. My legs were still too numb from the medication to stand, my body so racked by emotion and trauma, I knew I could not have managed it, and there was just not enough time. Still, my mind raced back to the first bath I'd given my son in the hospital, and forward to the thousands of baths I would never get to give his baby sister.

With our permission, the nurses had called in a birth photographer. Kelcy was a volunteer with Now I Lay Me Down to Sleep, a nonprofit organization designed to provide bereaved families like ours with remembrance portraits of their babies. I was concerned that it would be awkward to pose for pictures with Julia. I wondered if it would be morbid to take photographs of her. It ended up being the best decision we ever could have made.

Kelcy stood at a respectful distance and let our evening unfold, capturing both the tenderness and heartbreak of the too-brief time we had together. She worked with our nurses, and they all treated Julia, and us, with such dignity, such kindness. She took some posed photos of Julia, of our wedding bands on her tiny fingers and toes, of us holding her. They all raved about how gorgeous she was, and for at least those few moments, it seemed like we were just any other family, in any other birth photography session.

But, of course, this wasn't just any birth—it was a *still* birth. These photos were not just a nice idea—they were necessary. As much as I tried to memorize the dimple in her chin, her luxuriously long eyelashes, her tiny button nose—one night would never be enough to remember a face too precious to forget. And one night was all we had.

Chapter 4

I awoke to a nurse I hadn't yet met thrusting her open hands vigorously into my still-swollen abdomen to push out potential blood clots. She was asking me my name and other questions with obvious answers. It all seemed so strange. I felt like I was driving on a foggy highway, incapable of seeing what was in front of me. With each plunge of the nurse's hands, each question about who I was, where I was, my mind accelerated until I finally found my way into the clearing.

I remembered.

I sucked in a breath, frantically searching the room, my eyes wide with panic.

"Where is my baby? Where is Julia?!"

"Your mom has her; she's still here."

That's when I saw him. My strong, sensitive husband, his electric blue Oxford shirt, irreparably stained by my coal-black mascara, looking down at me with eyes so full of love, his face a mix of fear and a relief I couldn't comprehend.

"What happened?" I asked, my voice trembling, unsure whether I wanted to hear the answer.

The nurse looked weary, yet also oddly relieved. I watched as the three vertical lines between her eyebrows slowly stretched and settled back into her creamy chocolate complexion. Her lips parted to release a light exhalation before she spoke.

She calmly and professionally informed me that I had lost consciousness. When they could not find a medical explanation, they had called the doctor, who had reasoned that it was simply my overwhelmed mind and heart trying to catch up with the rest of my body.

"We will continue to keep a close eye on you," she said, "and we'll allow your family to come back in. Please let us know if you need anything."

Still trying to work through what I was hearing, I looked back up at Joe and saw all I needed to know in his face. "You just stopped talking and you wouldn't wake up," he told me, his voice high and wavering. "I lifted the sheet to see if you were bleeding out. I pushed the call button and screamed for the nurses. They couldn't get you to wake up either, and then more of them came running and cleared the room. There must have been ten of them working on you at the same time. They did everything they knew to do, but none of it was working. They all looked so scared."

I stared at him, my mouth agape, then looked around the rest of the room in disbelief as my parents, Car, Anthony, and Addie filed back in. Of course, I didn't remember any of it; how did this happen?

When I looked up at Joe, I watched the love of my life, my best friend, and the strongest man I knew, as tears spilled down his cheeks. His strong jaw trembled as he choked out the words I knew I would never forget. "I was so scared. I thought I was losing my whole family in one day . . . Please don't ever leave me." He buried his head into my shoulder, and we clung to one another. We sobbed silently, convulsively, in an unthinkable blend of gratitude that I was safe, and devastation that our baby was not.

My mom handed Julia back to me, and once she was safely in my arms, I couldn't imagine how I would ever let her go again. I stared at this perfect little bundle and pushed away the nagging reminder that our time together was running out. I wanted to hold her forever, never let her go, to somehow love her back to life.

Shortly thereafter, however, we knew it was time. We discussed undressing her—whether or not to remove the tiny ruffled gown with its pink satin rosettes and matching hat that we'd dressed her in, the outfit we'd brought to the hospital with us, when we'd naively believed we'd be taking her home with us. It was the one thing she had worn; I had to keep it, I reasoned, in order to keep a piece of her.

Yet the thought of swaddling her in a blanket and handing her to a stranger didn't feel right, either. None of it made sense.

We decided to leave her in her gown, unwilling to send her off with strangers wearing only a diaper. We did, however, agree to keep the matching hat with us, needing to hold on to at least this tiny piece of her, wanting so much more.

The room was silent for several sacred moments as we held Julia and tried to imagine a way to say good-bye. I heard my own voice as if it came from somewhere else as I began to softly sing *You are my Sunshine*. Joe quickly joined in. It was the song we had sung to her every night over the last nine months, its lyrics now taking on heartbreaking new meaning. How could we tell her how deeply loved her, how much we would miss her? She was our Sunshine. How could we let her go into the night? How would we navigate the darkness that would be left when we let them take her away?

I bathed her in kisses and regrets. I tried to drink her in, working to commit to memory each of her precious features, the silkiness of her skin, the pressure of her tiny body against my chest, for the impending lifetime I would spend without her. I would never hold her in my arms again. A part of me went with her that night. A piece of me died, too.

In those very wee hours of the morning, we gathered our strength to say good-bye to the daughter to whom we'd never even gotten to say a proper hello. Without hearing her cry, or nursing her to sleep, or changing her tiny diaper, I forced myself to kiss my baby girl one last time and let the nurses take her to the funeral director, a man I had never met, waiting outside our room.

And then she was gone.

Chapter 5

I woke up early the next morning to the nightmare that had started less than twenty-four hours before. I surveyed the darkness of my predawn hospital room. The monitors were quietly humming. Joe was making quiet breathing sounds on the couch beside my bed. There was only one conspicuous absence: my baby. There were no hungry newborn cries, no rustling of sheets as I pulled her into position to nurse. Nothing but silence.

I was so utterly alone in that moment. How could I wake Joe? It felt selfish to do so. He, too, needed rest after the tragic events of the day before. He would join me in its aftermath soon enough. I could call the nurses—but why? There was no baby to examine. Not even the best medicine could numb my pain.

So, I sat alone in my grief. I recalled in excruciating detail the events of the day before. I stifled my sobs into the stiff hospital blanket as I relived each precious moment I'd had with Julia. My chest was burning, screaming for oxygen as I watched the film reel in my mind: seeing her for the first time, holding her, sharing her, and saying good-bye.

I was jarred back into reality by a soft rap on the door, followed by a quiet "Hello?"

I gasped and swiped at my eyes as the figure approached.

"Good morning," she began gently. "I'm just here to draw some blood for the lab. Is that okay?"

I nodded rigidly, not trusting my voice to answer.

She worked mostly in silence, but when she did talk, her tone was upbeat. Did she know what had happened? Did she know that the baby from this room, my baby, wasn't just down the hall getting typical newborn screenings? Had anyone told her before she came in here that Julia was dead, taken away in the middle of the night?

"All done," she said. A gentle squeeze of my forearm and a sad smile revealed that she knew.

I couldn't muster a smile. Instead, I forced my lips together and nodded, thanking her as she packed her equipment into a plastic tote and left as quietly as she'd come.

I rested my head back against my pillow and let fresh tears run like rivers down my hot cheeks, the unbelievable reality soaking into my consciousness.

How did this happen? *Why* did this happen? What had I done wrong? How hadn't I known sooner? If I had known, could I have saved her? My instincts to pray were met with a sharp, surging anger. Where *was* God? Why hadn't He prevented this? Why hadn't He saved her? I had no doubt that He had seen all of this before it happened, not even the tiniest hesitation in believing that He *could* have brought her back to life. So *why hadn't He done it?*

My thoughts were interrupted by another soft knock on the door. I drew in a ragged breath as Dr. Moshier entered. She noticed Joe still asleep on the couch and walked quietly but with purpose to my bedside.

"Hi, Maria." Her tone conveyed a depth of compassion that resounded in my ears. "How are you feeling?"

I wanted to be strong, to answer her with words instead of tears, but the words were stuck in my throat, and I could only shake my head.

A small, quiet breath escaped her. "I know," she said, nodding, then shook her head, too. "It's a terrible question. I'm so sorry for your loss."

"I—I just don't understand it."

"I know," she replied, nodding her head again, her chin-length brunette hair bobbing along in sympathy.

"I mean . . ." Trying desperately to hold back my emotion, I struggled for words. "I keep thinking, *She was just here.*"

She closed her eyes and bowed her head with visible empathy before looking back up at me. "I know. I am hoping that the autopsy will reveal something that will provide at least some answers—some sense of peace, if possible."

I tried to take in her words, but they kept getting jumbled around in my head.

"She was perfect." I said it as a statement, but there was a slight lilt at the end that indicated an underlying question, a request for reassurance, and she caught it immediately.

"Yes. She was." She touched my arm gently and took a deep breath before going on. "Like we said last night, we look for certain obvious causes for concern—a cord wrapped around the baby's neck, or a physical deformity that the ultrasounds didn't catch. But Julia didn't have any of those things."

I turned my face and felt my body shake with silent, uncontrollable sobs.

"I'm sorry," she continued. "I know it's so hard not to know. I am glad, for that reason, that you are opting to do the autopsy."

"I just keep thinking . . ." I was trying to push through the fear to admit the thought that had been tightening itself around my neck like a noose. "I just keep thinking that I should have known, I should have come in sooner, I should have—"

"No," she stopped me, absolute authority mingling with the empathy in her tone. "You did not do this. You were here the day before, and everything was perfect. You did everything we asked you to do. Do not do that to yourself." Her voice softened a bit. "This will be hard enough to live with without taking on that kind of unnecessary guilt."

I nodded because I knew it was the right thing to do, not because I believed her.

"I wanted to ask about milk donation," I said, attempting to gather my composure. I could see by the look on her face that the abrupt change in subject had surprised her. Or was it something else? I continued with a bit more apprehension. "I just . . . I've heard of people, moms donating breast milk to milk banks or something. And I just thought . . . well, I won't be needing mine now . . ."

Emotion stopped me there.

"Oh, Maria."

I couldn't read her tone at first. After a deep sigh, she went on slowly.

"That is so kind. And generous. I have never had anyone ask about that before." She paused for a beat, her lips making a tight line. "I can get you some information, but"—another beat—"I just want you to be careful. I can only imagine how difficult that would be to do, emotionally."

We talked about it a bit more—what would be happening to my body in the next few days as my milk came in, and how to get it to taper off should I choose not to pump and donate it after all.

We went on to talk about support. She emphasized that I was going to have to lean on others, to be gentle with myself.

I nodded my head, although I wasn't exactly sure what that meant.

She prescribed some medication to help me sleep, if needed, to help me cope. I nodded again, wondering what kind of magic it would take to help me cope with this. We talked a bit more, a few questions asked and answered.

And then, when there was nothing—and yet everything—left to say, she reached out and rested her hand on mine. It was cool, birdlike, matching her petite frame. She closed her eyes for several seconds, then opened them slowly.

"Please know that we are here for you. You can call at any time, for any reason. If you need to come in before your follow-up appointment, you just let us know." She tucked her chin and found my eyes with hers. "You are strong," she said, nodding her head in response as I tearfully shook mine. "Yes. You have had to be so strong to get through the past twenty-four hours. Don't be afraid to accept help when you need it. We are all here for you."

I felt sincere gratitude mixed with grief. "Thank you," I managed, barely above a whisper.

With a slight tilt of her head, she nodded. We moved toward each other to shake hands, but then, as if choreographed, we shifted into a deep hug instead. I wondered how far outside the guidelines this was as I cried into her shoulder. This woman had delivered both of my babies. Joey, alive. Julia, not. We had been through so much together. If this act of compassion was a breach of protocol, I was eternally grateful for it.

As we moved apart, she enfolded both of my hands in hers and gave them a gentle squeeze. She shared a kind smile, nodded, and turned to walk away.

When I heard the door close, the breath that I had been holding back rushed out of me, an explosion of raw emotion, erupting out of me like hot lava. Trying to be quiet, I clenched my teeth and let out a low groan. When I rolled onto my side to curl myself into a semi-fetal position, I was surprised and relieved to find Joe there, standing at my bedside. I pressed my face into the warmth of his body, muffling my cries.

I felt him pull me close, his hands placing gentle pressure on the back of my head and the space between my shoulders. I eased backward, making room for him to lie down next to me in the hospital bed. My mind raced back to just a few hours earlier, when we had sat just like this, with only one difference—we'd been holding Julia between us.

Chapter 6

Joe and I were communicating solely in a language of tears and physical touch. When our tears and the intensity of our emotions slowed, we just sat together, still holding each other, me resting my cheek on his chest, him resting his chin on the top of my head.

A soft tapping on the door brought us back to the present.

"Hello?"

We recognized the gentle voice of our nurse, Lauren.

I adjusted my face into the semblance of a smile in an effort to convey that she was welcome to come in. Our room was still mostly dark, only the tiniest glimmers of sunrise peeking around the edges of the closed window shade.

Lauren entered with two other young women in scrubs. "Hey. How are you doing?"

I looked around the room for a beat, trying to find the words, then settled on another half-smile and a shrug.

"I know," she said, resting her cool hand on mine. "It's time for your medicine. Are you ready for it?"

I nodded and sat up, taking the tiny plastic cup containing ibuprofen for pain. I took it and looked up into her face. I hadn't noticed it the night before, but she was stunningly beautiful.

"Thank you," I told her, handing the cup back to her, thinking that her almond-shaped green eyes and glossy chestnut hair made her look more like a movie star than a nurse.

"Dr. Moshier said you wanted to leave this morning?" The lilt in her voice indicated a question—*Are you sure?*

I nodded. Yes. Without Julia, there was no reason to be here. Was my stay in a maternity ward even appropriate anymore? A mother without her baby? If I did decide to stay, would they move me to another department? Make room for another mother with a *living* child?

I just wanted to go.

"Okay. My shift is ending, but I wanted to come and say good-bye, and let you know that you'll be in my thoughts and prayers."

"Thank you so much," I replied, wanting to say more, barely squeezing the words out.

"Thank *you*," she answered, and the sincerity in her voice drew my eyes to hers. "Thank you for sharing your daughter with me. She is beautiful. I will never forget her. It was an honor to take care of all of you. Julia will stay in my heart always."

The combination of hearing Julia's name spoken from another person's lips and the empathy in her tone stole my breath. I brought my hand to my chest, closed my eyes, and forced myself to inhale deeply, fighting to keep my composure. I had to tell her.

"The way . . ." I sputtered, "the *way* you took care of her. Your kindness and gentleness. It means the world to us. We could never thank you enough."

"It truly was my honor." She said it with such conviction that I believed her. It touched my heart in a way I knew I would never forget.

She introduced us to Jen and Jen—one blonde, the other brunette, our new nurses who would take over the morning shift. We smiled at the coincidence of their shared name. I wondered how it was decided to put them on our case. Were they assigned to us; did they draw the unlucky straws? Or did they volunteer to walk into our story?

I watched for signs of discomfort—that they wished to be in any other room but ours. But their eye contact was steady, their posture straight. They smiled warmly but not casually, with obvious respect for the trauma that had occurred in this room hours before.

"They are fantastic nurses," Lauren offered softly, perhaps sensing my hesitation to trust strangers after what we had endured. "And they are also my friends. They'll take good care of you." She reached for my hand and squeezed it gently. We talked through what we needed to do to be discharged and they went to get the paperwork started while we got dressed.

Joe went to the bathroom to retrieve all of our toiletries while I unzipped the suitcase and sifted through all the baby things we had brought for Julia. I looked with new eyes at all the onesies, the receiving blankets, the tiny turquoise hat with *Bed Hair, Don't Care* emblazoned in hot pink. As was typical for me, I had seriously overpacked. We'd brought so many clothes, so many things that she would never wear.

I shuddered at the thought of what we'd have to do with everything once we got home.

Going through each item, lovingly selected and carefully folded into the suitcase, I was overwhelmed with longing. Longing for Julia. Longing for the life we had planned but would never have together.

I reached for the hat we had kept from the outfit she wore when they took her away, the one we had planned to put her in to bring her home. I traced my fingers unhurriedly along the soft, creamy cotton with its delicate ruffle, the sweet blush-pink satin rose that matched the one near the hem of the gown. She had worn it last night when we had held her, when Kelcy took her photographs.

I closed my eyes and brought it up to my face. Was there a scent? Some remnant of her left behind in the fabric that I could transfer to myself?

Before I realized it, my hands were trembling, the tiny bonnet quavering. I looked up to the ceiling. "Why?" I asked imploringly. "Why? This is not *right*. *This. Is. Not. Right.*" My shoulders and faith slumping, I closed my eyes and dropped my head forward.

Suddenly, I felt someone watching me. I clutched the little hat to my chest as my eyes darted across the room to see Joe in the bathroom doorway, toiletry bag in hand. His head was tilted, his forehead scrunched in obvious concern. When our eyes met, I watched his chest fall as he exhaled. I felt shame at my inability to control my emotions and anger that I had been put in this position. I sank to the couch, rested my elbows on my knees, and hid my face in my hands.

I heard him drop the toiletry bag into the suitcase as he sat next to me and wrapped his strong arms around me. He pulled me close, turning me so I was resting again on his chest. I realized in that moment just how incredibly *tired* I was. My eyelids felt like they were as full as our suitcase, my sinuses packed tight, emitting immense pressure. How good it would feel to just close my eyes. But how could I? There was so much—and yet, I realized, *nothing*—to do. Yes, I needed to pack up a few of our things, but there was no baby to nurse, no diapers to change, no newborn outfits to repack; they would remain in the suitcase, unworn. *Newborn, but stillborn. Still born, but never coming home.*

I felt whatever resolve I had built crumble into a heap. Giving in to the grief, I melted into Joe, like a crayon in the sun, still composed of the same material but unrecognizable in form.

35

Chapter 7

We were roused from our waking slumber by a soft knock and the sound of the door opening. Jen and Jen stood hesitantly in the entryway, silently asking if they were interrupting, if they should come back later.

"Please. Come in," we assured them.

They entered with a folder, a small bag, and clipboard of papers to sign. The folder was full of information about support groups, the milk bank donation I'd asked about, and brochures about how to navigate the loss of a child. They also gave us Julia's hand- and footprints that Lauren had taken the night before. I experienced a sudden shortness of breath and quickening of my pulse. *My baby.* Evidence that she was here.

I carefully examined the tiny impressions, each exquisite ridge and whorl. This was her. This was Julia, no one else. *What a precious gift.*

"Thank you," I whispered.

They nodded, their faces revealing a million unsaid sentiments of sympathy.

Brunette Jen seemed to brace herself with a deep breath as she began to go through the instructions for my release from their care. My body, she explained, had gone through a "normal" labor and vaginal delivery of my baby, but it didn't know that Julia was gone. I would still have all of the soreness and discomfort that comes from the trauma of childbirth. They handed me a bag containing a perineal irrigation bottle, numbing spray, and soothing wipes. They also gave me prescriptions for painkillers, laxatives, and the antidepressants I had discussed with Dr. Moshier. They advised me about the incontinence, constipation, discharge, and contractions I should expect.

I had been given all of these instructions with my first child, too. Then, however, I'd had a beautiful baby in my arms to justify the impending discomfort. Now, I only had empty arms, adding the emotional agony of loss to my physical pain.

My breasts would get tender as my milk came in, they explained. I closed my eyes as I considered the cruelty of my body preparing to care for the baby that it, ironically, did not protect in my womb.

"You can, of course, use the resources here, to pump and donate your milk," Blonde Jen began gently. "It is such a kind and noble gesture. Just please . . . be careful. Try not to put too much pressure on yourself. You will be dealing with a lot already. Be gentle with yourself."

I nodded, hearing her words, feeling the sympathy behind them.

"You can expect mood changes as your hormones kick in," she advised, understanding evident in her tone.

I heard a sound a bit like a chuckle escape me. *No kidding.*

"I know," she went on with a halfhearted smile, before becoming more serious as she discussed postpartum depression. Our situation clearly exacerbated my risks, since depression is expected to accompany the loss of a child. She gave us signs to watch out for, most of which sounded like a roadmap for what to expect after having lost a baby:

Feeling sad, hopeless, empty, or overwhelmed. *Check.*

Crying more than usual or for no apparent reason. *Or for every apparent reason.*

Irritability and restlessness. *Yes.*

Anger or rage. *Yes and yes.*

Losing interest in activities that are usually enjoyable. *In that moment, I couldn't even remember the things that I used to enjoy.*

Having trouble bonding or forming emotional attachment to my baby. *Well, that decision was already made for me, wasn't it?*

Thinking about harming myself or my child. *Pause.*

I thought of Joey. I looked away and my eyes shifted out of focus. I would never hurt him intentionally. Yet I wondered what kind of mental or emotional effects my grief might have on him. I shuddered. How was I going to mother one child in the midst of losing the other? How could I live when my child was dead? How could I not, when the other was alive?

I blinked back to the present moment. The Jens were talking to Joe about the warning signs, the powerful drugs the doctor was prescribing, encouraging him to call if he became concerned about anything.

"You can call us anytime," they urged, "for any reason. We want to be here for you."

"Thank you," Joe replied. "We appreciate everything."

"Can we get you some breakfast before you go?"

I looked at Joe, but he tilted his head and raised his eyebrows in my direction, silently deferring to me.

"No, thank you," I said. "That's very thoughtful, but no." The thought of food made my stomach roil.

"Make sure you do eat something, though. You will need to take care of yourself," they warned.

"I'll take care of her," Joe promised.

The Jens smiled their approval.

I looked at Joe and smiled in gratitude. He smiled back at me, but the expression did not reach his eyes. I studied the dark circles that seemed to underscore his fatigue, and wondered again how all of this was affecting him. He was so focused on caring for me, but what about him?

"Is there anything else we can do for you before we see you out?" they asked. "Anything else you need?"

I need my baby, I thought. But I knew that wasn't what they meant.

"I think we just need to finish getting ready," Joe answered, filling in the silence.

"Of course," they agreed, nodding their heads. "Take all the time you need. Just hit the call button when you're ready."

When the door closed behind them, Joe and I were silent.

I wanted to go. Joey was with my parents. On their way home from the hospital late last night, they had picked him up from the home of our friends who had been watching him. I needed to see Joey, to hold him. Yet I wasn't ready to go home. When we had locked the door behind us and pulled out of our driveway yesterday, we had still expected we would have Julia with us when we returned. I couldn't imagine how I would walk through that door again without her.

"Maybe my parents would meet us with Joey for breakfast," I suggested.

Joe looked at me for several long seconds, drawing his lips into a tight line and narrowing his eyes slightly. "Are you sure you can handle that?"

"No," I answered honestly. "I just don't think I can go home yet . . . without her."

His face softened and he nodded his comprehension. "Okay."

I texted my family while he finished packing the rest of our belongings into our suitcase. If my family found it strange that I wanted to go to a pancake restaurant less than twelve hours after giving birth to my stillborn baby, they didn't say so. They agreed immediately, no questions asked.

We looked around the room once our bags were all packed. So quiet. Eerily so. No baby squirming. No car seat. No Julia.

"Do we have everything?" Joe asked.

No, I thought. *Not by a long shot.*

"I think so," I replied, and pushed the call button for the nurses.

The Jens came with a wheelchair and a cart to escort us out.

I eyed the wheelchair, remembering the last time I had been escorted out of the hospital after giving birth. Then, I had held Joey proudly in my arms as we wheeled through the halls, waving at the nurses' station, smiling and cooing at my long-awaited miracle boy. This, I realized, would be a much different experience.

"Did you want to walk?" Brunette Jen asked uncertainly.

I couldn't stop staring.

"I think the chair is a good idea," Joe interjected.

I blinked and looked from him to the chair, then to Jen, and nodded my consent. I sat and sighed dejectedly, not knowing what to do with my empty hands.

Jen mercifully headed left instead of right, wheeling me out to the staff elevator just steps from our room. This kindness saved me from the newborn cries, balloon bouquets, and happy families that would certainly have greeted us in the main hallway of Labor and Delivery.

"Thank you," I murmured, turning my head, unable to lift my gaze from the floor.

She squeezed my shoulder warmly as she pushed the down button.

When the doors opened again and we made our way down the hallway, I squinted at the sunshine pouring through the large plate-glass windows on the ground level. How was the sun still shining? I wondered. How were all of these people just going about their business? Didn't they know? I wanted to scream, to tell them *my baby had just died*. She was in a morgue somewhere, waiting to be autopsied. Didn't they care?

Instead I sat in silence as Jen parked my wheelchair near the door and Joe went to get the car. We engaged in the smallest of talk until our SUV pulled up in the driveway and the large automatic doors opened for our exit.

After Joe assisted me into the car and closed the door, I rolled down the window and turned to Jen again.

"You call," she advised. "Even if you think it's something small. We'll be here."

"Thank you. So very much," I replied, amazed and grateful for the compassion and thoughtfulness of the staff.

A few moments later, Joe shifted the car into gear and we pulled away into the real world, a world without our daughter.

Chapter 8

We drove straight to the nearby restaurant where we had arranged to meet the rest of our family. When Joe pulled into a space and turned the car off, we just sat, staring out the windshield in silence. The sun was shining brilliantly in a cloudless sky. There were cars driving back and forth on the busy street just ahead. A young family, happily chattering and carrying leftover boxes, jumped into their minivan parked in the next spot over, apparently ready to carry on with the rest of their day. *The world was going on as if nothing had happened. How was the Earth still spinning on its axis?*

I exhaled a shaky breath and looked down at the floor mat.

Joe reached for my hand. "Ready?" he asked, although I am sure he already knew the answer. "If you want, I could just go in and get Joey and we could go home. I am sure your parents would understand."

I sucked in a deep breath and shook my head. "No," I replied. "I can do this. Let's go."

He nodded, unbuckling his seat belt with a loud *click*. He opened his door and closed it, then made his way around the car to open mine. He reached for my hand to help me out of the car.

Standing up, I looked into his eyes. They were bloodshot and squinting slightly against the sunlight. He looked so tired. He squeezed my hand, though, and shot me a half-smile, communicating that we were in this—whatever it was—together.

"Daddy! Mommy!" We could hear Joey from across the restaurant as we made our way past the oversized booths and kitschy decorations to our table. My parents, Anthony and Car, and their two-year-old son, Mason, were already seated around the table, waiting for us. Their older boys, age seven and nine, were at school.

Joey was bouncing on his bottom in the wooden highchair, arms extended in an enthusiastic pick-me-up pose. In spite of myself, I smiled as I reached for him.

"Careful, babe," Joe warned, and I remembered the hospital guidelines about lifting heavy objects. "Here, you can sit right next to him and give him as big a hug as you want," he continued, helping me into the large wooden chair beside Joey.

"Mommy!" Joey was beaming, still holding out his arms to me. I enfolded him in my embrace, unable to contain the tears. *Would he ask about Julia? He's only one and a half. Will he even realize she's not here? Has anyone told him that she's never coming home?*

Seconds later though, he turned to Joe, requesting a hug from him, apparently oblivious to the trauma that had just devastated our family.

"Hey," Car began. "How are you doing?"

My head felt like it was full of sand. I couldn't answer, only nod.

I looked at all of them and realized how sad and tired they all looked. It wasn't until this moment that I realized they were all exhausted, too. They had all been up past midnight with us at the hospital. I felt selfish for asking them to come out this morning, and grateful that they had come.

We briefly caught them up. After breakfast, we would be picking up prescriptions at the pharmacy near our house. When the autopsy was complete, the funeral director would go to pick Julia up from the hospital and transport her to the funeral home. At that point, they would call us and we could schedule a meeting to discuss arrangements. My parents would come with us to that appointment; Car and Anthony would watch Joey. We didn't really know what else we could do yet. Just go home. *Home. Without her.*

Joey and his cousin colored happily on their kids' menus, a few more questions, a few more answers, and we silently agreed to go on with breakfast. I looked at the menu. *What was I doing here? How was I going to eat anything? How could I eat anything when Julia was lying in a morgue, surrounded by strangers? I should be with her. If I were really with her, it would mean I was dead, too. Maybe that's what should have happened.*

"And how about you, sweetie? What can I get you?"

I was jarred back to reality by the chirpy voice of our bubbly waitress, standing over my shoulder. I wasn't sure if it was my swollen face or haunted expression that startled her, but I watched her eyes widen slightly before she lifted her rounded chin, took in a sharp breath through her nose, and regained her cheery smile, now rimmed with visible compassion around the edges.

"Coffee. Please," I said, recognizing that caffeine restrictions could be lifted since I wasn't pregnant anymore.

The world around me blurred, shifting in and out of focus. My family was trying to respect my unspoken wish to act "normal." I heard their chatter, but the words were indistinguishable. Food tasted like nothing, settling like rocks in my empty belly. Wretchedly empty, I realized. Empty of food. Empty of Julia. Just *empty*.

Once all the food had been eaten or pushed around on our plates, it was time to go home. We said our good-byes. Our hugs were tighter and longer than usual, but words were harder to find. We packed Joey into the remaining car seat and made the trip home.

Chapter 9

We drove through the neighborhood where we had lived for the past seven years. We had been excited to purchase a home on the edge of this historic district. Established as a Union Army training camp during the Civil War, it was full of winding roads and eclectic architecture, and was considered a safe and prestigious place to live in our city. We drove past people walking their dogs and mowing their lawns, despite the fact that we were almost midway through October in Iowa.

When we pulled into the driveway I remembered how I'd felt when we moved into the white, two-story house with powder-blue shutters and a picket fence. It had seemed to be everything I had ever wanted in a home, the perfect place to raise a family.

That seemed like such a long time ago now.

As if in a dream, I walked through the gate into the backyard. Going past the apple tree, I was haunted by flashes of a not-long-ago gathering of friends and family for a gender-reveal celebration. *Pink balloons. Cheers. It's a girl.*

Joe carried a sleeping Joey in from the car. I carried no one.

Once inside I looked around to see that everything was just as we'd left it when we'd headed to the hospital with Julia safely in my belly. There were boxes of newborn-sized diapers. Baby girl clothes and big, elaborate hair bows. Blankets and burp cloths. She was everywhere. And yet, nowhere.

While Joe went upstairs to put Joey down for a nap, I marched to the downstairs guestroom. I couldn't bring myself to go upstairs to my own room, my own bed, where the white bassinet stood adjacent, the one where Joey had slept, waiting for its newest tiny inhabitant.

I sat down on the edge of the bed, sinking into the fluffy white comforter. I clenched my fists, my nails digging, digging into the soft flesh of my palms, fury beginning to overpower the shock-induced stupor. I wanted to run, but where could I go? I wanted to cry, to scream, but who would hear me? God? No. He hadn't heard. Or perhaps hadn't cared? In any case, I thought, He'd apparently already made His decision.

Cognizant of the fact that Joey was napping, I plunged my flaming-hot face into the coolness of the pillow beside me, wondering for a moment how many seconds I would have to go without oxygen before I'd pass out and the pain would stop, even if it were just for a few merciful moments of relief.

But then I felt Joe's arms lifting me up, turning me away from the pillow's alluring darkness.

Sunlight filtered into the room, despite the shades and floor-length pale gold curtains, creating an almost ethereal glow as Joe drew me close, placing his cool cheek like a compress to my forehead. He reached for the glass of water and medicine he'd set on the nightstand. I took the pills obediently, wordlessly, then lay down, acquiescing to my body's, if not my mind's, desperate need for sleep.

I woke up to find the light in the room different from what it was before I fell asleep. Panicking, my eyes flashed to the oversized wall clock. Late afternoon.

I vaulted out of the bed and raced to find my phone. I needed to call the funeral home. They were supposed to call me when they had picked Julia up from the autopsy. *What if I had missed their call? What time does a funeral home close?*

No missed calls.

I breathed a shaky sigh of relief that quickly reverted back to fear.

Julia.

Where was she? Was the autopsy finished? What had they found? Had they just forgotten to call me? Where was my little girl? I couldn't just not know where she was. A mother should know where her baby is.

Strangers. Morgue. Autopsy. Funeral home.

I forced my eyes to focus as I began punching numbers forcefully into the screen. My heart was banging against my rib cage, my breathing short and staccato, anxiety blurring the edges of my vision. *Pick up. Pick. Up.*

"Hello?" The voice coming from the other end of the line, sounded like it belonged to a grandmother, all sweet tea and honeyed biscuits.

"Hi," I began nervously. *What was I going to say?* The words felt smothered in my throat, but I needed to get this out. I needed to find out where my baby was.

"Hello? Are you still there?"

"Yes. Yes, I'm here," I finally managed, then, with all the strength I could muster, "My baby . . . her . . . her name is Julia. Julia Price. She was born last night . . . stillborn . . . last night." I cringed. Hearing the words coming out of my own mouth was like being pushed down a flight of stairs. "The man came to get her. The funeral director. She was supposed to have an autopsy, and then be brought there. I am just looking . . . just wondering . . . if you knew where she was?"

"Yes," her answer was slow, deliberate, as if wanting to spare me from any additional pain. "You're Julia's mom."

"Yes!" Despite my panic, I smiled. *Julia's mom.* As if we were talking about bringing a forgotten lunchbox to school. Another moment that would never be. "Maria. Maria Price."

"Yes, Maria. I'm Barbara."

"Hi, Barbara."

"Hi. Yes, Steve picked up Julia last night and drove her to the other hospital."

I marveled at how she made it sound like Steve was a dad in the carpool picking Julia up from soccer practice with her friends. It was shocking, yet comforting somehow. Her voice conveyed a dignity for my daughter I had not expected.

"So, the hospital hasn't called yet to let us know if they are ready for us to come back and pick her up. Have you talked to them?"

"Um. No," I replied sheepishly. "I'm sorry."

"Oh, no! Not at all. Don't be sorry, dear. I understand. You just want to know. I would guess that the hospital is not finished yet. Sometimes it just takes a while."

"Do you know how long it . . . usually takes?" I asked, desperation pinching my voice.

"Well, I sure wish I could tell you. Unfortunately, there are several factors that could influence how long it will take. Would you like me to have one of our directors call? I could have one of them call the hospital and when they find out, they can call you to set up an appointment to come and see her."

See Julia?

I opened my mouth wide, but I couldn't speak. I could not breathe at the thought of seeing my daughter again.

"Yes. Please. I would like that very much."

"All right, good. I will talk to one of them right away and have them call. It's late in the afternoon, so it probably will not be today. Okay?"

"Oh, okay."

"But I promise they will call as soon as they can."

I nodded, knowing she couldn't see me.

"Okay, dear. Please accept my condolences for the loss of Julia. I promise we will take good care of her."

The benevolence in her words struck me, their tenderness finding the most vulnerable part of me.

"Thank you so much," I managed, before hanging up, wrapping my arms around myself, and dissolving into a puddle on the hardwood floor.

Chapter 10

I stood barefoot, staring at my closet. What does one wear to an appointment to plan a funeral for one's daughter?

I closed my eyes and let my mind jump to period-piece films and novels where the characters dress in black for—how long? A month? Six months? I knew such societal customs were no longer relevant, at least not in twenty-first-century America, but I couldn't help wishing that they were. I wished there were a hat, an armband, or a piece of clothing that I could wear that would display on the outside all the emptiness and pain that I felt within. Something that would announce to the world that I was wholly consumed by grief and could not be bothered by the triviality of life. Maybe I needed a T-shirt that read: "Don't expect much from me. My daughter just died."

Looking again at my closet, I suddenly realized that my options were fewer than I remembered, as my postpartum body was not yet ready for pre-pregnancy clothes. I had a post-baby body with no baby. I closed my eyes, sucked in a deep breath, and settled on a pair of black maternity slacks and a flowy black cardigan.

"You look nice," Joe offered from the doorway, buttoning his shirt.

As I raised my eyes to meet his face, I realized how impossibly heavy they felt, swollen and weighed down by the emotion of the last two days.

"I know," he acknowledged gently, folding me into his embrace.

I stood like a statue in his arms, willing myself to return his hug, to wrap my arms around him, too. But my arms felt like they were encased in chains too heavy to lift. I realized I wasn't crying, and I wondered if perhaps all of my tears had dried up after the constant weeping of the past couple of days. As if on cue, however, more tears welled up and traveled down their familiar paths on my cheeks.

I stood up straight, realizing I was making wet splotches on Joe's clean shirt, remembering the mascara stain on his shirt the day we'd lost Julia. Was that just two days ago?

"I'm sorry," I sniffled, attempting to dry the spots by sweeping them with my fingers.

He gently held my hands in his, squeezing lightly. "It's okay." His unconvincing smile, the brokenness in his eyes, told me that he was talking about more than the wet spots on his shirt.

He tenderly bent his forehead to touch mine, communicating love and encouragement where words failed.

Finally, drawing my strength from his, I met his gaze and nodded, almost imperceptibly. I was ready to go.

As we pulled into the parking lot of the funeral home, we were greeted by lush gardens, brightly hued flowers, and a babbling stone fountain. All of this, I thought, must be an attempt to bring some peace to people suffering the loss of a loved one. A baby. A daughter.

I surveyed the path before me, the heavy oak doors with beautiful cut-glass windows.

She was in there. Julia was just beyond those doors. While my heart knew that seeing her there, in a funeral home, would only confirm what my mind still refused to believe—that she was dead—I was overcome by an urgency to get through those doors, to see my baby again, even if it meant seeing her in a casket.

My parents had joined us to lend support, and to offer advice. They had been through the process of making funeral arrangements for both sets of their parents, but not a child. Now they were here to help plan a funeral for their grandchild.

We walked into the pristinely kept foyer to be greeted by our funeral director. His presence was at once commanding and compassionate. He was a man of about fifty, his broad shoulders covered by a well-cut suit. The tanned skin peeking out from his crisp white shirt spoke of recent summer boat rides and barbecues. His salt-and-pepper hair seemed simultaneously meticulous and effortless in its styling, framing his face and kind blue eyes. A bit of a silver fox—not at all what I had expected from someone who worked in a funeral home.

"Mr. and Mrs. Price?" he asked. I had little doubt that my puffy eyes and cherry-red nose must have given me away as the bereaved mother.

"Yes," we confirmed, reaching out our hands to shake his.

"I'm Greg Carson. I'm the funeral director who has been taking care of your daughter." His handshake was warm and strong. "I am so sorry for your loss."

"Thank you," Joe replied, and I nodded, the words blocked in my throat.

We introduced my parents. Handshakes. More talking. I was actively trying to focus on his words, but they were getting lost in my desperate desire to see Julia. Where was she? What would she look like? Would we see her now, or have to wait? Could I stand to wait any longer?

"This way." With a slight bow of his head, Greg gestured toward one of the visitation rooms.

All of the air left the room. My mouth went dry as I surveyed the distance between us and the ornately carved oak doors. She was in there. Julia was in that room, waiting for me.

I swallowed hard and felt Joe's warm hand slip into mine. Tears were glistening in his eyes as he returned my gaze. A dip of his head silently conveyed his question: *Are you ready?*

Was I? What would I see when we entered that room? Laced along the edges of my anxiety was a nauseating, soul-gripping fear. What would she look like? We had held Julia for a couple of hours after her birth. Even then, we had worried about what the decomposition process would do to her precious body. We didn't even know exactly when she had passed, how long she had been dead inside me. Later that night, when she was taken from us, she was delivered to a different hospital for an autopsy, and then brought here.

It had been approximately thirty-six hours since we had last seen her, since we had last held our baby. What had the autopsy and passage of time done to the beautiful face that had imprinted itself on my heart? I wanted to share that face with the world, the face that had so unequivocally won my broken heart. But what should I expect? The only people I had seen in caskets had been adults, almost all of them either old, or sick. I had never seen a baby lying at rest before. How could I prepare myself to see *our* baby like that?

Our baby. My baby. Julia.

I recalled the biblical story of Lazarus, raised by Jesus, even after three days in the tomb. There was no doubt in my mind that if He could bring Lazarus back to life then, He could do the same for Julia now. But *would* He?

I tried to move gracefully, but it was all I could do not to sprint into the room where my daughter was. It was a sizable space, serenely decorated, filled with plush accommodations, designed for comforting the bereaved. Then, it all seemed to fall away as my eyes locked on the tiny white casket at the other end of the room.

I tried to draw in a deep breath but only managed a shallow gasp before making my way to where she was. I think I must have floated to her, my little girl. In the instant that my eyes fastened on Julia, every fear my mind had constructed instantly dissolved into dust. She was beautiful—just as gorgeous as I had remembered.

Pure maternal love and longing flooded up from the deepest part of me, past the dam in my throat, overflowing from my eyes in unrestrained emotion. I stood there, staring, drinking her in. Her hair was silky and thick, dark as the night she was born. Her plump cheeks, the tiny dimple in her chin, her eyes just closed . . . sleeping? No. Slowly, slowly, reality began to creep in, dismantling my carefully constructed walls of denial.

My body was fighting against me. I was engulfed by intense heat. My heart thudded in my chest, but my lungs would not expand to bring in oxygen. My face, my mouth contorted in agony with silent screams as my voice fought in vain to escape the heavy, muddy gravel that filled my throat. I wanted to close my eyes, but how could I? How could I block out one of only a handful of opportunities I had left to see my baby girl? I had only a few chances left to see her before they closed the casket and took her away from me forever. So I forced them to stay open, staring in a wide-eyed blend of adoration for my precious newborn daughter, and horror that she was already gone.

I felt Joe's arms envelop me. This time, however, when I tore my gaze away from Julia to look up at him, the anguish in his expression told me that this embrace was as much for his own comfort as for mine. We stood as one, convulsing in heavy sobs, heartbroken to be so close to our little girl, yet still a world away.

For several minutes, we remained in that world of our own. We turned to her, then back to each other, then back, again and again, attempting to make sense of what we were seeing. We would almost regain our composure only to lose it as cruel, relentless reality staked its unwavering claim.

Finally, exhausted, we looked at my parents. Their faces mirrored the suffering in ours. They had been waiting, giving us time and space. But our wordless invitation was all they needed to move in and surround us, mixing their own grief with the cloud of heaviness that covered us.

After another minute or two we moved away, allowing my parents privacy to mourn the loss of their only granddaughter.

We turned to Greg, who had been waiting silently, patiently, a respectable distance away.

"Thank you," I managed, just above a whisper. The look on his face told me this was not the response he had been expecting. "Thank you for taking care of our daughter."

Greg bowed his head low and took a couple of beats before lifting it again to look us in the eyes. "It was my honor," he replied evenly.

I felt new tears stinging my eyes then. A kind man, but still a stranger, was taking care of my daughter. My newly born daughter. *I* should be taking care of her. In *our* home. Not a *funeral* home. Not like this.

Too soon, it was time to say good-bye to her again.

Joe and I returned to her side for one more moment with her.

"I can't do this," I whispered, and I truly didn't know if I could. What if I just took her? Surely I could pick her up, box and all, and bolt out of this room. Would they stop me? Would they call the police? Where would we go?

Hopelessly I pressed my thumbs against the pressure building in my sinuses and shook away thoughts of escape.

I looked into her perfect little face. Could I touch her? Was I allowed? I recalled having touched a grandparent in a casket years earlier. Grandparent, not a child. His chest had been hard as stone. I had never forgotten the shock. It was not the last memory I had wanted of him, and it was certainly not the last memory I wanted to have of Julia. I closed my eyes and remembered snuggling her in the hospital, as soft, pink, and pliable as a baby should be.

I drew in as deep a breath as I could manage and slowly placed my fingers on her tiny hand. I closed my eyes and exhaled. Her silky skin both relieved me and broke my heart. My baby girl.

Her feathery hair tickled my nose as I leaned down to kiss her forehead and whisper a tender, "Good-bye, baby. I love you so much," into her ear. "I'll be back—I promise," I said, and then I turned and walked away.

Chapter 11

We made our way through a hallway to an office to discuss how we would move forward with plans for Julia's services. Greg directed us to oversized, upholstered armchairs with soft cushioned seats and sturdy oak armrests. He filled gleaming crystal glasses with ice water, serving each of us before seating himself behind a large, polished desk.

Everything began to feel surreal. Reality seemed to give way to fantasy and sanity-preserving denial. *What is happening? Why are we here?* Joe's warm hand reaching for mine, his sad smile at my bewildered expression brought me back to the present, heartbreaking task at hand.

"Again, let me begin by expressing my sincere sympathy for your loss," Greg said. "No parents should ever have to bury their child. Our job, at this point, is to do what we can to make this very difficult process as easy for you as possible. You are young. No one ever expects something like this to happen. Accordingly, in cases of infant death, such as yours, we waive all service-based fees. That's just not something you should have to worry about."

Joe and I looked at each other, then to my parents. We sat back a bit in our chairs as Greg went on to explain the details of this unexpected gift of generosity.

"Perhaps, then," he went on, "you could share how we could serve you in terms of arrangements for Julia."

"Thank you so much. That is so kind. So generous," we all said, gratitude choking our voices.

For an instant, Greg's gaze fell to the desk in front of him. Then, looking back up, his brows came together, and he nodded. "We want you to know that we are here for you."

"I . . . we . . ." I tore at the soggy tissue in my hands. My words started out slowly, clumsily, then tumbled out in a heap. "I guess we just haven't ever done this before."

"Of course," Greg nodded empathetically.

"I just don't really know what is available?" It was more of a question than a statement.

"Of course," Greg repeated. He went on to detail some options and ask questions to guide our discussion.

Did we want a visitation, where friends and family could come and pay their respects?

Yes.

Did we want an open casket? Joe and I looked at each other. Having seen her face just now, we had no question.

Yes.

Did we want makeup on Julia's hands and face to help restore a more natural appearance? I closed my eyes, remembering the contrast between her face on Tuesday in the hospital and the slight discoloration we saw today.

Yes.

Did we have an outfit that we would like to dress her in? At the hospital we had been given gifts for bereaved families. In one tiny package was a handmade one-of-a-kind satin gown, adorned with lace, tiny beads, and delicate sequins, an *angel gown*, lovingly created from donated wedding dresses by volunteers from a local charity organization, founded by other parents who knew too well the pain of choosing funeral attire for their children.

Yes.

A funeral service? *Yes.*

On a different day than the visitation? *Yes.*

At the funeral home or at a church? *At our church.*

Cremation or burial?

Before we lost Julia, I had always, with more than a hint of swagger in my tone, insisted that I wanted to be cremated. Why keep my body? Wasn't it just a shell of who I was anyway?

"Burial." The word had come out of my mouth almost before I had finished thinking it. I wasn't sure if my mind had changed about my own final wishes, but I knew with certainty that I could not bear to do anything to her body.

The next obvious, albeit painful question was where? Where would we *bury* our little girl?

"There are subdivisions of each of the local cemeteries set aside for babies," Greg shared. "They call them *Babyland*, or something similar. The costs of these plots are covered by the cemeteries." I felt a knot form in my stomach. A whole section just for babies? One at each cemetery? How many parents have been in this position, having to make decisions about their own children's final resting places, for there to be a need for Babylands?

Greg shared the names and phone numbers of the local cemeteries. We decided that we would go and visit each one before making a decision. Was it better to bury her with other babies? We didn't have plots for ourselves. Should we purchase them now? How long would Julia lay buried, waiting for us to join her there? I couldn't stand the thought of her being all alone, surrounded by strangers.

"Another option," he continued, "is to bury her with a loved one. If you have a family member who has already passed on and you would like to bury Julia next to them, or between a couple, that is something that some people have done." I thought of my grandparents, my grandmother, Julia. Could she be buried with them? Greg explained that we would need a signed letter from my dad and each of my uncles agreeing to have the grave opened. If they would be willing, that would be an option we could pursue.

After more questions and careful planning, it was time to choose a casket. We turned to see at least a dozen dark wood podiums displaying caskets of varying colors and materials. Greg led us back behind the larger displays where a tiny white box stood in stark contrast to the giant ones. Instantly, heat rushed to my face. I opened my mouth but couldn't draw a breath. Giant, glittery snakes slithered through my field of vision as I heard my heart pumping the blood *whoosh, whoosh, whoosh* in my ears. My knees buckled. I was going down.

Before I realized what was happening, Joe's arms caught me and held me up.

"Maria!" my mom cried.

"Get her!" my dad commanded.

Greg instantly had a chair at my side and gently helped Joe get me settled into it.

"You all right?" Joe asked, squatting to my level to look into my eyes. "Come on, breathe with me."

My mom brought a water glass to my lips. "Drink, baby," she urged.

While I appreciated what she was doing, it made me think of my own daughter, the relationship we would never have, and I felt so robbed.

I looked up and stared at that little box. I couldn't help but think of the white Styrofoam coolers you see at picnics and baseball games. They wanted to put my *daughter* in there?

"We can take a break," Greg suggested.

"No," I insisted. "I'm sorry. I want to do this."

I could see everyone looking at each other, asking the questions no one wanted to say out loud. I looked meaningfully at Joe. He turned to Greg and gave a small nod of assent. Greg went on. Slowly, respectfully, he explained that the miniature casket before us was the one that they typically used for infants. It broke my heart that such a thing was even in production—that there was anything *typical* about baby loss.

He showed us a second, larger, yet still heart-wrenchingly small box with shiny chrome handle details on the sides. I liked this one much better. Greg explained that, based on Julia's size, we may need to use this option, rather than the smaller one.

Is this what we were doing now? Shopping for a casket for my baby?

Greg went on to ask if we had a blanket or anything that we wanted to put in the casket with Julia. I blinked. I had not thought of this.

"Some people," he continued, "choose to use the hospital blanket—"

"No," I interrupted him. "We will get one for her."

There was so little we could do for her now. We would not be paying for her college, or her wedding. We could do this one thing.

Greg smiled knowingly and nodded.

We settled the rest of the details. We would write an obituary, send a picture, gather clothes and a blanket for our baby's casket. We set up appointments to visit the various cemeteries. It was happening.

Over the course of my pregnancy, there were so many things I had imagined planning for her: big, elaborate birthday parties, playdates with friends, graduations, eventually, a wedding. But, never once in the nine months she grew inside of me did I ever consider planning a funeral for my baby girl. Despite our hopes. Despite our faith. It was real.

Chapter 12

The next few days were a blur of activity. We visited cemeteries. We saw the Babyland sections Greg had told us about, and they were even more disheartening than we had imagined. Mylar balloons soared in the wind. Hot Wheels cars, colorful pinwheels, and fuzzy teddy bears seemed so out of place on grave plots. Worse were the plots that were bare, just tiny headstones to mark the presence of tiny babies lying beneath. I wondered about their stories. My heart ached for these babies, for their families.

Ultimately, with the blessings of my dad and surviving uncles, Joe and I determined that the best final resting place for our daughter was between my grandfather and my grandmother, for whom she was named. My parents generously took care of the arrangements and I felt the smallest bit of peace in knowing that my daughter would be safe between two people who would have loved her as I did. I knew she would be their littlest *m'ija*.

My parents took turns with my brother and sister-in-law watching Joey over the next several days. Joey was thrilled about this arrangement, spending hours on end playing with his cousins and being indulged by his family, who were still reeling from the loss of their littlest member.

Prior to losing Julia, I had loved our bedtime routine—bath time, stories, songs, and sometimes falling asleep together in the cozy swivel armchair and ottoman in Joey's room. But after we came home, I just couldn't do it. Everything reminded me of Julia. I felt so cheated and angry. Only days before we had talked and sung to her. I couldn't stop thinking of how she should have been there in that rocking chair with us. I couldn't reconcile the fact that she never would.

So, Joe would race Joey up the stairs to distract him from recognizing that Mommy wasn't coming with them. I felt simultaneously guilty for deserting him and relieved to know he was being spared from my emotional turmoil that would have certainly frightened and perplexed him. Instead, I sat at the dining room table, writing an obituary for my daughter, or creating a slideshow from pregnancy photos and the Now I Lay Me Down to Sleep birth photography from that night at the hospital. Mostly, though, I just curled up on our couch, sobbing into the throw pillows, wishing desperately for the life we'd almost had.

Over the next couple of days we shopped for the perfect plush pink baby blanket to line our daughter's casket, and the only accessories Julia would ever wear. I had an "I Like Big Bows and I Cannot Lie" Pinterest board, with full intentions of adorning Julia's head with crowns of flowers, bows, and headbands of every variety. But for her funeral, we chose an elegant, creamy rose with pearls and delicate feathers fastened to a soft lace headband. We chose ivory tights, and burnished bronze shoes with just a hint of shimmer, both in newborn size, to be worn with her angel gown.

We visited a florist to choose arrangements. A spray of delicate pink roses, fern, and baby's breath with a satin "Daughter" ribbon from Joe and me, and a matching wreath with a bow and "Sister" ribbon from Joey. We chose music and set the order of her service with church staff. We purchased picture frames, display boxes, dress clothes, and new black leather shoes for Joey to wear to the visitation and funeral.

Through all the haze, there were also a million kindnesses. We arrived home one night, our arms full of packages, to find a dozen shopping bags filled with toiletries, kid-friendly snacks for Joey, extra-soft tissues, and other thoughtful gifts anonymously left on our screened-in back porch from a sweet friend who wanted no thanks or recognition, only to show her love and support.

My best friend, Addie, knowing that I would be entertaining company, came over and cleaned my house. My brother made programs for the funeral service. Meals and elaborate food trays poured in from family and friends, filling our refrigerator and countertops.

My eyes were a curious combination of red puffiness and large, dark rings. The constant crying brought on dehydration. My lips were perpetually chapped. The skin on my nose was fiery, flaky and cracked, stinging from the use of too many tissues. My mom went to a makeup counter and bought me expensive face lotion to help soothe it, but there was only so much it could do.

Joe's parents, sister, and nephew arrived from their home, hours away. I knew how much they had wanted to be with us since we had made that awful phone call earlier in the week. But my sister-in-law had had to work; my mother-in-law was blind, and my father-in-law, legally blind, unable to drive. It was a relief to see them walk through our back door. I watched Joe and his dad grip each other in a powerful, silent embrace. I thought about how strong Joe had been, constantly protecting me. But in this moment, it was painfully clear how much he needed support, too.

Having lost her vision as a child, my mother-in-law had overcome many obstacles to become a strong, successful woman, a mother, and a grandmother. She was always full of unflappable faith and fierce love for her family. I felt guilty for my lack of faith, for disappointing her, for losing her granddaughter. She reached for me and I melted into her, breathing in her sweet, citrusy scent, and communicating in tears what I could not say in words. Not in a rush, without a hint of judgment, she held me and stroked my hair, silently conveying her love, support, and heartbreak.

My body however, was not so kind. Milk came in, ready for a newborn to nurse. Since there was no baby to drink the milk, I was left to suffer through the painful engorgement. Each hug, intending to ease my suffering, also then, unintentionally, brought with it intense, shooting pain, an excruciating reminder of the baby I had lost.

In addition to the physical discomfort, there were also times, as we went about our errands to prepare for Julia's services, when another mother's baby would start to cry and my body would respond by unhelpfully leaking milky wet spots on my shirt, heaping visible embarrassment onto my invisible misery.

The doctor's and nurses' warnings in the hospital about being gentle with myself and considering carefully the idea of pumping milk to donate slowly began to make more sense once I returned home. I did not want the medications I was sometimes taking to help me sleep to taint the milk I was producing. And pumping every few hours served as a heartbreaking reminder that I should be nursing Julia, bonding with my own child at those times. Throughout the day, I would constantly find myself looking at a clock, imagining what Julia should be doing at that moment, nursing, napping, bathing, snuggling, only to blink back to the reality that we would never do any of those things. So I endured the agonizing process of weaning a baby who wasn't there.

It was thoroughly exhausting. It felt like we were constantly making phone calls, running here or there, searching, making choice after unbearable choice.

Yet, we were propelled by the knowledge that the work we were doing was for Julia, honoring her life and her place in our family. Persistent throughout was the illogical thought that if I just kept doing these tasks, we would get to the funeral, and that after that I would get to bring Julia home—that she would be alive and all of this just a cruel lie. My conscious mind, of course, knew this was a delusion, but the denial was tenacious. Each time I had to remind myself that Julia was, in fact, never coming home, it was like losing her all over again.

Chapter 13

It seemed at once like years and mere hours since we had lost Julia, when in reality, it had been five days. It was time for the visitation.

We arrived at the funeral home early in the afternoon for the private viewing with our family. Barbara, the kind woman from the phone, greeted us at the door. I recognized her by her name on the gold badge she wore. Dove-gray curls framed a face that was as kind as her voice had been. We shook hands, but that didn't seem like enough, and we moved in for a hug.

"Thank you," I whispered, and I felt her nod against my cheek.

When we stepped back, Greg had joined us, and was shaking Joe's hand. It felt like I was in a dream, hazy around the edges, as my parents took Joey, and Greg led Joe and me into the room to see Julia again. The space was now full of blooming floral arrangements, verdant sympathy plants, and beautiful angel statues. And, right in the middle, was Julia. She was sweetly lying in the larger, more ornate casket, delicately laid with the rosy baby blanket. We approached her carefully, so as not to disturb her precious sleep.

She was stunning. Her lace headband with the satin rose and feathers topped masses of ebony hair, framing her angelic face. I fingered the delicate gown, all lace, satin, beads, and sequins, and shook away thoughts of a never-to-be wedding day. Her soft-soled bronze leather shoes peeked out from her dress with just a hint of shine. My baby, just as pink and perfect as the night she was born.

I looked up at Joe and we exchanged sad but approving nods. Together, we turned to Greg. My throat thick with gratitude, I whispered, "Thank you. She looks perfect."

Greg brought a hand up to cover his heart as he released a deeply held breath, in an uncharacteristic, albeit momentary, lapse of self-control. "I am so glad you are happy. I wanted to do right by her."

Touched by his sincerity, we nodded thanks and approval. "She is perfect," I repeated, and turned back to her. I could not stop staring. She was beyond lovely; she was captivating. She truly looked like she was sleeping. How was it possible that she would never wake up? How would we close the casket and put this sleeping beauty in the ground?

I hugged my arms against my chest, fighting the maternal instinct to pick her up and hold her in my arms. I knew there was an unwritten rule forbidding it. I knew even if I did hold her, the embalming process would ensure that she would not feel the same as she had the night she was born. But she was my *baby*. I had delivered her from my body just days ago. She was not yet in the ground, yet there was already a deep chasm dividing us.

If I couldn't hold her, I wanted to stay there with her for the remaining hours until they put her in the ground. I couldn't escape the invisible clock, its steady hand ticking away each moment we had together. Eventually, reluctantly, we tore ourselves away to allow the rest of our family time alone with her before we opened the door to our visitors.

I watched my brother's three sons, my nephews, their innocence trickling away as they said hello and good-bye to their littlest cousin. I watched as our teenage nephew comforted his mom, Joe's sister, normally witty and sarcastic, as her shoulders shook in uncontrollable sobs, standing at Julia's tiny casket. I couldn't watch any more.

Joe and I walked around three different rooms, perusing the dozens of floral arrangements, plants, and gifts, sent by family, friends, and colleagues. Joe held my hand as we touched each card, grateful for the kindness of each sender, stunned by the love that was being poured out on us.

When it was time to open the doors, we took our places, in a line just to the left of Julia's casket.

"You make sure you sit down," urged my dad. He had been so concerned since the first night in the hospital and the other day in the funeral home office. But I was fine standing. I wanted to greet each person, and to be as close to Julia as I could get. I wanted to show them how perfect she was, how proud we were of her.

A moment later, the carved oak doors opened and the faces of our family and friends filed in toward us.

"I am so sorry for your loss."
"She is so beautiful."
"I love her name."
"I can't imagine what you are going through."

For three hours, they kept coming.

"God has a plan."

"You are in our prayers."

"We'll be thinking of you."

"Call if you need anything."

"God just needed another angel."

"Call me anytime."

"You will see her again someday."

We were surrounded by love and heartfelt sympathy. We were astounded by the show of support for us, for our baby girl. Some of the visitors were people we hadn't seen in years. Some, like Joe's best friend, Dan, and his wife, Meghan, had traveled for hours to be with us only for a short time, having to turn around and make the hours-long trip back home for work the next morning.

"When did you get here?" I asked my eyes wide with incredulity. He pulled me into a deep hug, pressing my cheek against the starchiness of his plaid dress shirt.

"Just a while ago," he smiled, as if they had only traveled across town.

Dan was a big guy with a giant heart. Joe and I always joked that he had the beard of a lumberjack and the rosy cheeks and mischievous twinkling eyes of a little boy.

"Where are you staying? How long?"

"Oh no, we're leaving from here. We've both got work in the morning." He said it so casually. I looked to Meghan.

"We love you guys," she answered simply. Her eyes held tears behind her glasses, and I remembered the little boy that they had lost years before. I had felt such empathy for them then, but now, it was like waking up to a new level of understanding.

I watched as Joe hugged Dan, their faces buried in each other's shoulders, white streaks on his red fingers indicating the intensity of their embrace. I considered again how many people were checking on me, asking how *I* was doing, but Joe had lost his little girl, too.

"Thank you so much for coming," I said, hugging Meghan. "He needed this."

"We're only a phone call away. Joe was there for us. We just wish there was more we could do."

The majority of those who came through the line were crying by the time they reached us. They hugged us, holding us tight. A colleague, a kind man, always professional, who greeted us warmly, then stood, looking at Julia for several quiet moments, with an expression I couldn't quite read. His Adam's apple bobbed slightly and the tiniest glimmers appeared in the corners of his eyes. Watching him watch her, I truly understood what it meant to *pay respects* to someone, and knew I would never forget this kindness.

Another friend came through, the same friend who had left the grocery blitz on our back porch a few nights before. She was sobbing, almost uncontrollably. "You guys didn't deserve this. I am so sorry." I was taken aback, and yet felt so understood, so *seen* by her empathy. We hugged each other fiercely, neither of us having the words to express how we truly felt.

I was pleased to see a new friend, one whom I had recently made in a new teaching position at work, standing in the line. But as she approached, I could see her resolve begin to crumble. She hugged me briefly, but apologized with big hiccupping sobs. "I'm so . . . sorry . . . I have to—I have to go . . . I just can't do this."

I watched her walk away in wonder. She had always seemed so in control, almost stoic. What exactly was it about this situation that created such a dynamic change in her? Was it the sight of Julia lying at rest? Joe and I standing beside her? Had she experienced a loss like ours? Or was it simply the painful recognition that tragedies like this were a reality—that babies, long-awaited, much-loved babies—actually died?

"Do you need to take a break?" Joe whispered in my ear.

I shook my head slightly and moved on to the next person in line.

Another friend approached, one whom I had met when I had done some volunteer work a couple of years previously. She expressed her condolences and then said how great this was, that she hadn't ever been to a visitation for a *stillborn* baby before. Were we going to do a funeral, too?

It felt like I was standing still, but the room began to rotate. I understood what she meant. She was trying to commend us for ignoring the societal constructs that prevented other people from memorializing their babies, even if they were *only stillborn*. Even though I understood her intent, the comment still stung. Julia was my baby. We'd had an exam. We'd had an early induction appointment. She was scheduled to be delivered. But it was too late. We had discovered that she was gone fewer than forty-eight hours before that appointment. If we had made it to the appointment, if she had been induced, and *then* died—*then* it would have been acceptable? It would have been expected that we would arrange services to mourn her loss?

My mom brought me a glass of water, asking, "When was the last time you ate anything?"

"Please, baby, sit down," my dad pleaded.

I shook my head. I was fine.

I thought of Sally Field as M'Lynn in *Steel Magnolias*. "I'm fine, I'm fine, I'm fine! I can jog all the way to Texas and back, but my daughter can't . . ."

"I'm fine," I said evenly, taking the glass. "Thank you, but I'm okay. I want to keep going." I was afraid that if I sat down, people would come to see me and maybe overlook Julia. I needed them to see her.

"Mommy!" Joey's exuberant toddler voice came cutting through my thoughts as he ran past the line toward me, arms wide open with expectation.

"Hi, buddy!" I exclaimed, in spite of myself, picking him up and holding him close. Chuckles and appreciative notes rose up from the crowd, everyone grateful for a break in the tension, an injection of life into our focus on death.

I learned later that it was a setup. Joey had been playing with friends in the playroom next door, but was sent in by my family, with the intention of getting me to sit down for the first time in a couple of hours of standing. Whatever the reason, I found immeasurable comfort in his wide, toothy smile, the deep dimples he'd inherited from Joe, the dark brown eyes he'd gotten from me, sparkling with life.

Pulling his sturdy toddler frame onto my lap to snuggle, I nestled my nose into his thick hair, still a warm butterscotch from the hours spent playing in the sunshine during the recent summer. I breathed in his scent, a mixture of sweet baby shampoo and a hint of salty little boy sweat, and tried to blink away the ever-present thought that I would never do this with Julia.

The sympathies continued for another hour, like a merry-go-round of familiar faces, some fallen in pity, others twisted in grief.

"She's *so* pretty. I love her bow!"

The spirited voice of the five-year-old daughter of our friends seemed so incongruous with our mournful surroundings.

"Thank you," I beamed, knowing that the words of this child were the honest truth.

"Why are her fingernails so purply?" she continued.

Silence. Breathless, I worked to keep my voice calm as I attempted to come up with a response that would satisfy her curiosity without scaring her—without scarring me.

"I don't really know," I admitted with a weak smile.

She nodded, the understanding of a much older child coming through in her eyes. "She's still really pretty, though."

I observed her glossy black hair and her eyes, dark as espresso beans, full of energy and life. Her beautiful dress was as twirly and sequined as a little girl's wardrobe should be. *Should be.* I thought of my little girl, with her thick, wavy tresses, all of the carefully chosen outfits lining her closet, never to be worn, and closed my eyes.

"Thank you, sweetheart," I replied, with a smile that reached my eyes but not quite my heart.

Shortly afterward, my seventy-five-year-old great-aunt and cousin came back after leaving the funeral home to bring me a bottle of orange juice and a can of V8, purchased from a nearby convenience store, and brought back to "keep my strength up."

I smiled as I thanked them for these gifts, grateful for their thoughtfulness, guilty that I had inspired this level of concern. Once again, I was astonished by the compassion that seemed to surround us.

It came down to this: Even in the midst of the greatest tragedy of our lives, there was love—unconditional, unwavering, unquestioning love.

Chapter 14

As we received those at the end of the line, the giant grandfather clock in the foyer struck five, and it was as if the spell had broken. It was time to leave again. Time to say good-bye again.

Our guests filtered out slowly. Good-byes were accompanied by tight hugs and advice to call if we needed anything. We briefly confirmed plans for setting up the funeral the following morning with Greg and his associates. Our parents, siblings, and their children were heading to our house to share another meal, lovingly provided by friends. Joe took Joey out to get him buckled into his car seat.

Finally, we were alone again. I stood and stared at Julia, lying in angelic sleep. *One more day.* The thought pulsed through my head like a message scrolling on a marquee. I had one more day before they would close this tiny box and put my daughter in the ground.

How had the last week gone so quickly? How were we at this place in our story already? As excruciating as it was to live through the first time, my heart longed to go back to that first day. Even if I couldn't change anything, I would have given anything just to hold her again, to kiss her sweet cheeks. Slowly, gingerly, I lifted my hand to touch her petite fingers. My breath caught at the satiny smoothness of her skin, as creamy and delicate as the roses that surrounded her.

"I love you," I whispered. "I love you so, so much, baby girl. I'm so, so sorry. I'm sorry I couldn't save you, that I didn't protect you." My tears, having started as steady streams, were now rushing as violent torrents down my cheeks. "I don't want to let you go. I'm sorry I have to let them take you away.

"You will always be mine. I will always be yours. I am so proud to be your mama, and that will never, never change. I'm so sorry it has to be this way. I already know I will miss you every moment of my life. I'll carry you right here in my heart until I can carry you again in Heaven. And then, sweet Julia, I promise I will hold you, and kiss you, and never, never, never let you go again."

I paused to look up at the ceiling and draw in a deep breath before returning my gaze to her again. I rubbed soft circles into the inside of her palm, wishing desperately for more time.

"Mommy has to go now. I have to go home. I so wish I could take you with me. But I'll be back. I'll see you tomorrow, I promise. I love you, baby." I brought my fingers up to my lips for a final, tender kiss, and brought it down slowly to rest on her perfect little mouth. "I always, always will."

I flinched, startled by a quiet sniff behind me. I turned to see Car standing behind me with tears flowing down her face. She tilted her head slightly and reached her arms out toward me. I fell into her, sobbing into the sheer fabric of her blouse, the silkiness of her long hair.

"I'm so sorry," she whispered, her voice brittle with emotion. "It's just so unfair. We love her, too, and we love you. We will always remember her and keep her in our hearts."

We stood that way, bound to each other, desperately wishing for a different ending to this story that should be only just beginning. Car had been married to my brother for the past ten years and had three beautiful boys. I had come to love her as a sister, and I knew how excited she was to have a baby niece to love and dress and do all the girly things. We all loved Julia. We all grieved her and the life we should have had together.

As the flood of emotion began to gradually recede, we slowly stepped back. We shared a simultaneous final glance at Julia before Car squeezed my hand gently.

"Are you ready?" she asked. Her scrunched eyebrows and pursed lips told me she knew how unfair the question was.

I would never be ready. I wanted to stay there with her. How could I just leave my child in the hands of strangers *again?* How could I walk away knowing that the next time I'd see her would be the *last* time?

I felt bile rise up in my throat with the realization that even before they put her in the ground, even in that moment, we were not truly together. I could not stay there with her, and she could not come home with me. We would never be truly together in this life. I wanted to keep her, but she was already gone.

"This is not okay," I announced. "I am not okay with this."

"I know," she nodded. "It's not."

After one more longing look back at my baby, I nodded my head slowly and turned and walked out the door.

Chapter 15

When we arrived home, the house was already busy, family members pitching in to get dinner served. Joey was playing with his cousins. The adults pushed through the heavy fog pressing down on us to "act normal." This meant background music and small talk about everything except the heartache that had brought us all together.

"Eat something," my mom urged, and I could hear the concern in her tone.

"I did."

"No. You moved the food around on your plate," she continued gingerly. She reached over and placed her hand on mine, but I couldn't look at her, see the worry lines I knew were crinkling her forehead. I peeked down the long dining room table and saw the others, pretending not to hear.

But how could I eat? *Julia should be here*, I kept thinking. Here we were, surrounded by our loved ones. A family gathering, incomplete. Worse, I knew it would always be this way. We would never be all together again, I realized. And any food that had made it to my stomach was already begging to come back up.

A little while later, I stood in the kitchen, making conversation, when Joey, apparently inspired by the music playing, tipped his head back, bent his knees into a half squat, his little bottom sticking out, and swung his hips back and forth to the rhythm. It was hilarious; these were moves I didn't know he had. Before I could stop myself, a laugh escaped past my lips. My hand flew to my mouth. I felt my eyes widen and the air suddenly left the room.

What was I doing? What kind of mother laughs only hours after seeing her daughter lying in a casket, not even yet in the ground?

I was disgusted with myself and wanted desperately to run and hide, but I couldn't risk upsetting Joey, or any of the others who were already so worried about me. So instead, I swallowed the lump in my throat, gritted my teeth, anchored myself to the refrigerator door, and forced myself to stay.

Later that night, however, in the privacy of my bedroom, I allowed myself to cry hot, repentant tears for my transgression. I crossed my arms over my still painfully engorged chest and dug sharp fingernails deep into the flesh of my upper arms. I rocked myself back and forth and wished for Julia, begged for her. I pleaded to wake up to find her wiggling inside me, and that all of this was just some horrific nightmare. But as quickly as those requests went up, they seemed to shatter against the ceiling, sending shards of broken dreams crashing down around me again. God hadn't listened before, I reasoned. Why should He listen now? This nightmare was real.

I jumped at the sound of the door opening behind me. As if caught in a criminal act, I inhaled sharply and brought my hands up to wipe the tears away. I turned to see Joe stepping in, clicking the door closed behind him.

I exhaled the breath I had been holding in a series of staggered sighs. I closed my eyes and made room for him to sit beside me.

"Hey," he began softly, his voice tinged with apprehension.

"Hey," I returned, rubbing my hands against my legs to dry the tears.

"You did great today," he began, cautiously sitting down beside me.

"Yeah," I said, with a bit more sarcasm than was necessary.

"You did." He moved closer then, pulling me closer, too. "I know it was . . . incredibly difficult. The most difficult thing we will ever do. But we did it. We got through it."

"But now she's . . . Our time with her . . . We only have one more day," I protested. "One more day! It wasn't supposed to be this way!"

"I know," he agreed, and the sadness in his voice propelled me onward.

"And then we'll never see her again!"

"We will see her again," he said quietly.

My head swiveled toward him, my eyes flashing angrily. "You know what I mean. She'll be gone."

"I know what you mean," he continued with caution, knowing he was on dangerous ground. "But, Maria, she's . . . she's already gone. She's not going to be any farther away than she is right now."

"How can you *say* that?" I cried, accusation lining my tone.

"Baby, it's true. You miss her, and I miss her, too. I wish more than *anything* that I could change what happened and bring her back here. But . . . I can't."

His voice was breaking, his lower lip trembling.

I looked into his face and saw the tears rolling down his cheeks, and I believed him. He was so full of faith, and so logical. Just like in his work with technology, $a+b=c$. I admired that quality, and wished I could be more like him.

"But she's safe," he said. "She's happy. And we will be together with her again . . . someday."

I felt my body tense at this last statement. Walls of indignation, plastered thick with anger, went up in my heart. I knew the target for my fury was not really Joe. It was God. I didn't understand. I knew that bad things happened to good people, and good things happened to bad people, but *this?* Not that we were perfect, but hadn't we been through enough?

We had fought so hard to start a family. I had wondered, at times, how my marriage would survive it, but it had miraculously deepened to a new level of trust and understanding. And I thought it had done the same for my faith, but at this moment, I couldn't feel God. I felt abandoned by Him. I had never once doubted that He could have prevented Julia's death or brought her back to life. But He didn't do either of those things. And I just couldn't accept that.

"Well," I replied, lifting my chin in defiance, "that's just not good enough for me."

Chapter 16

I awoke the next morning in a panic. More than an hour remained before my alarm would go off, but I knew I would never get back to sleep. I buzzed around the house in a frenzy. Today is the day. Today is the last day. I could feel the adrenaline coursing through me like a freight train. Against my better judgment, I drank a cup of coffee, knowing it would only heighten my anxiety. I had to get everything done.

Greg was transporting Julia to the church for the funeral. I wanted the services to be beautiful, perfect, for her. I had to get there to see her. I wanted to spend as much of our few remaining moments together as possible. I raced around the house. Each minute away from her felt like a wasted moment in time that we could never get back.

Finally, we were dressed and ready to go. Joey looked so dapper in his toddler-sized herringbone pants and vest combination, his little button-down shirt freshly pressed. Joe was in his black suit, his tie in a perfect Windsor knot. I wore a simple black lace dress. Standing at my shoe racks, my fingers passed over the sensible black pumps, and chose instead the metallic fuchsia heels. *For Julia*, I thought. Walking out of my closet, my mind wandered to hers, all of those beautiful dresses. How many times had I planned family outfits, each piece perfectly chosen to complement the others for holidays and family portraits? In all of my imaginings, however, I'd never dreamed I would be choosing our outfits for her funeral.

"Ready?" Joe's voice startled me out of my thoughts, back into the moment. I pursed my lips together, and, after a deep breath, nodded my agreement and closed the closet door.

As we drove through town to the church, I was once again struck by all of the people going about their lives as if everything were normal. The sun was shining. Scenes were whizzing past, people chatting in coffee-shop windows, cars pulling into grocery store parking lots. *Didn't they know?* It was bizarre to watch a world still in motion all around me when mine had stopped so completely.

I felt my pulse quicken and my throat constrict as we moved up the small incline to the church parking lot. It felt like we were moving in slow motion, like we were running, but through thick, knee-deep mud. I needed to get inside, needed to see her.

When we entered the foyer, we were greeted by the familiar faces and warm hugs of friends who had become like family to us. Aromas of lunch preparations were already wafting in from the kitchen. Everyone wanted to help, and I was reminded, again, of how Julia's loss had affected so many. Over the past several months, they had celebrated and excitedly anticipated her arrival with us, but now it was time to mourn.

We discussed the last-minute details of the service with church officials. Friends came alongside to help us, to take care of Joey, and to make sure the music, the slideshow, the flowers, the pictures, and the shadow box that displayed her coming-home outfit were ready.

Then, at last, it was time. Time to see my baby.

My heart fluttered in nervous anticipation as Greg led us down a hallway to a private room to see her. *Time is running out. This is the last time you will ever see her face again.* The door opened. It was the nursery, the room where I had planned to rock her and feed her when she was too fussy to sit or sleep quietly during church services. Everything went swirly for a moment, until I saw her. There, in the corner, was my precious, sleeping Julia.

She seemed somehow even more beautiful than she had yesterday. A sharp intake of breath, and I was at her side. I wanted desperately to pick her up. I forced my arms around myself, hugging tightly to keep from reaching for her. *How could she be so close, yet so impossibly far away?*

I felt Joe's arm reach around me. I hadn't even noticed him there by my side. I was so lost in a world of my own imagining. Denial played games, suspending my mind and heart above the truth, only to drop them again, violently crashing them back into reality.

See, she's just sleeping. No. She's gone.
She will wake up! She is never waking up.
What is happening? Julia is dead.

My heart couldn't make sense of it. It wasn't right. Just one week ago, we had heard her heartbeat, felt her squirm, watched her move on an ultrasound screen. How were we standing here, days later, staring at her again, now unmoving? Now *still?*

Chapter 17

After Joe and I had had some time alone with Julia, he went out to get Joey from the adjacent toddler room, where he had been playing with toys and waiting with the rest of our family. I tried to prepare myself for having the two of them together, both of my babies. We had introduced Joey to Julia the day before, at the visitation, but I knew he hadn't understood what words failed to explain, especially in language that a toddler could comprehend.

"Mommy!" His voice was so full of vitality and enthusiasm. I turned from Julia to see his delighted smile, those sweet dimples at each end of it. His arms reached for me, and I reached back.

"Are you sure?" Joe looked at me warily, questioning my physical, if not emotional, strength to hold our son. I could not be offended. I knew I was a mess. I'd been shaky and weak, but I couldn't turn him away, and my heart needed him.

Joey almost jumped from Joe's arms to mine.

"Careful," Joe warned, and I wasn't sure if he was talking to Joey or to me.

"Mommy!" Joey repeated with as much earnest excitement as he had used the first time.

"Hi, sweetheart," I said, adjusting him on my hip. I was actively trying to keep my voice as even as possible, though even I could hear the wobble of my barely suppressed emotion. Joey didn't seem to notice, though, and only snuggled up closer to me. I let my kiss linger on his forehead as I closed my eyes, acquiescing to the tears that would not be contained.

"Mommy?" he asked, sitting up and furrowing his little brow at the sadness he saw in my face.

"Hey, buddy." I attempted a smile, but the look on his face told me he wasn't convinced.

"Mommy sad," he said, frowning, and reached out to touch the tears streaming down my face. Joe and I exchanged meaningful glances; this was going to be harder than we had expected it to be. I drew in an unstable breath, then let it back out, bringing my forehead to rest against Joey's tiny brow as I summoned my strength. Then, with a confidence I didn't feel, I straightened my back and looked directly into his rich brown eyes, pointing to where Julia was lying.

"Joey, who's this?" I asked, attempting to keep my voice light. "Who is this?"

"Baby," he said, his smile returning at the sight of her. Joe and I eyed each other again, neither of us really having any idea how to proceed.

"Yes. Baby." I affirmed. "Baby Sister." At the word *sister* his face perked up. He looked from me to Joe, then back to me. We had spent a lot of time over the last nine months trying to prepare him for the birth of his baby sister. We had read books and sung to Baby Sister. He'd rested his head on my tummy to feel her kicks, and given Julia baby-belly kisses. Of course, in all our preparations, we had never thought to prepare him for the *stillbirth* of his baby sister.

"Baby Sister," he repeated, quieter now, matching our tone, but still smiling.

"Yes, Baby Sister. Good job, buddy," Joe affirmed.

"Yes. Baby Sister," I repeated. Then, after a brief pause, "Baby Julia."

"Baby Julia," Joey imitated proudly. Joe and I closed our eyes and opened them again, smiling through the tears.

"Yes, buddy. That's right. Baby Julia," I told him, bouncing him lightly on my hip.

"Baby sleeping?" he asked, his head cocked to one side.

Silence.

Joe and I looked at each other helplessly. It was like being whacked in the stomach with a baseball bat. All of the air was forced out of me, and I couldn't get it back. Joe took Joey from me and walked to the window while I slumped into a nearby chair and rested my face in my hands. All my focus shifted to stifling my sobs to avoid traumatizing my son with the grief I felt for my daughter.

Yes, she was sleeping. Born asleep. An eternal sleep. But how did we explain that to him? How could we help him comprehend what we could not? At one and a half, it was hard to know exactly what he understood. We knew that eventually he would have questions about what happened to his baby sister, but it seemed, thankfully, that we were not at that stage yet.

I was grateful to spare him the pain the rest of us were feeling at having lost Julia. But my heart was heavy with questions. *Would he ever know her? Miss her? Love her? Would he grow up knowing that he had a baby sister? When he went to school and his teacher asked him if he had any brothers or sisters, would he say her name?*

I squeezed my eyes shut and tried to focus on the present. My time with Julia, the precious little time I had with both of my babies in the same room, was running out. I could feel the fuse of my anger burn shorter with each *tick, tick, tick* of the clock on the wall behind me, mercilessly marching forward, indifferent to my suffering. *It wasn't right. It wasn't fair.*

I forced a sharp, deep breath. I wasn't wasting my time on this. I could be angry later. I needed to be with Julia now.

I got up and smoothed my hands along the front of my dress and stood in front of my sweet girl. She truly did look like she was just sleeping, not *dead.*

"I love you, baby girl. I love you, Julia," I told her, my voice strangled high into my throat by emotion and all the words left unsaid. I felt Joe and Joey come to stand by my side. We all looked down at her, the missing piece to our family, now irretrievably lost.

Closing my eyes, I forced a sad smile and reached again for Joey. Snuggling him in my arms, I began to softly sing the song we had sung to Julia each night for the last nine months, knowing Joe would join in with me, and Joey would flash his proud big brother smile as he swayed along with the music.

Please, don't let them take our Sunshine away.

Chapter 18

When our families came in, I stayed close by and watched each of them say their last good-byes to Julia. Some cried quiet tears, some let out explosive, wailing sobs. Viscerally, I felt each one.

I watched as my mother-in-law, who is completely blind, took her first look at Julia. Greg had warned us that the makeup on Julia's hands and face would be extremely sensitive to touch and would easily transfer to Julia's ivory dress. So Joe's mom had waited patiently until now to "see" her granddaughter. She gently traced Julia's angel gown with its delicate lace and intricate beadwork. Her hands moved lightly but judiciously over Julia's face, her hair, her little hands, seeing for herself both the family resemblances and the beauty that belonged to Julia alone.

Before long, it was time. The church was full of mourners. It was time to start the service.

Our family filed into the hallway, preparing for the procession, and Joe and I were alone with Julia again. Greg waited patiently in the corner, giving us time to say our final good-byes. But how could we do it? Greg had told us that once her casket was sealed, it could not be reopened.

I stood before her, completely speechless, a lifetime of words jumbled up in a tight knot within my throat. In that moment, I wasn't even crying. For the first time in a week without her, my eyes were dry.

I felt the pressure of the ticking clock hanging on the wall beside us, but what could I say to my baby, knowing this was the last time I would see her face in this life? What could I do? I was breathless, panicked, and helpless to stop it from happening.

"I'm so sorry, Julia. I'm so sorry, baby. I just don't know how to say good-bye to you. I don't think I can.

"I know that you are safe, that you are happy in Heaven, that you will never feel this kind of broken heart. I'm glad for that. I just don't understand why it has to be this way. Maybe you can explain it to me when I get there. I miss you so much already. I don't know how to live a whole lifetime without you here.

"Even if. Even if I could not change anything about that day, Julia, you need to know I would do it all over again, just to hold you. Just to hold you one more time. I loved you from the very beginning. I always will. Even now. I love you still.

"I promise you that you will never be forgotten. We will remember you. We will say your name. We will love you with every breath we take, until we take our last, and then . . . and then, sweet girl, we will be together again. And I will hold you and never, ever let you go."

Feeling Joe's hand on my back, I lost all my resolve. I gripped the casket with white-knuckled intensity. My body, my maternal instinct just could not let her go. Sobbing. Heaving. Panicking. Gasping for air, I desperately tried to memorize our last few moments together. It was not enough. It could never be enough.

With a last kiss on her forehead and a final "I love you," I turned and collapsed into Joe. He surrounded me, drew me close enough to block out everything else as he carried me away. The door behind us closed, signaling to my brain that it was actually happening, the moment I had been dreading. As Julia was being sealed into her casket an impenetrable wall was erected between us. The world I had hoped for was gone; I was now forever living in a world without my daughter.

I tried to scream, to cry, but when I opened my mouth, only silent, inexplicable anguish came out. My whole body was on fire, suffocating, and Julia was my oxygen. In that moment, if I could not save her, I wished I could go with her. I was already dead. I wished that they would bury me, too.

I was digging, digging, digging my forehead into Joe's shoulder, convulsing in silent, tormented sobs. A lifetime of never-to-be memories rushed past me, just out of reach.

The next moments were like coming out of a dream. I felt the arms of my family members around me, stroking my hair. Slowly, shock moved in like a thick, dense fog, my mind's feeble attempt at self-preservation. Denial and numbness clouded my vision, reality fading in and out. My head and limbs felt impossibly heavy.

I flinched as Greg opened the door for my brother, Anthony, and two nephews, Josiah and Xavier, aged seven and nine, Julia's pallbearers, to come alongside her casket. I watched, breathlessly, as they walked past us in their crisp dress shirts with dark vests and ties. They looked so grown-up, as if this experience had aged them somehow, stealing bits of their innocence. They walked straight-backed and with visible nervous tension, vigilantly carrying that little white box to the front of the processional line. The silver details on the sides glinted in the sunlight that poured through the glass entryway. I was grateful that we had been able to use the larger-sized casket with those elegant details. The thought sickened me. I was *grateful* that my baby was big enough to need an upgraded box. It looked like a treasure box, and it was indeed carrying our precious treasure.

When the doors to the sanctuary opened, Joe and I walked arm in arm down the long center aisle of the church. It was the church where I had grown up, where Joey was now growing up. This aisle was the one I had walked the day I had married Joe. I watched as my nephews carefully set Julia's casket on the podium at the front of the church. She would not walk this or any other aisle as a bride. Joe and I sat where my parents had sat at our wedding; we would never sit here for hers.

I sat with my eyes trained on Julia's casket as the pastor read the obituary we had written for her.

"Julia Rachel Price, infant daughter of Joseph and Maria Price, passed away unexpectedly prior to her birth on October 11, 2016." Had it really been only less than a week ago? Six days since our lives had so completely changed? In that moment, it had felt like a lifetime since I had sat in that sterile triage room, an unimaginable distance from the night when we had last held her.

"Although Julia was with us for only a short while, and was born asleep, she brought much joy to her family and friends. We expected her arrival with great delight and anticipation, and mourn her loss with the deepest of sorrows. We cherish the brief moments that we held her in our arms, and will forever hold her close in our hearts." Nine months. One night. These were cruelly short snippets of time to carry a child we would love for the rest of our lives.

The lights dimmed and morning sunlight seemed to pour through brilliantly colored segments of the giant stained-glass window at the front of the room. We shifted slightly in our seats to view the remembrance video we had made. Happy photos and videos of our pregnancy announcement, gender reveal, and my ever-expanding baby belly filled the screen, only to give way to the exquisite black-and-white photography captured by Kelcy that night at the hospital. I caught my breath as Julia's beautiful face filled the screen. Candid shots of our family grappling with the tragedy were integrated with expertly posed shots of Julia's bath, her hands, her feet, and again, her precious face.

I felt a tremor in my arm and had to look to see that it was not me, but Joe. All of his self-control, his limitless restraint, was suddenly crushed by an onslaught of emotion rising up within him. Empathy slashed at my insides seeing him like that, yet there was an unexpected sense of relief as well. In that moment, my heart connected with his in a powerful way. I wrapped my arms around him, simultaneously grateful for, and pained by, his demonstrative show of emotion.

As the music faded, the lights were turned back on and the pastor prayed and gave a eulogy. He spoke of our love for Julia, our plans for her, and her wholly unexpected departure from this life to the next. He spoke of God's love. But I could not pray, and the only love I could focus on was my own.

I closed my eyes and allowed myself to meditate upon the events of the last nine months, the last week. A familiar tightness began to build in my chest. Oh, how I loved her! How I would give *anything* to have her back, to somehow travel back in time and change those fateful hours between seeing her on the ultrasound alive and well on Monday evening, and *still* on Tuesday morning. If I could have only known. If I could have only insisted, demanded that they take her when we had been at our doctor's appointment the day before. If only a premonition could have warned me, and I could have somehow followed some old wives' tale to induce labor myself.

Tears streamed out of the corners of my closed eyes. There were a million what-ifs, I knew. I had pondered all of them, and bargained for them a million times over the past six days, yet always unsuccessfully.

The music drew me back to the moment as the closing prayer began. My eyes came to rest again upon the tiny casket before us. To know that my baby was in that airtight box, no more than ten feet away from me, filled me with an overwhelming sense of helplessness. *Stop!* I wanted to scream. This was not how it was supposed to be.

I watched as if petrified, powerless to stop what was happening right before my eyes. The boys again took their places at Julia's sides. My brother and Greg walked behind them to provide support, in case they needed it. I felt myself stand up and begin to follow them. We filed out, as we had come in, in a somber procession.

I wanted to look up, to see who had come to her service. I wanted to see their faces and offer a silent thanks for coming. But I couldn't do it. My vision was distorted by the unending tears, and it was all I could do to fasten my eyes on that little box that held my baby.

I watched as they placed her tiny white casket into the glossy black limousine. My brother drove our car, as neither Joe nor I were in any condition to drive. Joey sat in his car seat, happily eating goldfish crackers, while I sat where Julia's car seat should have been. I watched anxiously out the window, my eyes trained on that limousine.

I closed my eyes in gratitude as oncoming traffic stopped and pulled to the side of the road to allow our cortege to pass. I had participated in funeral convoys before, and I knew the protocol, yet I felt so personally touched by each person who paused and moved aside. It felt like so many nods of respect for my little girl, the princess of her own solemn parade.

My breath halted in my chest when we pulled up the hill and saw the giant stone pillars and wrought-iron gates that marked the entrance to the cemetery. Established in the 1850s, the historic cemetery had always been intriguing to me. Massive sculptures marked the graves of the founder of our city and his wife. Rolling hills were full of old, weathered headstones that marked the resting places of people, families who had died more than a century before. I had always wondered about their stories. Today, I realized, they would make room for another. Would anyone remember her story? One hundred years from now, would anyone look with wonder at the little stone for a little girl with only one date instead of two?

We followed the winding paths, lined by ancient trees to a more modern section of the cemetery. I thought rainstorms and gray skies would have been more fitting for the occasion, but we stepped out of the car into an unseasonably warm October day, by Midwest standards. Bright blue skies and a brilliant golden sun overhead, lush green grass beneath our feet. It won't be long, I thought, before the trees lose their leaves and the green lawn turns to yellow and brown. *Everything dies*, I thought. *Everything dies.*

Once we reached the tent and saw the rows of white wooden folding chairs facing the podium with that familiar white casket, I released the captive breath I hadn't realized I had been holding. In front of my grandparents' shared granite headstone was a little mound of dirt covered by a green blanket. Joe sat me down and took my hand in his.

I looked at him as if in a trance, in a wide-eyed, unblinking stare. *This is it*, I thought. *This is the end.* My breathing was shallow; my skin was clammy. *Cold as death*, I thought. I was dead, too. I needed to go with her. I could not let them put her in the ground. I could not let them take her away.

The pastor's voice pierced the silence, welcoming everyone who had traveled across town from the church to the cemetery. There were more words, an acoustic guitar as we all sang "Jesus Loves the Little Children" together. *Why my child? Why did He have to take my baby? My. Baby.*

A prayer. And then, it was over. There was an announcement about a luncheon back at the church, a statement of gratitude on behalf of our family to all who came.

Then, silence.

Nobody moved.

What about my baby? I couldn't just leave her there. Outside. Alone. How was I supposed to just turn around and walk away and *leave* her there?

I sat and stared in the silence for a long time, considering my options. Could I just stay here? Couldn't I just be alone with her? Couldn't I just crawl into the empty space and let them heap the dirt on top of both of us?

The tension of the moment was thick. I felt it in my throat, choking me. Nobody moved, nobody breathed. Out of respect, out of pity. I felt their respectful eyes watching, waiting for my decision. The moment was eerily *still*.

On trembling legs, I stood, and Joe stood with me, one hand on my arm, the other bracing my lower back, and we walked together to the podium where her casket silently waited for us. Slowly, apprehensively, I reached out and gently rested my hands on its smooth, cool top. Rivers of tears rushed down my cheeks, faster and faster, my silent hiccuping sobs contrasting with the otherwise peaceful stillness of the moment.

"I love you, Julia," I whispered. "You have had my heart from the very beginning, and you always will. It's good-bye for now, but I will see you again. I promise." Then, drawing in as deep a breath as I could manage, I leaned down, pressed my lips on that cool, polished surface, and kissed my baby girl good-bye.

Chapter 19

I spent the rest of the day trying to be the perfect hostess. The ladies of our church had prepared and served a mouthwatering hot meal, complete with every kind of decadent dessert you could imagine. I knew that it was an act of service, an act of love. I thanked them, and I thanked everyone for coming. Despite my family's insistence that I "sit down," "eat something," "drink this," I tried to make it to every table. I tried to personally greet each person who had joined us that day. It was all I could do. I had to honor Julia in at least that way.

I remember my aunt's gentle words: "Make sure you get some rest, honey." My only answer was a weak smile and nod. I heard the whispers, "She looks so tired." "Has she been sleeping at all?" "We should make her sit down." I was tired, but I couldn't rest. Julia was really gone. I couldn't be alone with my thoughts. I had to keep moving, or I might not ever get back up again.

When the final guests were leaving, we packed our car with plants and the pictures of Julia we had put on display. We gathered gifts and cards. *Everything but her*, I thought.

Back at our house, I continued to bustle about, setting things in order, plants and floral arrangements, sculptures and the framed photo collages. I needed to fill the house with Julia, to "see her" everywhere I looked.

I retrieved the glass ball ornament on which our nurses had gently captured Julia's footprints at the hospital. I carefully lifted it up to a tiny hanger on a shelf above my head, and then I dropped it. Glass shattered violently on the hardwood floor, along with my fragile composure. The crash, followed by my anguished screech, stopped everything and everyone around me. I felt the screams grate against the insides of my throat in devastation at the loss of something so precious. I had been careless, not appreciating how delicate it was. It had been a priceless, irreplaceable gift, and now it was gone.

Before I knew what was happening, Joe was at my side, pulling me away from the shards. He pressed my body into his, as if trying to physically hold me together. My mom was already wielding a broom and dustpan. My dad held Joey, who was now also crying, fearful and perplexed at why Mommy was so upset. The guilt was overwhelming.

Joe walked me upstairs to our bedroom and closed the door. He let me scream and cry.

"I'm so stupid! Stupid! Stupid! Stupid!" I screamed, pounding closed fists against my head and face.

"Stop! Maria, stop!" he demanded, grabbing my forearms just below the wrists and holding them tightly. "Stop!"

I dissolved then, sinking onto the bed into tears of pure grief and self-loathing. I sobbed loudly, finding no words to express the torment in my heart and mind. And despite the torturous pain, it felt good to just let the screams come out of me, to release them into the world.

Eventually, exhaustion quieted my cries to sniffling sobs and whispers of regret. My head rested heavily on Joe's leg as he silently stroked my hair.

"I would like for you to get some sleep," he ventured tenuously.

"I can't. There's so much to do. Our family—"

"They will be fine," he stopped me in a tone of gentle insistence. "They don't need you to entertain them. Nothing needs to be done today that can't be done tomorrow."

I cried harder as I realized he was right. The funeral was over. Julia was buried. The urgency was gone. He squeezed me and pulled me up to sit, leaning against him. Tilting his head to find my gaze, he tenderly lifted my chin with his finger,

"We're all worried about you. You need to rest. After that, whatever you want to do, I will help you do it. I promise."

I closed my eyes and dropped my head. "Okay," I breathed after a moment, "But . . . I don't know if I can."

He leaned over and kissed the top of my forehead then, and I could hear the relief in his voice when he said, "Good. Let's get you settled in."

He tucked me in and pulled the shades against the bright afternoon sun. I asked for the prescription from my doctor, and he brought it back with a glass of water. I drank as if I had been lost in the desert, feeling the coolness trace its way down my raw, scratchy throat and spreading into the rest of my body. Minutes later, my luxurious sheets and comforter pulled high up around my neck, I closed my eyes and succumbed to a deep, merciful sleep.

Chapter 20

After the funeral, our out-of-town family went home. Joe stayed home for few more days, but he needed to get back to work as an information technology network and systems administrator in the same school district where I taught. The district had been exceptionally gracious in their support, and in allowing us time to grieve. Many individuals, departments, and whole school staffs sent flowers, cards, and gifts. Many even attended Julia's services.

For Joe, it was comforting to get back into a routine where he felt like he could do something helpful. After a week of dealing with circumstances that were so out of our control, he needed to be back in a place where he could regain some power and productivity.

I stayed home. Joe took Joey to daycare and I was alone. My doctor had advised that, as I had endured all of the physical aspects of childbirth, my body would need time to rest and recover. I would need all of this time to grieve. This consideration was not mentioned in her notes, but was, thankfully, understood by all. She ordered me to stay home, and the school district and elementary school building staff where I worked thankfully accepted this with generous compassion and understanding.

In addition to the physical trauma I had endured, of course, there was the incalculable damage that had been done to my mind and heart. My breast milk was slowly drying up, but in the meantime I was still uncomfortably and embarrassingly engorged. As the soreness began to slowly dissipate, another kind of tenderness took its place as I came to terms with the finality of our loss and all the secondary losses that came with it.

We made an appointment with the funeral home to settle our account. As Greg had explained in our initial consultation, the funeral home had generously waived some of our costs. Greg had also told us about a local charity, Kennedi's Kisses, which was created to help shoulder the costs of funeral expenses for babies of grieving families, in loving memory of the founders' own daughter, Kennedi, who had also been taken too soon. We sent in our application with a summary of our story and were filled with gratitude and relief when we received a reply letter informing us that the remainder of our account had been paid in full.

We had received so many thoughtful gifts and acts of kindness, heartfelt cards, beautiful plants and flower arrangements. Someone had shared with us that when they went to order flowers for a baby girl, the florist had asked if they were for "Julia," as so many of the floral shops in our city had been inundated with special orders for one "special little girl."

Even after the funeral, flowers, plants, gifts, and cards with generous monetary gifts continued to pour in. A beautiful autumnal arrangement of flowers was delivered. The card indicated that it was from our OB-GYN office physicians, nurses, and staff. I closed my eyes and wept humble, grateful tears for the thoughtfulness and compassion that prompted these gifts.

I created thank-you notes using the photos from that night in the hospital. I spent hours each day handwriting notes to friends and loved ones who had shown us so much love and kindness.

As grateful as I was for the overwhelming show of support we had received, and as much as I wanted to let each person know how much their kindness had meant, I did not want to see anyone. I didn't return phone calls; I declined invitations to go out to dinner or to "catch up sometime." I loved everyone for asking, but just couldn't be socially appropriate.

It hurt to breathe, to exist. I saw the discomfort on people's faces when they saw my red swollen face, my inability to fight back the constant tears. I felt guilty for my lack of self-control. It was frustrating to hear them try to make me feel better, to cheer me up with platitudes, as if "this too would pass." I knew they felt helpless—what could they say? So raw was my pain, so exposed was my heart that even the cool breeze of a kind word sent shock waves through me. Isolation seemed like the safest solution.

I cried and screamed, or stared silently out the window for hours at a time. I was consistently fatigued, physically and emotionally.

I scoured the Internet for statistics and stories of families who had experienced losses similar to ours. I was surprised to find a community of bereaved parents, often moms, who reached out online to give and receive support. I had not realized that these groups existed, though, of course, it made sense that they did.

I read story after story of loss and pervasive loneliness. They lamented about the insensitivity they suffered, the support they needed, the lack of awareness for their plight. I was ashamed of my own lack of awareness. How I had not known to support these women, until I had become an unwitting member of their ranks? "Loss moms" they called themselves. Now I was one of them. I was a part of that club now, the club no mother would willingly join.

I wept for the women who wrote these posts, and wished there was no need for these kinds of groups. It felt somehow comforting, though, to know that there were other women who, if they had to endure it, had the same thoughts and feelings as me. It validated and normalized the thoughts and feelings that I did not want to acknowledge.

I did not find stories exactly like ours, but they were enough alike to evoke a sense of belonging. I wasn't alone—and that made me feel simultaneously better and worse.

Chapter 21

I saw Julia everywhere. Not only when I closed my eyes and remembered the day we lost her, but in everything we did. It was the Baader-Meinhof phenomenon, or frequency illusion. Similar to when we had bought a new car a few years earlier and immediately started seeing the brand and model everywhere, my brain was searching for patterns and consistencies. Even my subconscious mind was looking for traces of Julia.

Everywhere I looked, I noticed pregnant women and babies. More than I ever had before, I would hear the name "Julia" spoken aloud, or see it in print. When we did go out, I would inevitably see a sweet baby girl with a big bow headband, like all the ones lying unworn in my Julia's closet. I dissolved into tears in the middle of a store, more than once, lovingly admiring dresses and outfits that I would have bought for Julia. The words *dying* and *dead* even in reference to a battery or innocuous idiom were sensitive to my ears.

I had to take breaks from social media. It seemed like every time I logged in I saw a beautiful baby girl or happy pregnancy announcement. There were advertisements for an upcoming daddy-daughter dance that I had once imagined Joe attending with Julia one day, with dreams of dinner, dancing, and a sparkly little dress.

Every sleeping baby was a trigger to the post-traumatic stress. They confused my conscious mind, which was still struggling to keep up with the trauma we had endured. I saw sleeping babies and my mind immediately thought they were dead. I had to explicitly remind myself that no, these babies are just *sleeping*. Julia was *born* asleep.

Even at home, I was not safe from the assault on my consciousness. Every movie or television show or commercial seemed to be about babies, or even loss.

It was November 1, a Tuesday. Three weeks after Julia's death. We were watching game six of the World Series between the Chicago Cubs and the Cleveland Indians. We were not really baseball fans, but it was the closest the Cubs had come in more than one hundred years to winning the championship. Living just across the Mississippi River from Illinois and only about 180 miles from Wrigley Field, it was all anyone around us was talking about, and it seemed important enough to at least acknowledge the moment in history.

Yet as I watched, it seemed so frivolous to care how many times a ball hit a bat and men ran around a bunch of bases amid the tragedy we were living. For me, it was another reminder that life was moving forward, history was being made, without *her*. I recalled all the not-long-ago moments when Joey was a newborn, when Joe and I would watch TV quietly at night while I nursed and rocked him to sleep. My arms ached for Julia, for her to be a part of all of these moments—whether history-making or not.

There was a pause in the action for an ad—a diaper commercial that seemed to play every time I turned on the television. A new mom in the delivery room reaches out for her newborn baby—her screaming, wriggling, *living* newborn baby. A voiceover promises to take as much care with her baby as she does. As she takes the pink little girl in her arms, her joy is unmistakable, and, to me, heartbreaking.

"I hate this one. Seriously? They play it every time!" I growled to Joe as it began to play, the gentle lullaby background music now instantly familiar and grating to my ears.

"I know, baby. I'm sorry," he said.

"So rude!" I seethed. "Don't they know not everybody gets that stupid fairy-tale ending?!" In a fit of rage, I hurled the remote violently against the wall. Despite the minimal exertion, I was panting hard. I closed my eyes, hot, angry tears beginning to burn under my eyelids. "I'm sorry." I whispered.

"It's okay," Joe replied evenly. "Do you feel better?"

My eyes darted to him, but I didn't hear any sarcasm in his tone. Eyebrows raised, he lowered his chin and seemed to be genuinely asking the question. When I could not ascertain any further information from his face, I looked back over to the long black remote, its batteries and the cover that held them in place sprawled out on the dark hardwood floor.

"A little," I admitted.

"Good," he replied.

I still couldn't make out his tone. Concern, yes. Also, relief? Perhaps he was expecting this? Or hoping that I had gotten something out of my system?

"I don't understand you," I murmured under my breath.

"What?" he asked, as he retrieved the pieces and put the remote back together.

I knew I was treading in a dark, potentially dangerous place, perhaps off the safer path of this grief journey, but in the moment, I didn't care.

"I don't understand how none of this even seems to bother you."

"What do you mean?" His voice was calm and quiet, but his question was unmistakably pointed.

Too far in to turn back, I kept my eyes trained on the floor in front of me and continued.

"I just feel like I am processing this thing so much differently than you. Like, I miss her so much I can't breathe. And . . . I know you miss her, too . . ."

It was a statement, but there was a question lying in wait beneath its surface. I closed my eyes, wondering if he would catch it.

He was quiet, silent for several long seconds. When I risked looking back at him, I saw his jaw trembling.

"Of course I miss her," he said slowly, his voice breaking, and instantly I was flooded with shame and white-hot regret, knowing how much I had hurt him.

"I know. I'm sorry," I whispered, shame reddening my cheeks.

A heavy silence settled over us, each lost in our thoughts and feelings, until we were jerked back to the moment by the sudden *crack* of a bat, followed by the raucous cheering of Cubs fans coming from the forgotten television. I watched as Joe slowly lifted the remote and pressed the power button, bringing the screen from full-color vibrancy to total, silent darkness in a single moment.

Neither of us moved, like bookends at either end of the couch. Each silent minute that passed felt like adding a block to a precariously high tower between us. I shifted uncomfortably on the cushions, unable to think of what to say, or how to say it. I wondered what he was thinking, how angry he was with me. He'd been so patient, so forgiving all this time. Had I finally done it? Had I finally pushed him away?

When he finally spoke, his voice was soft, almost imperceptible. I had to hold my breath to hear him.

"Mia," he began, using his nickname for me, "I know that it's hard for you to see the differences in the way that you and I grieve."

"I know, I—" I stammered quickly, but he held up his palm in a stop gesture, silencing me.

"I know it's hard. But you have *got* to believe that I *love* Julia, and I miss her, and I wish to *God* that she were here with us."

I nodded my head forcefully, desperate to convey to him that I did know that.

"But she's not here," he continued, his voice breaking again.

I closed my eyes at this simple yet powerful statement, not wanting to hear it. But when I looked up, I watched his face twist in inexplicable pain.

"She's gone, and I hate that. And I have to face that there is nothing I can do to change that—and I hate that, too. And I hate that I can't make this pain go away for you, either. There is nothing I can do for you—and that kills me." He raised his arms and dropped them again, helplessly. "But if she has to be gone," he straightened his shoulders and stiffened his jaw, "I am comforted in knowing that she is safe, she is loved. She will never be sick, or know fear, or the pain of a broken heart. And I will see her again someday."

I had to look away and exhale the breath I was still holding. I felt sweaty and nauseated, hot bile rising in my throat.

"I know that's hard for you to hear, Mia. And I'm sorry. It doesn't make us miss her less, but it does provide some sense of . . . hope. For me, at least."

Another long moment of silence elapsed between us.

"I do believe that. Of course," I told him, sliding my fingers along the seam of a throw pillow. "And I'm sorry. I'm so, so sorry. I *know* that you love her and you miss her as much as I do, and I'm sorry that I insinuated otherwise. Can you forgive me?"

"Of course." He smiled weakly. "I love you."

"I love you, too."

I expelled a staggered breath and closed the distance between us on the couch. I felt the prickle of a day's growth of whiskers on his jawline graze my forehead as I nestled into him.

"You're right, we just . . . see it differently. I just don't understand *why* it had to happen in the first place. I don't understand why she had to go."

"I know," he murmured.

"I don't know why He *took* her, when He could have just *healed* her," I said.

I felt his chest tighten as he held his breath, and I feared he would be angry or disappointed in me and my lack of faith. But when I twisted nervously to look back up at him, I saw only love and grace welling up in his eyes. When he opened his mouth to speak, his voice was slow and soothing.

"I know. We don't know now. But one day we will. Or we won't—but it won't matter because we'll be together again."

I had to look away.

"I just—I want to be strong, but I just—I need her *here*. I don't *want* to wait my whole life to hold her again. I want her *now*."

There was nothing more to say. He held me through the swelling wave of emotion that crested high before it came crashing back down, settling into a gentle ebb and flow. I rested my forehead against his temple, and he lifted my hand and kissed it gently, reassuringly. We settled back into the couch, wordlessly shifting into more comfortable positions.

I rested my head inside the crook of his neck, where I could feel the steady beat of his pulse. Steady. That's what he was, I thought. Of course he loved Julia.

I recalled a night a couple of weeks ago when we'd sat on this same couch together watching the Julia movie—the one that we'd created from photos and videos of our pregnancy and that night in the hospital. I recalled feeling numb, staring at the screen as if entranced by it. Suddenly, I felt the cushions behind me begin to shake.

Confused, I turned to find Joe, in an uncharacteristic outpouring of emotion, sobbing for his lost little girl.

Of course, he missed her just as much as I did. Everything he did was a demonstration of the love he had for his family. He was steady, secure, and strong in both his faith and his love for Joey, Julia, and me. Even when I had hurt him—and I knew that I'd hurt him, that I did not deserve him—he continued to love me with that strong, steady love. *Still.*

Chapter 22

I couldn't pray. Even at mealtimes, I was consumed with anger. I would sit quietly and seethe while Joe or even little Joey would say a blessing over our food. I went to church on Sunday mornings, primarily for Joey. He loved church. I knew it was good for him, and I did not want to cause any more confusing disruptions to his routines.

When I got there, though, I felt like walking right back out. Everyone was so kind, hugging me and asking how I was doing.

"We are praying for you."

"She was so beautiful."

"Her services were so touching."

"We're so sorry for your loss."

"God loves you."

The church was one of the few places I had seen Julia, the last place I had seen her face. I saw flashbacks everywhere I looked. Her funeral. Her casket. Saying good-bye.

The faith-filled music and the messages of hope were impossible to reconcile with the pain in my heart. I cried from the moment I walked through the door to the moment I walked back out again.

I set up a counseling appointment for Joe and me to meet with a church leader and his wife. I had faith that Julia was safe and that I would see her in Heaven one day, but I had so many questions. I needed to know *exactly where* Julia was, *what* she was doing. I would never let one-and-a-half-year-old Joey, let alone newborn Julia, out of my sight without knowing where they were going and what they were doing, I reasoned. I felt like everything was so far outside my control, and, of course, it was.

There were the obvious questions: Why had this happened to *us?* What had *we* done (or not done) to deserve this tragedy? How could we have prevented it? I knew in my soul that I had not once doubted that God could have healed Julia, either inside or outside my womb, or that He foresaw her death and could have prevented it altogether. So why hadn't He? Why did my daughter die, and others live? Why did I have to say good-bye before I could even say a proper hello? Was it my fault?

It felt personal, unjust, to have to suffer the death of my beloved child, one that I would have loved and walked through fire to save, when so much evil—child abuse, sex trafficking, neglect, and other atrocities against children—seemed to go unchecked.

I knew what I believed, what I had known since childhood—that God was good, loving, and merciful—but it was difficult to see in the haze of soul-crushing grief.

We discussed all of this—theology, prayer, and where faith meets feelings. I was grateful to feel no judgment, no condemnation for the anger that seemed to be consuming my faith. We talked about grief, society's discomfort in supporting grievers, and the importance of self-care.

"Jesus loves you both," they said, "and we do, too."

I gulped back the tears that had been flowing freely for the past hour, and we thanked them extensively for their time. As we walked out into the parking lot, the sun was shining brightly, and I had to hold my hand up to shade my eyes.

"How are you doing?" Joe asked as we got into the car and buckled our seat belts.

"I don't know," I confessed, looking at him after a long pause.

He said nothing but extended his chin and nodded knowingly. He reached for my thigh on the seat next to him and squeezed it gently in a silent show of support before moving his hand back to the gearshift and setting us in motion.

Watching the Iowa farm country on the outskirts of town skip by outside my window as we headed back across the city, I didn't know if the philosophies and theological ideas had been especially helpful. I realized I probably already knew most of what I needed to know. I knew that Julia was loved and safe and that I would, some sweet day, see her again. What I didn't know was whether or not that was good enough.

Chapter 23

A few weeks later on a Sunday morning, I stood, as was our faith tradition, during the worship music segment of the service, but I did not pray, sing, or raise my hands. I stood and stared at the wall where the words to the song being played were projected so that anyone who didn't know them could sing along. So many of the songs I had sung for years made me crazy now. Singing about trusting Jesus with my crisis, and letting him solve it, or even how Christ's sacrifice had defeated the grave, now left my stomach feeling like a gnarled tree stump.

I still believed in the power of God, in the reality of his presence, and even His love, but I just didn't want to feel it. I was so angry at Him, so hurt by the loss of my daughter when I knew He could have saved her. So I shut him out. I stood silent and still, often I sat, ignoring the words on the wall and the worship going on all around me.

But this Sunday morning, I felt the inexplicable tug of the Holy Spirit, known to believers, inside of me. I tried to squelch it, to push it away, but I felt His love reaching for me. The song was one of my favorites from *before*. Metaphors of God's love like a hurricane, an ocean, a jealous lover who would go to any lengths to win back His lost love.

How? How could you still love me? When I have pushed you away and screamed at you so many times?

But He did. I felt his overwhelming love like an ocean wave rushing over me. I heard His voice, not audibly, but inside my heart, not reprimanding or condemning, but *wooing* me back to Him.

Still, I resisted, tears dripping off my nose and quavering jaw. I didn't know if I *could* let go of this anger, if I could learn to trust Him again.

Yet, He called to me still.

I didn't deserve Him. I didn't know how I felt about reconciliation, but, slowly, I felt myself begin to pull back on the steel barrier I had used to cover myself, to keep Him out. Like a cleansing summer thunderstorm, I felt His Spirit lovingly rain down on me, soaking into the parched, dry ground of my hardened heart, restoring me.

This did not mean that my faith was instantly restored and my heart was healed. I didn't know if that was even possible, or if it was even what I wanted to happen. My anger was not gone, yet He loved me anyway. My questions had not been answered and doubt lingered. Yet, despite how I felt, what I thought, or even how I treated Him, the God who created me persisted in loving me—in spite of these things. He loved me. *Still.*

Chapter 24

I have always had vivid, colorful dreams. Pregnancy intensified my dreaming with both Joey and Julia. I had never been one to know I was dreaming in my dreams and try to wake up. However bizarre the dreams were, they always felt completely real at the time. Silly or scary, I usually remembered my dreams, at least for the first few minutes after waking up.

After we lost Julia, the intense dreaming continued. In the first few months afterward, I had the same dreams—or the same kind of dreams—almost every night. I had no idea, at first, what they meant, but the frequency was concerning.

One especially puzzling genre of dream was one where I desperately needed to find a bathroom. I had this persistent, urgent need to urinate, but I could never find a bathroom. I would search through places I knew well, my church, schools where I had taught, even restaurants and stores we frequented, and inevitably the bathroom was closed for renovation, or just missing altogether.

Sometimes I would find a bathroom, but there were no doors on the stalls, sometimes no stall at all, and always lots of people all around. Often the people around me were strangers, but sometimes they were acquaintances, and I had to make small talk with parents of my students or random people that I knew, but not well enough to breech protocols of polite conversation. I could not tell them what was happening inside of me.

After weeks of having this dream almost every time I slept, I searched online for answers. I was surprised to learn that I was not the only one having these kinds of dreams. Apparently, enough people have these kinds of dreams that there are multiple sources of interpretation. According to the wisdom of the Internet, this kind of dream is common when you are frustrated by a lack of privacy. The urge to go to the bathroom symbolizes an inner struggle with emotions that need to be purged or relieved.

Well, *yes*. This, of course, made perfect sense to me. I was so grateful to have medical leave from work to heal from childbirth, which also afforded me time alone to grieve during the day. Despite this blessing of privacy, I did feel this inability to be honest with others about my feelings. The grief, the all-consuming loss, would certainly qualify as an "inner struggle."

I didn't feel like I could be honest with anyone. Joe loved me, and his patience with me far exceeded my expectations for anyone. I believed God could understand my pain, but I was often still too angry to pray. Friends called, texted, a couple visited. But the truth was, as much as I wanted to share how I was feeling, I didn't *want* to let anyone in. I *wanted* to be alone. I didn't trust that anyone would or could understand what I was feeling. I was convinced that this was true, primarily because I didn't understand it either.

Many people sent their thoughts and prayers via social media or in brief conversations at church or other social situations. They encouraged me to let them know how they could help and to "call anytime," and I knew they meant it. But I typically didn't call.

I did go to one support group meeting. It was a local group that I had joined online months earlier, ironically, in an attempt to support others while Julia was just beginning to wriggle around inside of me. I'd had no idea then that I would need their support later.

When I pulled into the parking lot for their November meeting, I nearly circled around and drove right back out.

My hands shook like the wings of a hummingbird beneath the round plastic table. I looked around at these women who seemed to be holding it together so well. Could I be honest, vulnerable, with complete strangers? I cried the whole time while they told their stories, and especially while I told mine.

I wondered what they would think of me, if they would roll their eyes at each other while I reached for my sixty-third tissue of the evening, but they didn't. They wept with me. They told me they had been in this stage of fresh grief, too, and that I had no reason to feel ashamed. They told me their own excruciating stories of stillbirth, miscarriage, and infertility. Though our experiences were different, I saw threads of my story in each of theirs. They told me that Julia's death was not my fault and that it was okay, even good and healthy, to grieve her loss. They told me that I would survive, and that that would be a good thing. I wasn't sure if I believed that last part, but I left feeling grateful I hadn't circled the parking lot to drive back home. It did feel good to tell my story, and to hear the stories of other moms who had lost their babies and loved them still.

Usually, though, if I had conversations with people, it was because *they* reached out first. My best friend, Addie, would stop by after work. She brought cards my students had made, news from the elementary school where we both worked, and well wishes from everyone there. I always cried pretty much the entire time. I felt bad about this. It was somewhat humiliating—I knew what my ugly cry looked like by now, and it was called *ugly* for a reason. But I also knew that big displays of emotions made people uncomfortable. Addie, although passionate in her beliefs and love for others, was someone who was always in control of her emotions, especially sad ones. She rarely cried, usually preferring to deflect her own sadness with humor or by just ignoring it altogether. For others, including me, she was a fixer, generously giving of her time and energy to do whatever she could to help. Not being able to *do* something to alleviate my pain was painful for her, I knew. I felt both guilty and immensely grateful that she kept coming.

"I have an idea," she said one day, with a mischievous twinkle in her expression that, despite the tears in my eyes, still put a smile on my face.

"What?" I asked, chuckling as I squeezed and wiped my nose with a new tissue.

"Okay," she said, clapping her hands, excitedly, her charcoal-lined eyes widening enthusiastically. She gathered her dark hair up into a messy bun on the top of her head—this was serious. "So, I heard of this place that opened up where people pay money to break dishes."

I put the tissue I had been holding down on my lap and stared at her for a moment, my eyebrows drawn together in a question. "What?" I asked finally.

"Right," she said, shaking her head, but still smiling. "So, the point of it is to just let out your frustrations in a safe place. Like, you can be violent, but nobody gets hurt."

"Oh yeah?" I asked, raising one eyebrow in interest.

"Yes! So, that place is actually kind of far away, *buuuttt*," she continued, drawing out the word, "I was thinking that maybe I could go to a thrift store or something and get us a bunch of old plates and dishes and we could break them into a dumpster somewhere!"

I couldn't suppress a giggle. "That's awesome."

"I know! I would totally do it! Or," she continued, lifting her eyebrow, "you know if you did want to just be violent, I would totally find someone for you to punch. Trust me, I have a long list of people who have it coming."

A huge burst of laughter shot out of me.

"Girl, you know I would do anything for you." She said it with her eyebrows raised and lips protruded in a pseudo-serious "tough chick" expression that was as endearing as it was funny.

"I love you," I told her.

"Love you, too."

We continued talking until the sun was starting to set.

When it was time for her to leave, I walked her to the door, and she wrapped me in a tight hug. As I closed it behind her, exhaustion fell on me like a weighted blanket. Joe would be home with Joey soon, but I knew I had enough time for a brief rest before they got there.

I walked a few steps over to the couch and covered up with the fleece throw I had folded over the back in preparation for our visit. Fluffing the throw pillow under my head, I closed my eyes, grateful for true friendship in the midst of true suffering. Sleep came swiftly as I considered how much harder this grief would be without Addie and the other friends—and strangers—who loved at all times, even still.

Chapter 25

My phone rang and caller ID showed it was my doctor's office. I sat back and felt concern start to tighten my chest. Were they just calling to confirm our visit in a few weeks? Did we forget to do something? I cleared my throat and answered quickly.

"Hello?"

"Hi, may I speak to Maria, please?" came a familiar voice.

I tried to sound natural, but my voice was small and taut, pinched even to my own ears. "This is Maria," I responded, anxiety stealing my breath.

"Hi, Maria, this is Dr. Moshier." I knew it was her before she introduced herself, and I was genuinely thrilled to hear from her. But *why* was she calling? Was she personally checking up on me instead of a nurse? Was this something they did for all the mothers whose babies had died? Were there enough of us to demand a protocol?

"Yes. Hi!" I replied, a bit too brightly. I scolded myself for entertaining all the distracting thoughts instead of paying attention to the doctor.

"Hi. How are you doing?"

Pause.

I wasn't sure how to answer.

"Umm, I'm okay." My voice rose a few octaves, revealing that this was a lie.

"I know that's an unfair question. Are you taking care of yourself, though? Are the medications working all right for you?"

"Yes. Umm, yes. They're fine. I pretty much don't need anything anymore. I only take the Xanax occasionally, because it knocks me out," I replied nervously, pacing laps around the long dining room table as I spoke, and still wondering as to the purpose of her call.

"Good," she said in her calming, even tone. "Maria, I am calling because we got the results back from Julia's autopsy. Do you have time to talk about them now?"

Immediately all the air was sucked out of the room, and I felt like I was shot backward through a long, underground tunnel. My knees buckled and I reached out to lean against a sturdy wooden chair for support. I sat down and closed my eyes, but that made the spinning motion worse, so I forced them open again.

"Yes. Yes, please. Th—thank you," I choked out the words hoarsely, desperate to focus on what she was saying, to stay conscious long enough to hear it.

"So, as you know, in cases of stillbirth, we look for obvious causes of death, such as a cord wrapped around the baby's neck, or a physical deformity that we didn't catch earlier on in the pregnancy. We didn't find any of that with Julia. So we decided to do an autopsy to determine if there was anything internally, within Julia, which would have caused her death."

I nodded my head vigorously, then, realizing she couldn't see me, whispered "Yes," urging her onward.

"So we ended up doing two autopsies."

"Okay." I swallowed, not sure what that could mean.

"The autopsy of Julia's body did not reveal anything internally that would have led to her death."

Short, forceful exhalations came out of me, chased by an onslaught of fresh tears, and I didn't know if I was relieved or disappointed.

"So, she was healthy?" I asked between sobs.

"Yes, everything we can see says that she was perfectly healthy," she acknowledged.

I closed my eyes, grateful for this. But then *why did she die?*

"But you did a second autopsy?"

"We did," she confirmed, and then paused briefly. "We did an autopsy of the placenta, which includes the umbilical cord. It appears as though there was a slight narrowing of the cord at one point, and there was a small clot of blood behind it."

My vision swirled in and out of focus. My mouth was wide open, chest burning, but I could not get any air. *Breathe—you have to breathe.*

"Maria, I am so sorry."

Rivers of tears rushed down my cheeks and my lungs finally opened, taking in all the air all at once.

"I don't . . . I don't understand. What does that *mean?* How did it even . . . get there?"

"I'm sorry, we really don't know. We know that the clot in the cord came from the placenta. It would have cut off her access to the oxygen and nutrients that come from your body to hers. For her, it would have been like going to sleep, and just not waking up."

"No. No, no, no, no, no. *No!* My *baby!*" I wailed, unable to control myself any longer.

It felt like a thousand knives stabbing me all at once to hear about Julia's final moments, to know that I was oblivious, that I did nothing to stop it, or to say good-bye.

"So what did I—what did I do wrong?" I asked, remembering that the doctor was still on the line.

"Maria, you did *not* do *anything* wrong. You did everything that we asked you to do. I am so sorry. It is tragic. It happens, unfortunately, and we just don't know why. But please do not blame yourself. You did *nothing* to cause this."

"She didn't suffer?" My voice was high, brittle, childlike.

"No," she answered definitely, "she would not have suffered."

I let that statement hang between us for a long time, perhaps to absorb it, perhaps wanting to convince myself of it, before speaking again.

"Thank you," I whispered finally.

"You can certainly call anytime . . . Do you have any other questions for me now?" she asked gently.

It felt like I was swimming, drowning in this new information. I waited a moment before answering "No."

"All right. Again, if questions do come up, you can call anytime." She paused, and it seemed like she wanted to say more. "Please know that we are all thinking about you, Maria."

"Thank you," I whispered again, barely finding the strength to speak past the enormous elephant in my throat. We said our good-byes and I dropped the phone onto the table with a loud *clack*.

A cry began in the pit of my stomach, rising in intensity, swelling and slashing as it screamed out of me like a giant howling windstorm. Destruction was everywhere. It felt like I was back to that first day, losing Julia again. It was like ripping off every bit of skin that had just begun to grow over the wound. My daughter was dead. There was a scientific reason for it. And I wanted nothing more than to join her.

Chapter 26

"What's this?"

I asked the question aloud, although there was no one around to hear or answer me. Standing barefoot on the cold sidewalk in front of my house, I looked quizzically at the nondescript white plastic envelope as I pulled it out of our mailbox. I squinted at it, turning it over in my hands. Something soft. The return address wasn't recognizable, but my name and address were clearly printed on the paper label. I wondered who had mailed me a package, and what could be inside.

Back indoors, I carefully cut the outer package open to find another package inside. Clear plastic covered a piece of folded brown fabric. *What was it?* I carefully pulled apart the adhesive seal and reached in to pull out the mysterious item. When I unfolded it, my mouth went dry and my heart slammed into my chest like a car crashing into a tree.

The dress. I had forgotten that I'd ordered it. Several weeks before she was born, I had ordered this Thanksgiving dress for Julia.

Without thinking, I clutched the little garment in my fists and brought it to my face. I knew she hadn't worn it, yet somehow it seemed like a piece of her, something from *before*.

I closed my eyes, pushing out the tears that had already begun to gather there, while my shoulders convulsed in unexpected sobs. *My baby*.

With a deep, staggered breath, I opened my eyes and let my hands drop slightly. Still holding tight to this tiny time capsule, I moved to the couch. I sat back and drew my legs underneath me. As I carefully unfurled Julia's little dress I recalled sitting in front of my computer, Julia still wriggling around in my belly as I carefully chose this specific dress from others offered by the online retailer.

My fingers bumped along the gathered neckline, slowly tracing the smooth A-line bodice. The chocolate brown was richer than I had expected, decadent, a perfect contrast to the turkey appliqué with brightly hued feathers of hot pink, turquoise, and orange polka-dotted fabric, outlined in shiny embroidered scallops. The hot-pink hem and matching bow screamed *girly girl*, as did the puffy sleeves that gathered at the elbows, then flared outward dramatically. I smiled in spite of myself as I noticed that even the little turkey wore a shiny bow. As I touched it gingerly, I thought of the oversized hot-pink hair bow and bright leggings with tiny ruffles across the rump that Julia would have worn to complete this look.

I let the tears roll down my cheeks and reunite under my chin as I remembered the other items still left in my cart, awaiting my final decision. A tiny onesie that read, "My family is thankful for me" would have been an outfit change, perhaps after dinner when Julia would have been passed around like a gravy boat from member to member of our family, who would have, indeed, been thankful for her.

We were still thankful for her, I realized. We would forever be thankful for her little life, for the lessons she'd taught us. She had taught us the value of each moment, the fragility of life, and not taking any of it for granted. Even now, she was teaching us to be brave in her absence, to live, even when we wanted to die. She taught us, in a way no one else could, what true love really is.

I looked back down at Julia's dress to find that two puddles had formed, darkening the fabric like dirt turning to mud. I closed my eyes, gulped back my emotion, and shook out the little frock, holding it up to examine it more fully. It would now hang in her closet like all of the others, unworn.

I ran my fingers along the cold, damp spots, so incongruous with the bright happy little turkey girl smiling back at me. One more piece of evidence of the paradox of our lives: forever thankful for what we had, forever longing for so much more.

Chapter 27

I visited Julia's gravesite every day. We had ordered Julia's headstone the week after her funeral, a beautiful combination of steel-gray and pearl-white granite to match the shared headstone of my grandparents, with whom she was laid. We had asked that it be engraved with her name, the single birth and death date, and "Our Precious Daughter." The text would be flanked by an elegant Botonee cross on one side, and a baby, sleeping in the hand of God, on the other. The memorial company had warned us that by the time the stone was finished and ready to be laid, it was possible the weather might delay its installation until spring.

As the days began to get colder and shorter, I brought blankets and extra layers. I would sit or lie in the prickly grass, sometimes for hours, sometimes until it finally became dark and the cemetery would close. Each time, it broke my heart to turn around and walk away. I felt like I was abandoning her, again. Despite believing that her spirit was already free, I felt like I was just leaving her there in the bitter darkness, and guilt squeezed the breath out of me.

Through bleary eyes, I drove through the curving paths. As I glimpsed a large tree, as if for the first time, a thought began to emerge from the darkest place. Tall and majestic, it rose to the night sky . . . just as I wished to do. How long had it been here? The cemetery itself had existed for well over a century; had this tree been here that long? Half in the grass, half in the road, I wondered if it could be my salvation, an end to the suffering, the pain of separation from my daughter, buried so many feet away. If I started far enough back, removed the seat belt's promise of safety, gave enough acceleration, would it work? Could I leave this world for the one beyond? Could I finally see her again?

I closed my eyes and drew in a deep breath. Clenching the steering wheel, I pressed down on the accelerator. Staying well on the right side of the narrow road, my gaze never left the tree as I drove past it, and it moved from my windshield to my driver's-side window, and finally, to my rearview mirror.

Despite the hours of weeping, new tears stung my eyes. The congestion in my nose blocked the deep breath my lungs needed, forcing my mouth open to receive it. Slowly braking and pulling over to the side of the path, just inside the gated entrance, I thrust the car into park and rested my head against the leather-bound steering wheel.

It hadn't been a plan. I wasn't suicidal. I just missed my baby. I didn't want to die, but I wanted desperately to be with her.

Even still, the fact that those thoughts had taken shape within my vulnerable, broken heart scared me. I thought of my family. How could I selfishly escape this unbearable pain, only to inflict more of the same upon them? What kind of mother would I be to heap that kind of burden upon my son? To deny him a childhood, a lifetime without a mother? I thought of Joe and his pain in the delivery room that night when we had already lost Julia, and then I had, inexplicably, lost consciousness. I recalled his eyes, full of tears, and his face, full of terror, and I had to turn my head away from the memory. My husband, who had already lost a child; would he even be able to survive losing a wife, his life partner? How hypocritical would it be for me to expect my own parents, who were also already grieving their granddaughter, to also endure the same pain of child loss that had brought me to this low place?

I tilted my head back against the headrest and looked up through the moon roof at the night sky, now fully dark, studded with a million sparkling stars, light years away. I felt gravity like a giant iron, pressing me down against the leather seat. Although my feet were fixed as ever to the earth, my heart painfully straddled both worlds: here with my son, and, far beyond my grasp, with my daughter.

Chapter 28

I sat motionless in the passenger seat as Joe drove. We were going back to the hospital to visit my OB-GYN office for my six-week checkup appointment, and for the doctor to release me to go back to work.

I stared out the window, remembering the last time we'd driven to the hospital. *Before.* Everything was different then. Unlike today's gray, overcast skies, the day had been brilliant and warm. We had just installed Julia's car seat in the back with the naive intention of bringing her home with us. It was the day we learned that she was already gone, never coming home.

My mind skipped back further to my six-week checkup appointment after delivering Joey almost two years earlier. Joe had been working, and I'd convinced him that I could take Joey with me without his help. I wanted to show Baby Joey off to the staff and nurses who had taken care of us during our pregnancy. I have a picture of Dr. Moshier holding him in his cozy fleece pants and matching striped vest with a big embroidered gray elephant. Joey and the doctor both seemed to be smiling into the camera. What a different experience that was from today.

The baby's car seat was gone. The baby was gone. It was only Joe and me. With empty arms.

As we crested the top of the hill, I felt the familiar tightening of my chest, the quickening of my breath and pulse. When we stopped at the traffic light at the parking lot's entrance, I gasped involuntarily. Joe turned to me, his eyes flashing with concern, then giving way to a sad understanding. He reached for my hand and rubbed gentle circles into my palm with his thumb.

I closed my eyes and clenched my teeth as we made the wide turn into the lot. As we walked up the curved sidewalk I glanced at the white exterior with its long dark windows, then ahead to those wide automated doors. It looked exactly the same as it had before. This should not have been a surprise. Of course it looked the same, even though my life now looked completely different, darker than it had on that sunny morning six weeks ago.

Nausea roiled in my stomach and I swallowed hard against it, grateful for the gust of bitterly cold late-November air against my burning face. I leaned against Joe, appreciating his sturdy frame and strong arm. He pulled my hand up to his chest, linking my arm in his as we had at our wedding so many years before. What a journey it had been since then, I thought. How could we have known that *this* heartache would be part of the "for better or for worse" clause in our wedding vows?

The doors opened, revealing the lobby, a bank of wheelchairs, the long hallway with the wall of windows that looked out to the gazebo where we had called our families, the wide steps we had traveled so many times up to Labor and Delivery—*before*. My feet stopped as if cemented into the floor. Bending slightly, I tried to catch my breath in a series of quick short inhalations. My head felt like a bucket full of water, sloshing with each step, releasing tiny trickles of sweaty condensation on my face and down my back.

I clutched Joe's forearm. I couldn't do this.

"You can do this," he told me, reading my mind. "You can do this. I am right here, and we are doing this together."

I closed my eyes and everything seemed to move away from me; I was sinking.

"Keep your eyes open, Mia. Come on. Stay with me."

We sat on a bench outside the gift shop, *It's a girl!* pink Mylar balloons stretching, swaying high in the window display. *Why are we doing this?*

"Do you want some water?" he asked, twisting my hair back away from my face.

"No," I replied, shaking my head, working to loosen some of the pressure. "I just want to go home. I can't do this."

"I know, baby," he replied slowly. "This is hard, but you *are* doing it. We'll go in and get this done, and it will be one more thing that you didn't think you could do, but you did it anyway."

What had I done to make him have so much confidence in me?

I looked at the intersecting diagonal lines of the monochromatic gray carpet, getting lost in its hypnotic pattern. I squeezed my eyes shut and let out a long, slow breath before returning my gaze to Joe's face, worry lines like exclamation marks between his eyebrows.

"Okay," I agreed simply.

He helped me up and we walked through the frosted glass door to the OB-GYN office where we were once again assaulted by memories. Joe's hand supported my back as we moved forward to the desk. I knew I would have to tell them my name and date of birth, but how could I do it like this? I wanted to be calm, "normal," but I could not control my trembling hands or my incessant tears.

My eyes connected with the kind dark-haired receptionist, Vanessa. She saw us walk in and guided us over to her station.

"Hi, Maria." She said it with so much compassion, I knew she wanted to say more. "I'll get you checked in. You can go ahead and have a seat."

I nodded gratefully and turned toward the seating area, near the television. We sat in the comfortable leather armchairs as happy morning-show hosts talked about the latest trends in winter fashion. Another couple was already waiting there. The woman was fully pregnant, rubbing large circles on the giant cocoon at her middle where her baby rested safely.

I felt her eyes watching me, a no-longer-pregnant woman with puffy red eyes and chapped lips and nose in an OB-GYN waiting room. Did she know? Had she ascertained the reason behind my devastation? Did she know that just six weeks ago, I'd been sitting in her seat, still pregnant, still so full of excited anticipation? *Still.*

I opened a pregnancy health magazine and held it up in front of my face, enjoying the intense pleasure of resting my tired eyes.

Just moments later, however, we heard my name. I put down the magazine and looked to the door. It was Ana, Dr. Moshier's nurse. We stood and walked toward her, past the other couple, who must have been happy to see us go.

Ana let the door close behind us.

"Hi, guys. It's good to see you," she said.

I tried to smile my thanks for her genuine tone and compassionate expression. I liked all of the nurses in this office, but Ana had always been one of my favorites. She was tall and blonde, with a runner's frame and a serene demeanor. She was approachable yet professional, capable yet supremely kind.

She led us to a room down the long hallway, past the nurses' station and the bulletin boards full of happy birth announcements. I scanned all the happy drooly baby faces, some bright-eyed, some peacefully sleeping in posed positions. *Sleeping.* I wondered about the card I had sent with pictures of us in the hospital with Julia. They wouldn't want to upset expectant mothers by posting it here, I understood. I wondered if it was posted anywhere.

We walked into the room, past the examination table and the posters that illustrated female human anatomy and an infograph warning about the hazards of smoking while pregnant. We sat down together in the cushioned bench chair across from Ana, and answered questions about how I had been doing over the past six weeks.

She listened attentively, then blinked her eyes closed for a moment before opening them again and saying, "I'm so sorry, you guys." Her compassion was visible, and I was grateful that someone was acknowledging Joe's grief, too. So many times in the last six weeks, people completely overlooked and ignored him to ask how I was doing. To be fair, my face was typically the one that was red and swollen, but Joe had lost his daughter, too. I was thankful to Ana for remembering him.

She took my blood pressure and my temperature and logged the numbers into her computer for the doctor. When she had finished, she gathered her clipboard and supply tote, then swiveled on her stool back over to us. Letting her shoulders relax, she leaned in toward us, intimately.

"I hope you know that we are here for you guys. If you need anything at all, or if you have any questions, you have our number." She made eye contact to emphasize her point. "Please call."

Joe and I nodded together.

"Thank you," he told her.

She nodded back with a small, tight-lipped smile. "Doctor will be in shortly," she told us before leaving the room.

I changed, donning the periwinkle cotton gown with its tiny diamond-and-dot pattern for my examination. My mind flew back to that night six weeks before, ripping off my gown to hold Julia close, skin to skin. Holding her—

"Hey," Joe said, touching my arm, bringing me back.

I looked up at him, swallowing hard, words not necessary to communicate what I was feeling.

"Come here," he said, drawing me close to him.

I rested my cheek against his chest and felt the buttons from his dress shirt pressing into my face. I remembered the bright blue one he'd worn that night, the mascara stain that had still not come out of it.

The triggers were endless, I thought. Especially here. Everywhere I looked I was reminded of Julia—how I had had her, and then lost her. How I wanted nothing more than to hold her again.

Chapter 29

A light rap on the door let us know that Dr. Moshier had arrived. She came in and sat across from us, tilting her head slightly.

"Hi, guys," she began. "How is it going?" She asked the question with a pained expression that told me she recognized how difficult this was to answer.

I couldn't suppress a breathy, humorless laugh. I looked at Joe and his eyes twinkled, despite the sadness in them. He nodded at me, imparting a silent message of encouragement.

Squaring my shoulders, I looked at Dr. Moshier and replied, "It's been . . . as good as you might expect, I guess?" I was conscious trying to keep the sarcasm out of my tone.

She closed her eyes and nodded her understanding. "I would imagine that's true."

We exchanged more technical questions and answers about my physical healing, which was all fine. My milk had dried up, and all of the soreness was gone. Little physical evidence remained of the trauma my body had endured.

There were a few silent beats between us as we each prepared ourselves to discuss the pain that did still very much exist.

"And how are you coping?" she asked, drawing her eyebrows together in a serious expression.

I looked down at the collection of soggy tissues I had already accumulated in my lap, then up to the tiled ceiling, searching for the words.

"I . . . I don't know," I finally admitted, shrugging and pulling one side of my mouth up into a crooked grin.

"That's fair, too." I watched the canned light from the ceiling reflect off her shiny dark bob as she nodded in agreement. "Does the medicine seem to be helping at all?"

"I don't really take the Xanax," I told her. "It just makes me really tired, and I really don't need that. I already feel like I sleep all the time."

"Okay. And that is totally fine not to take it. Some people have a hard time sleeping, and some don't. We just wanted that to be available to you if you needed it. But if you don't need it, and you can do okay without it, we certainly would prefer that route anyway."

She did the physical examination and we talked more about medication and depression, and strategies for coping with the loss, and now the additional stressors of going back to work and the upcoming holiday season.

"I just wish we could skip over the holidays altogether," I admitted.

"That makes total sense," she said. She appeared to be weighing her next statement. After a brief pause, she said, "It will be important for you to be gentle with yourself."

"People have said that. I just don't really know what it means," I confessed.

She nodded. When she continued, I appreciated that her explanation was informative without being at all condescending.

"It will be important for you to not be too hard on yourself, to not put too many demands on yourself. I don't know if you usually cook during the holidays?"

"She does," Joe answered, in a tone that left no room for debate, which evoked smiles from all of us.

"Maybe let somebody else do that this year," she suggested. "You focus on you. If you need to take a break, if you need to leave early, if you need to stay home altogether from some of the celebrations, any or all of that would be okay. You have a great husband," she said, gesturing to Joe with an open hand to emphasize her point. "Your family seems to be very supportive as well. Let them take care of you, and you just take care of you."

I considered this. I had always loved baking, trying new recipes, and cooking huge feasts, especially for Thanksgiving and Christmas. I realized, however, that I couldn't remember the last meal that I had cooked for my family since Julia died. Guilt, sadness, and anger all swirled up together in my belly, punctuating the longing I had for the life I'd once expected to have—the one I would never have again.

I blinked slowly and realized I had drifted for a moment. I straightened nervously, wondering how long I had been lost in my daydream.

Without a hint of hurriedness in her voice, Dr. Moshier asked, "Do you have any questions for me?"

We had already been talking for a long time. She was a well-loved doctor, and I knew she was busy. I truly appreciated that she never tried to rush me. She seemed content to stay with me for as long as I needed her.

"I just don't understand it," I said slowly. "I know you explained it to me—I so appreciate that you called me yourself, too—I mean, I know there was a clot," I continued, the word sticking in my throat. "I just—I just don't understand *how* it happened."

I thought I caught a pained expression in her eyes before she bowed her head for a moment. She paused and exhaled slowly, seeming to weigh her words before answering.

"I wish I had a better answer for you," she said. "The truth is, we aren't really sure. I know that's not good enough, and I am so sorry about that."

"I just . . . I—I need to ask . . ."

I could feel my sweaty palms shaking despite my effort to hold them down as I worked to ask the questions that had been haunting me for weeks.

"I started a new teaching job this year and it has been really, really stressful. I've also been taking grad classes, and I was writing final research papers the week we lost Julia . . ."

From the perplexed expression on her face, I knew I needed to get to the point.

"Anyway, it's been really stressful, and I wondered if that could be the reason? All of the stress? Could that have—hurt Julia?"

"Oh, Maria, no," she said, shaking her head quickly, her forehead crumpled in visible concern. "No. Absolutely not."

"Okay," I replied, somewhat relieved, but not finished. "But I also—I know I had a coffee the weekend before. I try not to drink any coffee while I'm pregnant, but it was a frozen blended thing, and I just didn't know—" My throat seized, putting an abrupt end to the words that had been tumbling out.

"No," she said, shaking her head again.

I couldn't read her expression. She seemed frustrated, but not with me.

"Maria, you did everything we asked you to do. Coffee, stress, or anything you did would *not* have caused this. I promise you."

"I tried to look online. I tried to find statistics, numbers, some information about how often this happens, or just stories about other families, and I couldn't really find anything much, not that really matched our experience. I just—" My voice faltered again. I paused to draw in a breath and tried to start again. "I just need to know if this happens often? To other people?"

"It does happen," she replied slowly, and the mournfulness in her tone made me pause. I wanted to believe her—that it wasn't my fault—but I just didn't see how that was possible.

I thought of all the other families who experience this sudden, unexpected loss.

"It's just so unfair."

"Yes. You're right," she agreed. "It is."

"Are you going to try for another one?"

It was the question we had been asked even before we had buried our child in the ground. No matter how many times it was asked, it never lost its sting. The question was deeply offensive. It assumed that Julia was simply a dud, an unsuccessful attempt to have a baby.

No. We had a baby.

She was conceived, carried, and birthed in love. And she was beautiful, perfect, just . . . still. Our hearts were destroyed by the loss of our child. It felt as if we were being encouraged to simply replace her with a new baby, Julia 2.0. The insinuation was that another child could take her place in our hearts, make everyone feel better, and, essentially, hit the reset button on our lives.

"I don't think we are ready to think about that now."

The question of whether or not to attempt to conceive another child was, for us, fraught with emotions and considerations that we could not even bring ourselves to discuss.

Would having another child replace Julia? Would I get so busy in the day-to-day care of a new baby that I would forget the one who came before? Even if *I* remembered her, would others forget that she had ever existed? Would the erroneous, offensive notion that a new baby could erase the hurt in my heart, the absence of my child, simply be perpetuated with the birth of another child? Would I become a self-fulfilling prophecy? If I had another little girl, would she wear the clothes and bows I had lovingly chosen for Julia, the ones that still hung in the closet, waiting to be worn?

Truthfully, at the top of my list of fears was that I could not love another baby, even if I tried to do so. It felt as though all the contents of my maternal love tank were solely reserved for Joey and Julia; there was simply not enough left for anyone else, not ever.

Even if we eventually wanted one, would it even be possible to conceive another child? Julia was conceived with miraculous ease. Prior to that, though, it was only after five years of devastating infertility before we had conceived Joey. The autopsy results revealed that Julia was perfectly healthy. Could we be so lucky again? I wasn't getting any younger, and we knew with distressing clarity how the probability of complications increased with maternal age.

The painful truth was that we *were* a statistic. I had learned from my involvement with the online bereaved parents support groups that one in four pregnancies in the United States end in loss. Could this happen again? *Would* it? My heart knew I would never survive losing another child.

Before we left the appointment, I had to broach one more important topic.

"So, *if* we were ever to decide to have another baby, would this loss put us at an increased risk for—losing that baby, too?"

"No," Dr. Moshier answered with definitive kindness. She shared that however tragic Julia's passing was, it was truly an accident. It did not, in any way, increase the probability of a subsequent loss. Knowing this information, and based on my history, we could reasonably expect that future pregnancies would be healthy and unlikely to result in the same kind of loss.

"I'm not saying that I'm ready. I am *not* ready."

"Of course," she empathized.

"I don't think that I even want to have another baby, ever," I told her honestly. "But I want to be informed, just in case."

"Sure," she nodded. "That makes sense."

"I cannot . . . I *will not*," I began, wrestling with my emotions as I fitfully shredded the already fully sodden tissues in my hands, "I will not even *consider* bringing another child into this world unless I know that we can deliver earlier than thirty-nine weeks."

Joey was born nine days ahead of his due date. Julia's last ultrasound, where we'd heard her vigorous, healthy heartbeat and watched her wriggle around in my belly, was nine days before her due date. The next day, she was gone. Whether it made sense scientifically or not, my heart could only surmise that *nine* was the magic number.

I knew from previous discussions, which led to the scheduling of Julia's early induction appointment for October 13 (that ended up being two days too late), that Iowa physicians could not induce labor more than one week early, at thirty-nine weeks' gestation, without medical evidence that it was necessary to do so. I needed to know that my history would provide enough reason to deliver early.

As it did the day we'd lost our baby, visible compassion filled Dr. Moshier's face as she closed her eyes and nodded gently.

"I understand," she said. She briefly shared the policy that guides their practice, but quickly followed up in reassuring tones with their firm commitment to excellent patient care and their shared desire to deliver a live, healthy baby. If in the future Joe and I decided that adding another child to our family was something we wanted to do, we would most certainly address our concerns with the team at that time.

"Thank you so much," I said, "for everything."

I was exhausted, like I had just run an obstacle course.

"Yes, thank you, Doctor," Joe added.

I watched as she looked down at her lap and then back up at us, shaking her head slowly.

"You're welcome," she said, though her eyes conveyed much more. "Thank you. I can only imagine how difficult it must have been for you to come back here today. Please take care of yourself. If there is anything at all that we can do, any questions you may have, please know that we are still here for you. You can call anytime."

It was my turn to look at my lap and then back at her. But all I could manage was a quick nod and a small "Thank you," quietly said, but profoundly felt.

In our quiet moments together on the way home, Joe and I agreed that it was far too soon to begin discussing another baby during these early weeks after losing Julia. We needed time to grieve the loss of our daughter, and to learn how to live without her.

We agreed to table the discussion for several months, at least until the summer, before we would even consider having conversations about the possibility of enlarging our family.

Chapter 30

Despite my days looking very much the same, despite how desperately I tried to hold on to them, the six weeks I had at home passed so quickly, it was like trying to catch water from a garden hose in my hands. Thanksgiving came and went, unremarkably so. And the week after the break, it was time to return to my classroom.

At the end of July, I had been informed that my previous position as a teacher of the deaf and hard of hearing had been eliminated due to a decline in enrollment within a low-incidence population. I had been devastated. More than six months pregnant with Julia, my mind immediately panicked with fears of unemployment and how and where I would find a new teaching job at this point in the summer, especially when I was visibly pregnant and would be needing maternity leave so early in the school year.

Thankfully, I had already signed a contract and my school district had a provision for situations like mine that allowed me to stay employed, just within a different position. Out of a pool of choices, I opted to take a position as a special education teacher at an elementary building where I had some previous experience.

From the very beginning, the position was extremely demanding. I signed a new contract with the agreement that I would apply for a conditional license until I could take the graduate classes I needed to earn my endorsement. The learning curve of new curriculum, assessments, and expectations was steep. I was doing my best to manage significant learning needs and behaviors that were largely new to me. Coping with all of this, on top of the fatigue that comes with the last trimester of pregnancy, had me exhausted.

Then we lost Julia.

As the weeks of my maternity leave dwindled to days, panic began to rise out of the pit of my stomach into my chest, then my throat. I was suffocated at the thought of returning to a classroom of children after burying my own child. Designing lesson plans, implementing quality instruction, and managing aggressive behaviors while attempting to walk through the all-consuming grief seemed impossible.

On my first day back, I felt like I was walking through a fog. The car door was jarringly loud as I closed it behind me. All of the other noises of a normal day came in pulsating waves, as if through a seashell—the buses in the drop-off lane; the parents shouting last-minute instructions to "Remember your instrument today!" and "Be good!"; the children's voices playing on the blacktop. I was desperately trying to hold back tears by the time I made it to the giant glass doors. Even the enormous metal-art eagle mascot hanging in the atrium stared at me knowingly as I attempted a deep, calming breath, in and out, before entering the main office.

Immediately, I was greeted warmly by colleagues. Our school secretary, Steph, came around the desk to greet me with a warm, full-bodied hug. I remembered hearing how, when she had been told of Julia's unexpected death, Steph, who was unabashedly outgoing and vivacious, had silently turned around, walked into a nearby office, and closed the door behind her to cry alone. I held my breath, attempting to draw my strength from hers, her long, dark hair tickling my cheek and nose. I heard the fluid sounds of my own saliva in my own ear as I attempted to swallow hard and regain some measure of control of my emotions before letting go. Heat flushed my cheeks as we stepped back slowly. Her hands moved from my back to my elbows, then down to hold my hands, squeezing gently.

"You okay?" The protectiveness and concern in her voice melted my tenuous resolve. I felt my face crumple, and she pulled me back in. "I'm so sorry," she continued in my ear, rubbing my back with the strong palm of her hand. After a moment, we pulled back again, so she could look me in the eyes.

"Do you want to use one of the offices for a minute?" she asked. "Mitch's is empty."

I managed a sharp intake of breath and tiny shake of my head.

"No," I began. "Thank you, though. I just want to go to my classroom."

She blinked and exhaled slowly before nodding her head. I found so much comfort in the lightly golden bronze of her skin, the dark cocoa of her rounded eyes reminding me of my own Mexican roots, my Grandma Julia. *Julia.*

Still holding my hands, she rubbed little circles with her thumbs.

128

"Be gentle with yourself. We're all so happy to have you back. We've missed you, but go easy. You don't have to tackle everything in one day. Whatever you need, I am right here for you. We all are. Okay?"

I swallowed hard, remembering all the colleagues who had come to pay their respects at Julia's visitation and funeral. My mind flashed to the beautiful angel statue and floral arrangement that had been placed only a few feet away from her casket, and all the cards, meals, and plants that had arrived in the days afterward. I had felt so blessed to be surrounded by such a caring community. Still, it felt strange to consider myself "blessed" when my daughter lay buried beneath the ground.

A gentle squeeze of my hands brought me back to the present. I nodded gratefully and went in for one more hug before moving away from Steph to others in the office. I felt like a fragile egg, my thin shell fracturing bit by bit with each hug and heartfelt word.

Gathering all the courage I could muster, I braced myself as I opened the door to head down the highly polished hallway to my classroom. Student artwork lined the walls, glittery snowflake mobiles spun from the library ceiling; it all seemed like remnants of another life. *Before.* Was this the right move? Was I ready for this? No. But did I really have a choice? Would I ever be ready to reenter the life I'd had before I'd lost my daughter? *How* was I going to do this?

Chapter 31

Opening the door to my classroom felt like stepping back in time. The geometric-patterned area rug was still in its place directly in front of the interactive whiteboard, waiting for our daily lessons. The plastic and metal chairs were neatly pushed in at each child's workspace. Colorful crayon boxes, writing folders, and art supplies lined the shelves. Bright, morning sunshine poured in through the floor-to-ceiling windows that looked out onto the playground. It was all so perfect, as if nothing had happened.

I had worked up until the day Julia died. When I had left, I had been fully pregnant, happily on my way to our final prenatal checkup appointment. I closed my eyes and raised my face toward the ceiling, desperate for wisdom and strength to make it through this day.

Over the past week I had connected with my team via e-mail, getting updates in preparation for my return. When asked what they could do to help ease my transition back, the only request I could think to make was that someone please get in touch with the classroom families, to prepare my students. The students in my special education classroom were from all grade levels in our elementary building, kindergarten through fifth grade, and exhibited a wide range of cognitive abilities and social skills. Some of them were especially excited and intrigued by the little life growing inside of me. We had used the opportunity to talk about how to ask for permission before touching someone else's body and practiced when and how to do so.

One little girl, Sasha, had been particularly excited, as she had "lots of baby dolls at home," she'd told me in her most grown-up voice. I couldn't suppress a smile as I watched her raise her shoulders, rub her hands together, and gently place her palms on my belly. "Hi, Baby!" she'd sung, her face so close it was almost touching my rounded stomach. "I can't wait to see you! I love you!" Julia had intuitively chosen that moment to kick hard, and I watched as Sasha's bright blue eyes grew wide in childlike awe; we'd both felt it like an electric current connecting all three of us in that moment.

I opened my eyes and exhaled slowly. Had anyone told her? How had she reacted when she had been told that she would, in fact, *never* get to meet that precious baby? That our baby had never even made it home? I gulped back tears for Sasha as I imagined her heartbreak, her disillusionment upon learning, too soon, how unfair life could be.

The shrill school bell rang loudly, startling me back to my empty classroom. I looked up to the industrial black wall clock, its long, red second hand moving in sharp *tick, tick, tick*s around the white face. The students were at breakfast, but they would be coming in soon, I knew. I had to be ready for them.

I pressed the heels of my palms into my eyes, willing the tears to stop their incessant flowing. I tucked my chin, inhaled a shaky breath, and walked to my desk, preparing myself for the day ahead.

The click of the door latch a few minutes later jolted me to attention. *They are coming. I'm not ready.*

But then I admitted to myself, *I'll never be ready.*

I stood up from my desk, consciously straightened my shoulders and my favorite black cardigan, and walked, with more confidence than I felt, across the polished linoleum floor to greet my students at the door.

Winter coats had replaced their fall jackets. Their locker routine was smoother than it had been six weeks earlier. One by one, they closed the blue metal doors to their lockers and came in the classroom, just as I had remembered them, only quieter. Some of them were looking down, focused on making the sharp right turn from the doorway directly to their seats. One little girl pushed up her glasses with one hand and gave only an inconspicuous wave at her hip as she walked past me. *Strange*, I thought, until I realized that they had likely been reminded just before coming in to "behave normally," which, of course, meant that their behavior would be anything but normal.

I felt a sad smile cross my face as I realized that this was yet another part of life after the death of my child. People, even adults, didn't know how to act, what to say. I was sure that they had probably had a class meeting, maybe a social story about how to behave, what to say, what not to say to Mrs. Price when she returns to school. I felt guilty that these children, who already struggled with nonverbal cues and the unwritten rules of social etiquette, would have to be exposed to these circumstances so early in life.

"Hi, guys!" I began with a forced brightness. Fighting past the pinch in my throat, I continued. "I'm so glad to see you. I've missed you."

The tension in the room was palpable. I could see the paraprofessionals standing behind the students, holding their collective breath, hoping for the best.

Finally, the awkward silence was met by one brave little voice. "I missed you, too, Mrs. Price."

Some of the tension broke loose in my chest and the rest of the room, then. A subdued chorus of greetings gradually began to crescendo into exuberance as they talked about what they had been learning and doing in my absence. I released a small held breath as I listened to them and closed my eyes in silent thanks for having made it through that moment.

We completed our calendar routine and began our writing activity, but Julia was always at the forefront of my mind. When we began a music and movement activity, one of the girls chose a song from a popular movie about a princess. I had never seen the movie and I remember thinking, *before*, how when Julia was born I would need to familiarize myself with all of those girly things. I gulped back the emotion rising in my throat and blinked hard at the threatening tears. *Before*, but not anymore.

Later in the day, we all sat around a large table for a social skills activity. We pulled large photo cards out of a box and discussed what was happening in the picture and looked for clues that would tell us how the people in the picture were feeling. We came to a card with a little boy with his head hanging down, his lower lip puckered out, and a broken truck in his lap. I held it out and asked, "How do we think this little boy is feeling?"

"He's sad," answered a boy with brilliant blue eyes and a round, cherubic face.

"Yes," I validated. "I think you're right. I think he is sad. How do we know that?"

"Because he is not smiling," called out a little girl with creamy hazelnut skin and hair styled in an intricate pattern of long braids and colorful beads. "He's frowning. Like this," she continued, dropping her head and pouting her lower lip dramatically.

"That's right. His face is giving us clues that he is sad. Let's look for other clues in the picture. *Why* do we think he might be feeling sad?"

There was a beat before another little girl ventured, "Maybe because his baby died?"

Instantly, I felt heat rush to the surface of my skin. I tried to swallow, but my mouth was completely parched. I tried to take a breath, but it felt like I was stoking a fire in my throat and lungs. I couldn't lose control now, not in front of the children. But the room started to move away from me, as if I were traveling backward through a tunnel. A hand came from behind me to rest gently on my shoulder, grounding me. I looked up to see one of my paraprofessionals looking down at me, her face crinkled in sympathy. I turned my back to my students to look up at her, and the tears that I had been blinking back all day finally began to overflow.

"Why don't you take a break for a minute? We've got this," she said.

The hesitation stuck in my throat, and I ended up nodding my head in agreement.

Without looking back at my students, I stood up and walked out of the room. I walked the few steps around the corner to the end of the hallway by the recess door and rested my face against the wall, and let loose an agonized, silent scream. I pressed my fists hard against the painted cinderblock walls, needing the sensory input, the physical pain, to match the emotional anguish inside of me.

I turned around, leaning the back of my head against the wall, drawing in a breath and holding it tightly. I couldn't stay there, weeping in the kindergarten hallway.

I can't do *this*, I thought, and I truly didn't think that I could.

I looked at the door that led out to the playground blacktop, the jump ropes and basketballs ready for recess. I thought how good it might feel to take in a breath of clean, fresh air. But it was almost December. I didn't have a coat or a key to get back into the building. I'd have to walk all the way around to the front and face more people, more questions, to get back in. I didn't want to have to tell the story and relive what had just happened. I considered how much I just wanted to go back home and put my head under the covers and not come back out.

But my students needed me.

I peeled myself off of the wall that had been holding me up and quickly made my way to the staff bathroom twenty feet down the hall. As the door closed itself behind me, I was slightly shocked by my reflection in the mirror above the industrial sink. I looked so tired. I *was* so tired, I realized. I placed my hands against the cornflower-blue laminate countertop and leaned in heavily. I was exhausted and it wasn't even lunchtime. How was I going to make it through this day, and all the others after it? How was I going to *live* like this?

I bent over the sink and splashed cold water on my red swollen face, only to stand up, see my reflection, and revert back into uncontrollable sobs. I had to get myself together, but—how? My child had *died*, and I didn't know how to go on without her. Her loss had changed me. Looking at myself in the mirror, I knew I looked the same on the outside, but inside I was different. How was I supposed to come back to work and continue my life from before, when I didn't even recognize myself?

By the third attempt of washing the redness out of my eyes and cheeks, I resigned myself to the fact that I was not going back into the classroom fresh-faced and happy—because I wasn't either of those things. I was broken. I dried my hands and my face with the thin brown paper towel that seemed to disintegrate in my hands. I used another one to open the door and dropped them both into the little plastic waste can by the exit.

I opted to take the long way around the hallway back to my classroom, hopeful that the change in scenery might help distract me from the fear of returning to my classroom, and my own expectations for "normalcy," expectations I could never fulfill. Over the last six weeks many people had encouraged me to find a "new normal." I rejected the idea that anything could feel "normal" about my child being dead. But, I also recognized, I would have to learn to live with that reality, learn to be okay with not being okay.

It was a tough lesson to learn, I thought, as I passed by a group of giggly first graders on their way to the library. I thought again of the students in my classroom, waiting for me to teach them social skills. Someday, perhaps I could have a conversation with my students about how it was okay to not be okay. How it is all right to be sad when bad things happen to us. But, I thought, sucking in a breath and pushing down the door handle, today was not that day.

Chapter 32

After making it through the rest of the morning without having to leave the classroom, I held my breath as I dismissed my students to the playground for recess. The three paraprofessionals would supervise them as they played and then escort them to the cafeteria for lunch.

I was exhausted. The past six weeks had taught me how draining constant emotion was for my body. Yet, as it turned out, stifling all of these emotions was just as tiring. I couldn't eat my lunch; my stomach felt like a wrung-out, twisted-up rag. I fell into my rolling desk chair with a heavy sigh. I rested my elbows on top of the ungraded spelling tests and spiral notebooks and covered my face with shaky hands.

This is only day one, I thought. How in the world was I going to make it the remaining six months of the school year? Desperation pinched at the edges of my sadness, squeezing, making it feel more like unchecked anxiety.

I closed my eyes, desperate to calm my body to prevent a full-blown panic attack. I pushed aside the clutter and rested my forehead against the sturdy wooden teacher's desk, willing the fast, hard breaths to slow. But the more I tried to focus on peaceful thoughts, the more my mind raced with turbulent ones.

It's never going to get better. Julia is gone. She's never coming back. You work with kids. They will always remind you of her. You will always—

My upper body bolted upright at the click of the latch and the slow creak of the classroom door opening. My tears paused for just a moment, defying gravity while I held my breath, wondering who was coming, and why. When I saw Addie's face peek around the barely open door, relief and gratitude reopened my airways.

"Hey, friend," she said, stepping in slowly, "Can I come in?"

I nodded vigorously, not trusting my voice to convey my desire for her company.

"Hey," she started again.

I lifted my chin and pressed my lips into my best attempt at a smile.

Addie and I had become friends four years earlier, but ours was the kind of friendship that felt much longer. She had been with me through some of the darkest places in my battle with infertility, and was one of the first people to find out that I was pregnant—first with Joey, then again with Julia. She had been at the hospital the day Joey was born, and on that dark night six weeks ago, she was one of the few people to ever hold my baby girl.

We were somewhat unlikely friends. She was the effervescent extrovert; I was the shy introvert. We both knew that my emotional outbursts made her uncomfortable. I sometimes wondered why she stayed.

She would say something outrageous, to try to make me laugh, and I would end up laughing through my tears. She believed in me, and I trusted her.

I told her about my morning—about the kids coming in and acting weird, about the social skills lesson, about all the times I wanted to walk out the door and never come back.

"But you didn't," she answered. "You didn't leave. Because you are strong."

"Strong?" I scoffed.

"It's true. It's hard. Of course it is! No one would expect it to be easy. But you are doing it. You're still here, because you are so much stronger than you give yourself credit for."

I felt my face crumple at this. Hot, salty tears ran down my cheeks onto my dry, cracked lips. I didn't want to be strong. I wanted my baby.

"I know this day sucks," she said, softening. "But I'm proud of you for making it this far. Pretty soon you'll get through the rest of it, too. And you don't have to do it alone. How can I help?" she asked, shifting from side to side, hands out, as if she were a basketball player, ready to catch an invisible chest pass.

I smiled at this. Addie was always most comfortable when she was doing something. When I called her from the hospital gazebo the day Julia died, she had come immediately, then driven straight to the pharmacy, bringing back soft tissues, bottled water, and anything else she thought we might need. In the days leading up to the funeral, she and her family had brought us food trays and essential items so that we wouldn't need to make any extra trips to the store. While we were out running errands and buying the shoes Julia would be buried in, Addie had come and cleaned my house in preparation for the out-of-town guests we were expecting.

"Seriously, give me a job," she said, bringing me back to the moment. "Do you want me to go get you some lunch? Do you want me to do an activity with the kids so you can have a little more time? Do you want me to flash you?" she asked, tugging at her button-down shirt, bouncing her eyebrows upward and batting her long, dark eyelashes suggestively.

It was enough to shock me into a little laughter, in spite of myself. I knew that it was Addie's coping mechanism. She turned to humor, usually silly, sometimes dark and irreverent, as a way to break the tension and avoid becoming emotional herself. I smiled at the irony that someone who was so uncomfortable with big displays of emotion could be best friends with someone like me, and I loved her for it.

"Well, you know that always does make me feel better," I returned drily, wiping my nose again and forcing a small, lopsided smile.

"I'm here to help," she quipped. Then, turning more serious. "I love you, friend. I'm so sorry this is happening to you. Is there *anything* I can do?"

My eyes searched the room as if I might find an answer there. Finding nothing, I looked back to her and shook my head.

"You know, you've taken some big steps today. Maybe you could talk to Mitch? Take the rest of the afternoon off? I'm sure people would come and fill in. Lots of people want to help."

Mitch was our principal. He had come to Julia's visitation and funeral. I knew he and so many other staff members wanted to help me, but how? I had already taken so many weeks off. I didn't want to be a slacker, or to confuse my students any further by leaving again.

"I'll be okay," I answered quietly.

Addie dropped her chin to her chest and raised one brow to look at me disbelievingly.

"I will. Seriously." I laughed.

She closed her eyes slowly, her long, dark curly lashes resting for a moment on her high cheekbones. She pressed her lips together and breathed out deeply through her nose. "I love you."

I looked down at the floor and nodded quickly, giving myself enough time to swallow the lump in my throat before answering, "Love you, too."

Chapter 33

The pressure in my chest lifted enough to allow the first full breath of the day. Finally, miraculously, I'd made it to the end of my first teaching day. My eyes were heavy and achy when I looked up to see my co-teacher, Angie, walk through the door. Hired a few weeks into the school year, Angie's primary responsibility was to float among several special education classrooms in three different buildings in our district, to allow the teachers in those classrooms to have a prep period. In my case, she taught social studies to my students at the end of the day. I had been so relieved when she had joined us in late September, and we had worked it out that she would finish out the day teaching social studies to my students, allowing me a much-needed break to complete paperwork and all of the other tasks I couldn't accomplish while responsible for instructing a room full of students.

Angie was another aspect of my *before* life, I realized. We had only met about a week before Julia had been born, and I had been grateful to have a chance to sit down after being on my feet all day, and to have a plan in place before I left for maternity leave. At the time, I was relieved to be able to check one more box on my sub plans, to know my long-term sub would also have prep time, and that my class would be in capable hands, which meant I would be free to relax and enjoy getting to know Julia during our six weeks at home together. But that was *before*.

Her heavy teacher bag slung over one shoulder and her mouth on the straw of the cup she carried in the other hand, Angie bounced across the room to my teacher's desk.

We both startled slightly when our eyes met. I watched as sympathy softened her hazel-green eyes.

"Hey, welcome back!" Like so many others today, I felt the weight of what was left unsaid hanging in the air between us.

"Hi. Thanks," I replied, grateful that this would be one of the last awkward interactions I would face today. "They're just finishing up," I went on, nodding toward the students as they began cleaning up their math supplies and preparing for the transition to social studies.

"Great!" she said, a bit too brightly. She shook her head nervously and her coppery red topknot bobbed along vigorously. A brief awkward silence fell between us, and I could see the red splotches begin to creep up her fair, freckled neck and face. I could feel the heat rise in my own complexion, too. I felt guilty. People didn't know how to act around me, and I didn't know how to help them. I was too focused on surviving each moment to find a way to ease their discomfort, the discomfort we shared.

After another beat, I turned away, breaking a bit of the tension that had built between us.

"I think I'm going to go to the office and check my mailbox," I offered.

"Sure!" she said, again, with more enthusiasm than was required for the interaction.

I grabbed my water cup—the small pitcher with a reusable plastic straw that the hospital had given us the night Julia was born. I clutched it tightly against my chest, hearing the fragments of barely frozen ice cubes slosh against its sides. I inhaled and forced my lips into a tense smile before sticking the straw in my mouth and sucking in hard, willing the water to cool my burning face and neck. As I made my way out the door a chorus of little voices sent me on my way.

"Bye, Mrs. Price!" "See you later!" See you tomorrow!"

"I'm just going to the office," I assured them with a genuine smile. "I'll be back." I put my hand up for a halfhearted wave and quickened my pace out the door.

Tomorrow, I considered with a heavy sigh. What a daunting thought.

I made my way down the hallway, darkened until automatic ener-gy-saving lights clicked on as I walked. The brightly polished floors reflected bits of sunlight through classroom windows, gleaming up at me as if lighting my path.

It was a long trek around the building to the office. I remembered walk-ing, or waddling, this course multiple times a day when I was pregnant with Julia. Inevitably, I'd be stopped along the way by the wide, knowing smiles of my colleagues. "Getting close, huh?" they'd ask. "When are you due again?" I closed my eyes and swallowed hard, pushing back the memories. The halls were empty today. No more friendly faces, no more questions, no more baby.

My hands were tingling as I reached for the shiny metal lever to open the office door. I paused to draw in a stabilizing breath before pulling open the heavy wooden door and walking through.

"Hey, Mrs. Price!" Steph's voice sounded intentionally chipper, but not falsely so. Memories of my entry from the outside door this morning came back, recalling the difficulty of walking back into my old life.

"Hey," I tried to match her tone, but didn't quite reach it.

The office was quiet at this point in the afternoon, one reason why I had avoided it until now. Another friend, Diane stood at the copier as I came around the corner, and I braced myself for the interaction.

"Hi, Maria," she began, and I could already feel the tightening in my chest and the prickling in my nose that signaled I was in danger of dropping my threadbare veil of composure.

"How are you doing?" she asked, with the concerned head tilt and furrowed brow that everyone seemed to use to greet me now. I recognized it because I saw it all the time. I recognized it because I, too, had used it, *before*.

I didn't dare breathe. I focused on her forehead, tortoiseshell glasses resting like a crown on top of her head, her sparkly snowman earrings, anything but her dark, kind, knowing eyes.

"I'm fine." My response was too quick, too high-pitched to sound credible. Desperate, I tried for a convincing bob of my head, but it was too late. Tears had already pooled in my eyes, and when I blinked they came spilling over onto my cheeks.

"Oh, hon," she said, almost sounding relieved at my emotional release. She reached out and touched my arm halfway between my elbow and my wrist. "I'm so, so sorry." Without a conscious thought, we moved together into a deep hug, her hand pressed between my shoulder blades, my face deep in her coarse, silver hair. She smelled clean, an indistinguishable blend of shampoo and fabric softener. Although I did not know her well, I felt safe somehow in this embrace, relieved to finally let go of the feelings I had attempted to keep caged all day.

When the emotion began to gently ebb, we took simultaneous steps backward, but her head was still in that tilted position.

"I don't know how you are doing it," she went on. "You are so strong."

I opened my mouth and exhaled a small, humorless laugh.

"I am *not* strong," I told her. "Not at all."

"Maybe you don't *feel* strong," she said dropping her chin to her chest to meet my gaze, "but you are a *lot* stronger than you think you are."

She reached out to me and pulled me into a maternal embrace.

"I'm so sorry," she whispered in my ear, gently stroking my hair.

What was I doing? I barely knew this woman, but it felt so good to be seen, validated, it felt so much like love.

As I came up for air, I could see the tears in her eyes, too. She reached for a box of tissues on a nearby shelf and offered them to me before taking one herself. I watched her dab at the corners of her eyes lightly, the way women do when they are trying to avoid smearing their mascara.

I took one of the tissues in my hand and swiped in broad strokes at my eyes, cheeks, and nose. There was no hope for even the best waterproof mascara today. Whatever feeble attempts I had made this morning to cover up the red puffiness in my complexion had been washed away hours ago.

"Can you go home?" she asked.

I felt my eyes widen as I looked at her past the soggy tissue in my hand.

"I just mean, it's almost the end of the day. Maybe you could ask Mitch if you could just take the rest of the day?"

I closed my eyes and dropped my head. I wanted to go home, but I felt like I had already been given so much, I was afraid I would be perceived as lazy or taking advantage of that generosity.

"I don't know," I replied weakly, shaking my head. "It's almost the end of the day."

The hesitation in my voice seemed to only propel her further.

"Come on. Let's go find Mitch," she said, her voice a mixture of authority and nurture. She turned on her heel and I felt compelled to follow her.

We stopped steps away at Steph's desk, and the conversation turned to how many days of leave I had left to use. Being a teacher, my contract did not include vacation days, and I had already exhausted my maternity and bereavement leave allotments.

As Diane, Steph, and I were talking, Mitch walked out of his office and joined us.

"Hey, guys, how's it going?" he asked, looking at me, his concern evident in his sympathetic voice and expression.

"We are looking at leave options for Maria," Steph said.

As they talked about HR and logistics, I desperately wanted to escape, to compose myself, tell them this wasn't necessary, but their kindness seemed to draw the emotion out of me.

Mitch pushed his dark-rimmed glasses up his nose and straightened his back.

"Let me call HR," he said, looking up at the clock. The bell would ring soon, signaling the end of the day. "Do you have time to come back after dismissal so we can discuss what I find out, and we can develop a plan? Maybe Angie can come with you?"

I held my breath and nodded my head in agreement, pulling the edges of my cardigan and wrapping it tightly around myself. Diane, Steph, and Mitch seemed to feel some relief that at least this much was settled.

I exhaled and offered a silent smile of gratitude to everyone in the small circle. They returned small sad smiles and nods, which seemed to grant me permission to end the encounter and search for a place to regain some of my composure.

As I walked through the door into the relative privacy of the hallway, I drew in a deep, staggered breath. I kept my head down and made my way quickly to the staff restroom just around the corner. I pulled hard on the door, struggling against the heavy vacuum seal, praying I would be alone.

Relieved to find it empty, I made my way past the sink to the larger of the two stalls and closed the metal door behind me. Aware that my privacy could be interrupted at any moment, I slammed myself back against the painted cinderblock wall and let out an anguished, silent scream. My daughter died. Wasn't that enough trauma for one person? Why must I live every day, every moment with these secondary losses, reminders that my life *was* not, and *would not ever*, be the same again?

Minutes passed, and the piercing trill of the school bell jolted me back to the moment. It was the end of the day and the restroom would soon be inundated by teachers who had been waiting too long to use these facilities. I did not want to face them, their questions, and their pity. I couldn't do it.

I unlocked the stall door, hurried over to the sink, and turned on the cold water. After splashing water on my face, I stood and sighed at my tearstained, swollen reflection. Not for the first time that day I had to resign myself to the fact that I could not wash away the redness, the dark circles, or the sadness from my face.

Pushing out a heavy sigh, I felt some of the tension loosen in my neck and shoulders. My eyes stung as I closed and wiped over them with the rough paper towel in hard, heavy strokes. Dropping the towel in the tall industrial gray trash can, I took one last look. I barely recognized myself. Not because I looked so different, but because I felt like a completely different person than I had been *before*.

Chapter 34

The busyness of the end of the day in an elementary school had evened out to a steady hum as Angie and I walked together to the office to meet with Mitch.

Steph led us into the conference room to wait. When I sank into a cushioned armchair, I suddenly realized how heavy my eyelids had become. I rested my elbows on the long wooden table and brought my face to rest on top of my closed fists. I pushed hard against my eyelids, rubbing in large circles, hoping to inspire energy back into them.

I flinched at the sound of the door opening and watched Mitch walk in, yellow legal pad in one hand and a pen in the other. He moved quickly, with his characteristic confidence and authority, pulling out a chair and sitting down at the head of the table. Steph followed him, closing the door behind them and coming to sit in the chair next to mine.

I sat up straighter, feeling my pulse quicken and finding it a bit harder to breathe in the enclosed space. I looked across the table to Angie, who shot an almost imperceptible nod of encouragement. I swallowed hard and wondered what Mitch had learned from his call to HR—what it would mean for me.

"So," he began, concern rounding out the edges of his tone, "how did it go today?"

I felt my eyes dart over to Angie, then back down to the table. I exhaled a shallow breath before I began.

"Good," I said, suddenly aware of how dry my throat had become. I closed my eyes, then looked up to meet his gaze. "It went okay," I amended.

"Great," he replied after a beat, nodding. After another brief pause, he looked down at his paper, with notes in his block handwriting, a bit too far away for me to read. He clicked his pen a couple of times before beginning again.

"So, we have been in contact with HR, and it looks like there are not any more paid days of leave available. If you want, though, we can talk about finding some extra time, if you feel that is what you need."

I shook my head, feeling heat rise to my face. This was what I had expected. It hadn't been my idea to ask about this. I felt silly, like a child being told that the ice cream truck had sold out of my favorite flavor.

"That's fine," I returned. "It's fine. Really. Thank you for asking. That was kind of you. All of you."

My words hung in the air for a few moments before Mitch moved forward in his seat. Clearing his throat, he continued more gently.

"We'd like to help in whatever way we can—to make it easier for you. Can you tell us what we could do, how we can help?"

My breathing became shallower, and lightheadedness began to overtake me.

"I—I don't know," I admitted with a weak smile. "I . . . I think I'll be all right."

I felt Steph's hand rubbing gentle circles on my back.

"Do you think it would help to take more time off?" she asked. "I mean, we've missed you, and we love having you here, but we want you to do what's right for you."

The prickling in my nose and my fingers returned as I fought the losing battle against yet another onslaught of embarrassing tears.

"No. I'm okay. Thank you. You have all been so great, so kind to me. I want to do my job."

I closed my eyes and opened them again, still staring down at the table.

"I mean—I'd love to stay home, but I'm not sure if that would help. I don't know that I will ever really be *ready* to come back. And I don't want to confuse the kids any more than I already have."

I couldn't look at them, but I imagined they were looking at each other, asking silently whether or not I was to be believed. The tension in the room rose with each unspoken word.

Angie quietly cleared her throat. "The kids will be okay," she said in reassuring tones. "We all just want *you* to be all right."

All right? They wanted me to be *all right?* I knew what she meant, and I appreciated the sentiment. They were all being extraordinarily kind, but my heart thudded with the reality that *my daughter was dead.* The truth was that there was nothing they could do, nothing I could do, to make everything better, normal. I had lost hope that I would ever be *all right* again.

"Is there anything that you can think of, anything we could do to help make it a little bit easier for you?" Mitch said.

I opened my mouth to speak but nothing came out. Not sure if this was because of the lump in my throat or the fact that I simply couldn't conceive of a response, I closed it again. I held my breath and dug my fingernails deep into my palms, making little half-moon indentations in my skin. But it wasn't helping. I was beginning to lose control.

"I'm—okay," I lied. "I'm . . . fine."

"We want to help you," Mitch insisted, raking his fingers through his sandy-colored hair in obvious frustration. "We just need you to tell us what to do."

I could hear the exasperation in his voice and it made me want to crawl into a hole. I felt stupid and small and unprofessional. I knew he wanted to help. He wanted to fix it. Everyone just wanted to fix it. I wanted to fix it, too. But there was no *thing* to fix. What was *broken* was—me. Julia's death had shattered into tiny shards the person—the mother, the wife, the friend, the teacher—I had once been. What was broken was *me*.

"I'm sorry," I cried, and the intensity in my voice surprised even me.

Sweat broke out on my forehead and upper lip. My hands and legs were shaking uncontrollably under the table. The tears that had already been a steady stream began to gush out as if from a fire hose. I felt ashamed at breaking down in front of my boss and my colleagues, and I wanted to stop, but I had to get it out.

"I'm sorry. I really am. I know you just want to help me, and I wish I knew what I needed. I really do. But I just don't. I don't know. The only thing I know that I need is the one thing you can't give me. I need my baby. I just—I need my baby."

Exhausted, I dropped my head and covered my face with my hands. I didn't hear any sound, any voices, any movement. I was afraid, ashamed to sit up and face them again.

When I did manage to open my eyes and chance a brief glance, I saw Mitch, his dark-rimmed glasses in one hand, pinching the bridge of his nose with the other, exhaling a deep but soundless breath.

In the end, we decided to see if Angie could arrange her schedule with the other teachers on her caseload so that she could come earlier in the day and take over for me in my classroom. I would spend more of the afternoon catching up on paperwork in a private office and finding a way to transition back into my old life. Or, perhaps it would be transitioning into a new life altogether.

I was so grateful for their kindness, their thoughtfulness in making these changes for me. I felt undeserving and feared that at some point I would exasperate their patience and their sympathy. It was humiliating to need their help, to admit that I couldn't just get it together and do my job. Would it always be this way? Embarrassed, grateful, and exhausted, I could not articulate any of this, and settled for, "Thank you so much. I really appreciate all of you and your willingness to help me. I'm sorry."

As soon as the next day, I realized that having time to myself to work in a quiet office, away from the bustling noise that constantly butted up against my grief, was actually a huge relief. I found solace and respite in my time alone at the end of each day. I was able to ease into my work and get caught up on the never-ending mountain of paperwork required of special education teachers. I was deeply grateful to my team, who gave me the space I needed to find my way forward.

Chapter 35

For years I had seen the posters in the teachers' lounge advertising the Employee Assistance Program but had disregarded it as something for someone else, not something that pertained to me. Now, it felt as if this program had been created with me in mind. Participants were granted a handful of mental health services, including grief counseling, by a partnership between my school district and a local health organization.

When I put my car into park and stared up at the white, box-like, soulless building with dark rectangular windows, I rested my head on the steering wheel and cried. It was so unfair. *I should be at home holding my baby right now*, I thought miserably.

But I wasn't at home cooing with my newborn baby. I was at a therapy appointment. On an overcast early December afternoon, I had come to this office building to talk to a stranger *about* my baby, who had died.

I lifted my body up from the steering wheel and slumped back into my seat. When I flipped open the little door to the mirror on the inside of my visor and the light came on, I sighed at the reflection I saw. The dark circles beneath my eyes had deepened and darkened over the last seven weeks. It looked like a permanent burglar's mask, even though I was the one from whom something precious had been stolen. The whites of my eyes were red and bloodshot. Despite the high-end facial lotion my mom had gotten me, my nose was still prone to dryness and cracking from the constant use of tissues to wipe it. I closed my eyes and smacked the mirror shut.

It's not going to get any better than this, I scoffed inwardly.

Reaching for my purse, I made sure that I had my wallet and a couple of packs of tissues before opening the door to the outside.

Once in the building, I stepped into the elevator with an older gentleman. I stared at the door, willing it to close and get us quickly to where we needed to go. It was only seconds, but the awkward silence made it feel much longer.

He stood quietly in his beige trench coat and blue plaid scarf, also watching the numbers light up as we ascended each floor. He did not have a briefcase or anything else in his hand. Did he work in one of the offices here? I pulled my purse more tightly against me, hugging myself, the wool collar of my winter coat scratching against the side of my neck. I knew he must have noticed my tearstained cheeks, my swollen eyes and nose. Was he wondering about me, too? Or was he also receiving counseling? Had he lost someone he had loved, too?

A loud *ding* signaled our arrival on the third floor, pulling me back to the moment. I braved a sideways glance and he held his hand out in a "you first" gesture. I nodded politely and quickly exited in front of him. Following the signs with large black arrows to my destination, I turned tightly to the left. I peeked behind me to see if he was following. But he wasn't. He had turned to the right. *Good for him.*

When I arrived at the door to the therapy office, I rested my hand on the lever, pausing before I pushed it down. *Could I do this?* I looked to my right, back down the long hall. The man in the trench coat was gone. I considered leaving, too, going home. But that felt inconsiderate. I would have to call and cancel the appointment, wasting busy people's time. Would I reschedule anyway? *Just get it over with,* I told myself, and forced down the lever to open the door.

The waiting room was empty and silent. Even the receptionist's desk was vacant. It was an eerie feeling walking through, as if I were somewhere I wasn't supposed to be. I raised my eyebrows in realization that I *wasn't* supposed to be here. I was *supposed* to be with my daughter, who *wasn't supposed* to die.

I closed my eyes, shook the thoughts away, and walked forward. The office was neat, but outdated. It reminded me of one of those silly sitcoms from my childhood, the ones where they play slow, melancholic music while the characters have heart-to-heart chats and wrap everything up in a neat bow at the end of each episode.

"Hello!"

I winced as a middle-aged woman with spiky blonde hair and oversized cat earrings dangling from her ears slid open the glass partition to the check-in desk. My palms were sweaty, but my mouth was dry. I looked at her silently, forgetting what I should say, what I should do.

"Are you here to see someone?"

"Yes. Yes, sorry. I am. I am Maria Price. I have an appointment."

"Okay. Do you remember who you are seeing today?" she asked.

"Umm, no—I'm sorry, I don't remember her name."

I can barely even remember my own name, I thought, making a pretense of looking through my bag to find the name of the counselor they had assigned to me when I'd made the appointment a couple of weeks ago.

"I'm sorry," I said finally, giving up and returning my gaze to her.

"Okay. That's fine. Why are you seeing us today?"

Seriously? Didn't they have this written down somewhere? Shouldn't she be able to pull up my file on her computer and find "Daughter is dead" in the notes next to my name?

I trained my eyes on the clock above her head, begging the tears to, this once, stay in their ducts.

"Grief counseling," I replied, the familiar prickle in my nose and dampness in my eyes letting me know that the tears had no intention of staying away from this interaction.

"My daughter—my daughter was stillborn. . . . She died," I managed, before dropping my eyes to the dull beige laminate countertop.

"I'm sorry," she replied quietly. She handed me a clipboard of forms to complete and sign.

After I'd filled them out and handed them back, she invited me to have a seat while I waited to be called. I noticed the rough upholstery on the chair, and despite the fullness in my sinuses, I could smell a strange mustiness that I couldn't quite place. I started to wonder again if I had made a mistake.

Just then, however, a bubbly woman peeked around the corner. She had straight strawberry blonde hair that stopped halfway between her shoulders and her waist. She wore glasses that framed her eyes in bright plastic rims. As she pushed them up the bridge of her nose, I noticed a silver bracelet loaded with dangly charms.

I felt my shoulders relax a bit. She was younger than I'd expected her to be. Probably about my age. She was curvy, and her jeans and purple cable-knit sweater were not sloppy, but casual, not a professional suit that might have felt intimidating. She seemed approachable, less like a therapist and more like an old college roommate, and I wondered if this was by design.

"Hi, Maria," she said, reaching out a hand. "My name's Tracy. It's nice to meet you."

She led me down a narrow corridor and into her office. The small space was neat, but overwhelmingly full. Every shelf was crammed with books and topped with knickknacks that seemed to have sentimental meaning. Even the wall space was covered by inspirational posters and a framed diploma from a school I didn't recognize.

I scanned the room and stopped at the windowsill where one of those solar-powered animated desk toys, a daisy with a yellow face and sunglasses, stared back at me. Its chartreuse leaves waved outward like arms as it swayed back and forth in a dancing motion, seeming to not have a care in the world. I felt my eyes narrow as I stared down that daisy for being so blissfully unaware, so indifferent to the real pain that existed in the world.

"All right," Tracy began, and for a moment, I sat, blinking, thinking that the voice had come from that flower. "So, we can go ahead and get started."

I pressed my lips into a tight smile. They were so dry I could feel the chapped pieces of skin poking out, and I felt myself biting them self-consciously as I nodded my agreement.

"Good," she smiled.

Despite the pounding in my chest, her calm demeanor inspired a sense of ease. Tracy started by telling me about herself. I had expected this. It seemed like a good plan, an attempt to gain my trust before she expected me to share intimate details about myself.

When she had finished, she let the silence fall between us for a few moments before continuing, audible caution encasing her casual tone.

"So, would you like to tell me a little about yourself? Or what brings you here today?"

I stared again at that stupid, smiling daisy and felt tears approaching hard and fast. I opened my mouth, but my throat was thick with emotion and could produce no words, so I closed it again. I looked down at my hands and started to reach for the plastic-wrapped packs of tissues in my purse, but Tracy reached out and handed me a box with a single white tissue sticking up like a flag, offering itself to me. I attempted a smile of thanks as I took it and set the box down beside me.

"I'm Maria," I started, realizing that this was dumb, as I knew she already knew my name. Then, simply, "My daughter died." It was a statement that somehow felt like a confession. Once it was out, it was followed by a deep, heaving sob. I felt ridiculous, ugly-crying in the tiny office of this professional I had only met two minutes before. I wondered if it had been a huge mistake to even come here, to expect any good to come from this.

When I finally gathered enough courage to look back up at Tracy, I saw concern but no judgment in her face. Her expression conveyed sympathy, but without the head tilt to which I had become accustomed. She nodded gently, spurring me, without pushing me, onward.

I swallowed and used a new, dry tissue to wipe my nose before continuing our story. I told her about Joe and me, about Joey and how we had wanted another child. I told her about our perfectly normal pregnancy. And then, I told her about the day we lost Julia.

It felt good and terrible to talk about it. Good to share Julia's story, to say her name, to acknowledge her beautiful existence. But terrible to know that there was so little story to tell.

I looked at her and saw more compassion, but still no judgment.

"I'm sorry that happened to you. Thank you for telling me your story," Tracy said after a pause, and I knew she meant it. She let another long, deliberate pause hang in the air, and then she asked, "Why did you come here? What do you hope to get out of our time together?"

I sat back a bit in my chair and felt my face scrunch up a bit in concentration. Of course, I had thought about this, but apparently not enough to construct a response.

"Maybe you're not sure yet, and that's okay," she followed up. She sat quietly, allowing me more time to think.

"Well, I guess I'm not completely sure. My family and friends think I need to see someone," I answered honestly. "And I guess I agree with them. I have just hesitated, I guess. I just—I know that it won't bring her back. Nothing will bring her back. So everything feels kind of pointless." I suddenly thought better of that. "Not that I don't think you are good at your job; it's not you."

Tracy smiled reassuringly. "I know what you mean."

I swallowed again and nodded, my gaze returning to the tissue I was twisting in my hands.

"I thought it might be good, though, to talk to someone different. Someone who I don't know and who doesn't know me. Someone I don't have to pretend with. Someone I can tell my honest feelings to and who won't judge me or try to make me feel better by saying things like 'Everything's going to be okay.' Because it's not okay. It will never be okay."

I looked at her briefly to get her reaction. When I saw her nodding in what seemed to be agreement, or at least comprehension, I continued.

"I know people want to make me feel better, but they tell me to 'count my blessings' or 'Everything happens for a reason,' and I just—I don't believe that," I said, my nostrils flaring. "I just don't feel like I can be honest most of the time, without making people worried or upset. And that's just—really hard."

We talked for a long time about people, about Julia, about me. I admitted to Tracy that yes, I was sad, but I was also angry. So very angry. We talked about my anger at God. I knew this was a critical component in my grief, but one that I didn't feel comfortable sharing with most people, for fear of their judgment.

"Hmm. Why do you think you're so angry at God?" she asked, sitting back and pulling one leg up to rest her ankle on the other knee.

"I don't know. I know everyone tells me He loves me, and I have always believed that, but it doesn't *feel* like that right now. I believe that He could have prevented Julia's death. I know in my soul that He could have healed her, and saved her. But He didn't. I don't know why. In my head, I know I don't *have* to know, but in my heart—I just don't know if I can be okay with that. I know in my heart that God is big enough to take my big feelings. He made me with emotions and gives me the ability to express them. He even gives me the choice to reject Him. I believe that. I am just having a really hard time reconciling what I *know* with what I *feel*."

"Hmm," Tracy said again, scratching her nose. "Have you tried talking to God about it—praying?"

"Yes," I started. "And no." I took a deep breath. "I'm having a really hard time with that."

"That's understandable," she replied.

She looked away and scratched lightly in her hairline before reaching her arms to her crossed leg, making a "V" shape across her chest.

I could feel her discomfort rising like a partition between us. I wasn't sure if I was imagining it. It seemed like she was trying, but it felt like she was uncomfortable with the conversation turning to faith.

"I just miss her," I said finally. "And I don't know what to do about that. I feel so helpless," I shared, hoping to steer the conversation into more-neutral territory.

"Of course!"

Tracy seemed to brighten at this—probably not because she was happy to hear it, but because she was relieved to be headed away from faith talk and back into her comfort zone. This was my assessment. I had dealt with this a lot in the past several weeks. It seemed an irony that part of my role as a griever was to ensure the comfort of those who were trying to comfort me. Don't talk about this, don't bring up that, don't cry too much, don't express how you *really* feel, or you might scare them off.

"I know it's not the same as losing a child—I can't imagine that . . ." Tracy began.

I braced myself for what would come next.

". . . but I lost my grandma last year." She began sharing some practical things she did to help her feel connected to her grandmother, de-stressing techniques, and strategies for self-care. She handed me a tiny keychain like one that had become a sort of talisman for her, a little plastic cat with a local insurance company's logo on the side.

"Keep it in your pocket," she suggested. "Perhaps when you feel especially lonely, you could reach for it and feel closer to Julia."

I appreciated what she was trying to do for me. It was kind of her to share her own story and this practical advice. She was trying to help, I knew that. But what I wanted to tell her, what I wanted to scream, was that I didn't want to be comforted. I didn't want to carry a keychain in my pocket; I wanted to hold my daughter in my arms.

"Thank you," I whispered, taking the tiny tabby cat in my hand, squeezing it gently. "I appreciate that."

We concluded our visit by scheduling another appointment for the following week.

I dropped the squelchy globs of tissues from my lap into the little plastic can she had offered me early in the session and reached for my purse.

As I stood up, I felt off balance, my sinuses congested from crying for the past hour. She walked me back down the hallway, my head and eyelids so heavy that it felt like it took all of my energy just to keep them up.

"Thank you."

"You don't have to thank me," she said, shaking her head.

"Maybe not, but thank you," I repeated, meaning it.

She responded with a smile and a nod, stopping at the entrance to the waiting room. She signaled that I should continue the rest of the way out of the office on my own.

I put my hand up in a simple good-bye gesture and walked out the door.

Once safely out in the hallway, I took in a huge gasp of air. I walked quickly to the elevator, desperately hoping to make the journey back down alone. I held that breath until I walked through the lobby and out the glass doors, the brisk, wintry air striking my burning skin.

The cloud-filtered December sunlight had given way to darkening twilight during my visit. Yellow parking lot lights glowed, illuminating my way back to the safety and privacy of my car. As I approached, I hit the fob's unlock button harder and more repeatedly than was necessary. I pulled the door open and tucked myself inside before slamming the door shut again.

Discovering Julia's heart had stopped, holding her lifeless body, burying her body beneath the ground—those were all hard things. But living every day afterward without her—that was hard, too, I realized. I thought about the events of the last hour, the empathy and genuine concern of a stranger, the relief of sharing thoughts and emotions that I did not feel I could share with my friends and family. That was a gift.

Ultimately, my faith was at the crux of my grief journey. I would talk about it again in the next session, but it felt awkward and uncomfortable again, so I didn't bring it up after that. I would complete the two remaining sessions provided by the Employee Assistance Program, but would not set up any more. She was a nice person, and I appreciated being able to vent to someone whom I didn't have to face in future social situations, but it just wasn't a good fit. It wasn't her, it was me. Setting up future sessions felt like a long-term commitment to a relationship I wasn't sure would go anywhere.

I knew I needed to find someone with a similar faith background, but I was also just so tired. Tired of talking, and tired of staying silent about the things that were important to me. I was too exhausted to make myself vulnerable again. Too tired to seek out the help I needed.

Chapter 36

A little over one week after this first counseling appointment, I woke up on a Sunday morning with the same thoughts I'd had the night before: It had been two months. Two months since that awful, wonderful day when I had delivered and held Julia for the first and last time.

It felt like an important milestone, and I wanted desperately to pull the comforter over my head and let the weight of it sink into me. I stared up at our vaulted ceiling in the predawn December morning. Could I just stay home from church?

I closed my eyes with the realization that Joey would hate to miss Sunday school. He'd grown up so much in the past few weeks, and he enjoyed playing with his friends and all the toys in the nursery.

I was lying there waiting for the alarm to buzz when I heard rustling sounds from Joey's baby monitor on my nightstand. *He's up*, I thought, and turned to look at the empty bassinet, still beside my bed. Joe had asked me several times in the last few weeks if I wanted him to remove it, but somehow I just couldn't allow him to do it. Removing it was like removing *her*. It required more acceptance of reality than I was willing to give, a finality I just couldn't face.

I closed my eyes again and listened to Joey's waking-up sounds: a rustle, a yawn, and the beginnings of a day full of chatter. He went on to say something that stole my breath and made my blood freeze.

"Where Julia?" he asked no one. "Where Julia?" The innocence in his little voice, the earnest wondering over what had happened to his baby sister—the room started to spin and nausea began to churn in my empty stomach. Soon tears were rolling down my face. Guilt climbed up and sat its full weight on the center of my chest.

How were we going to explain this to him? I'd worried so much about this in the past two months. Where do I find a balance between honoring

Julia's memory and teaching Joey about his sister, without confusing or scaring him? We had talked to him and tried to prepare him for the arrival of our new baby. While she had indeed arrived, to him it must have felt as if she had just disappeared. We had tried to open up a dialogue with him in the days and weeks following Julia's death, but what could we say? How much did he need to know? He wasn't even two years old yet; how much was too much to put on his little heart?

I listened again and Joey was on to some new topic of conversation with his toys. I knew he would be calling for me soon. I rolled over onto my other side, and grieved for both of my babies, for our foiled plans of giving them each other.

Always a much heavier sleeper, Joe began to stir next to me.

"Hey," he said groggily, his long dark lashes fluttering open in the semi-dark. "What's going on?"

I breathed in and told him everything.

"I'm so sorry, babe," he said, his tired face crumpling. He reached for me and I started to nestle into him.

"I know. I just don't—"

"Mom-my!" Joey's little voice called through the monitor and we both paused, knowing what was coming next.

"Mom-*my!*" he cried out again, this time with more insistence.

I closed my eyes, rolled over. I reached for the monitor and pushed the little red intercom button.

"Coming, buddy," I told him, letting my gaze linger on the empty bassinet for just a moment longer before getting up and padding to the next room.

Chapter 37

"Hi, Mommy!" Joey greeted me from his crib. "Ho, ho, ho! Merry Christmas!"

"Hi, Jojo," I giggled. He didn't know it was Julia's two-month birthday. To him, it was December. The air was lighter and more festive as everyone's minds turned to Christmas. "Let's get you ready for church."

"Yay! Church!"

As I dressed Joey in a little red sweater and black corduroy pants, I thought of the dress Julia would have worn, the black-and-gray-plaid one with the satiny red bow, still hanging in her closet.

When the service ended, I was greeted by friends with warm hugs and promises to pray for me. I had learned to smile politely and nod my head when it was too hard to speak. This made everyone feel better—everyone else, anyway. I truly did appreciate their kindness. I felt their concern. They wanted to make me feel better; I wanted to make them feel better. In truth, what I really wanted was to just get through it and get home.

People in our congregation love each other, and they love to linger and talk after the service, catching up on each other's lives—anything from how their week was to making plans for going to lunch to catch up some more. I attempted to make my way inconspicuously through the crowded center aisle toward the lobby and around the corner to the south wing to pick up Joey from the nursery class. I hadn't even made it out of the auditorium, however, before I was stopped.

"Maria!" a woman said breathlessly, bringing her hand to rest on my forearm.

It was Jacklyn. I didn't know her well, and the familiarity of her gesture unnerved me. I took a step back; she was a lot to take in: a tall woman with giant platinum blonde curls that framed her mature, tanned face.

She wore a bedazzled Christmas sweater, tight pencil skirt, and dramatic stiletto heels that made her tower over me.

"I wanted to introduce you to my aunt! She's a ladies' ministry leader and she's here from Oklahoma for a visit. I hope it's okay—I shared your story with her, and she wanted to meet you."

I felt the stinging in my eyes and blinked rapidly, trying to keep up. I looked from her hand, still gripping my arm, to her face, alarmed by the volume and insistence in her voice. Swallowing nervously, I opened my mouth to protest but was interrupted by the introduction of a woman in her late seventies, about eight inches away from my face.

I instinctively took a step back but was trapped in place by her soft, yet surprisingly strong hand. She was all big hair, large hoop earrings, and flowery perfume. I felt consumed by her presence.

"Hi, Maria," she began in a strong but tempered Southern drawl. "I am truly sorry about your loss."

I felt a suffocating tightening in my chest. Unable to speak, I nodded and wished away the new tears already starting to prickle my tired eyes.

"When I heard your story, I wanted to tell you about a girl we know."

I looked at this stranger, not knowing what to say, but soon realizing she wasn't waiting for my permission to go on.

"There is a girl we know who lost her baby, too. It was earlier on than yours was, but she was real heartbroken about it." She shook her head and I couldn't decide if the gesture was dismissive or out of genuine sympathy. "Anyways, *then* several months later, she had a terrible car accident. The car was completely totaled and there was no way the baby would have survived it."

I felt paralyzed in the moment, confused. I was trying to process what she was saying, wondering what her point might be, why she might be telling me this story.

"So, it ended up being a *good* thing!" she explained.

Excuse me?

"A good thing! Not that she lost the baby, of course," she corrected, "but if she had to lose it, at least she did it *early*. If the baby had been *born* she would have *bonded* with it, and then if it'd died in the car accident, now *that* would have been *so* much harder."

She shook her head vigorously, her jewelry jangling as she moved.

I could not get air. I could see the sunlight pouring through the door behind her, the promise of oxygen just out of reach. I looked around but couldn't find Joe, or my parents, or anyone to whom I could have shot a look of desperation, asking for help. All around me were people chattering happily, but I was completely alone.

I needed to stop crying. I wanted to ask her what in the world she was thinking. I wanted to shout at her that just because this poor girl's baby wasn't *born alive*, it didn't mean that she hadn't already bonded with him!

I thought of Julia, singing to her in my womb each night, holding her in the hospital, kissing her face, and how I felt like I'd died, too, when they took her away from me. I wanted to get into this woman's face and tell her that I love my baby just as much as any mother loves her child, and that no amount of time spent with or without her will *ever* change that.

But I didn't. I just stood there and cried.

"I'll be praying for you, hon," she finished condescendingly, with another intrusive squeeze of my arm.

My hands clenched into fists and I shook violently as hot, angry tears streamed down my face. I wanted to punch that woman, but instead I cried. And in my silence, I let her think that I was crying because I missed my baby, which I did. But I let her walk away without telling her how obnoxiously misguided her philosophy was, and I hated myself for that.

Stifling my sobs, I pushed past everyone between me and the door with a bit more force than was socially appropriate. I thrust myself through the plate-glass doors as if I were a prisoner escaping captivity. I hurriedly made my way around the side of the building to get away from the small crowd that had gathered, despite the frigid December temperatures.

Once confident that I was relatively concealed, I leaned back against the building and allowed myself to breathe the shallow, staggered breaths that I had been suppressing. Little white clouds quickly formed and dissipated in the cold, dry air and a bitter gust of wind froze my tears to my flushed cheeks. I pounded my fists backward, then turned and grated my face hard against the rough textured brick, pushing into it, willing the physical stimulation to distract me from the searing pain that was boiling up inside of me.

How was this my reality? Why had God taken her from me? Would I spend the rest of my life trying to justify my grief—my love?

I moaned against the wall, aware that I needed to stay as quiet as possible to avoid drawing attention to myself. I jumped when I felt a large hand on the back of my shoulder.

Gasping, I turned to find Joe standing behind me. His eyes were wide, searching for an explanation for my obvious distress.

"What's going on, Mia?" he asked, protective concern palpable in his tone. "I saw you run out the door. Are you okay? Did somebody say something?"

I closed my eyes and fell into his arms. I melted into the warmth of his body. I felt his tension rising with each passing moment, his struggle between wanting to help me and patiently waiting for my explanation.

"What happened, baby?" he asked, pulling me closer. I looked up at him, observing how worry had creased deep lines into his forehead and knotted his brow. His blue eyes flashed and I could see him trying to make sense of what he was seeing, like trying to put a puzzle together with only a few of the pieces.

"Nothing," I told him, returning to the safety of his embrace, grateful that the differences in our heights allowed me to tuck my head under his chin, hiding my face.

I wanted to tell him, to share every infuriating detail. But I was just so tired. I didn't think I had the strength to relive it just then, even with him. I also didn't want him to feel the need to find her and clear up her misunderstanding himself. As detestable as it was to admit, this woman's intention was probably pure. She probably really did think she was helping me. I just didn't have the strength to fight it, to educate someone who, as a women's ministry leader, should have known better. I just wanted to rest, to find a place of forgetting, at least for now.

I felt his frustrated exhalation. "It's not *nothing*. It's something, Mia. What happened?"

I cringed, knowing my resistance was hurting him.

"Please," I asked, blinking back tears, "can we talk about it later? Can we please just go home?"

I watched his face as he examined me again for a long moment. Then he released a deep breath, squared his shoulders, and nodded.

"Okay," he said in a husky voice, just above a whisper.

He brought his hand up to my face and used his thumb and forefinger to tenderly tuck a piece of hair behind my ear. "Let's get you in the car, and I'll get Joey. Let's go home."

Chapter 38

After relaying the story to Joe on the way home, I took a long nap that afternoon. Soon afterward, we got ready for a return trip to the church for a special Christmas program that night.

It was a beautiful, live production of *It's a Wonderful Life*. The movie had always been one of my favorites, and it was my Christmas tradition to watch it multiple times each year. *Before*. I loved the production at church—the costumes, the message, each word as familiar as an old friend. Yet, as with everything else, I viewed it with different eyes, tired eyes, weary from missing Julia.

I watched the girls with their exquisite dresses and charming hair-styles from the period, and I thought of her. I remembered all the adorable dresses on white plastic hangers, waiting to be worn. Waiting in vain. I closed my eyes and shuddered as I recalled all of the sweet selections I'd forced myself to put back on the shelf, to *not* purchase for my baby girl.

I thought back to the night she was born, and all her gorgeous dark hair. I recalled how it felt on my fingers at the funeral home, perfectly fine and silky smooth, like so many feathers, as she lay in her tiny white casket, her precious spirit having already flown away to be with Jesus.

I miss you, Julia, I thought. *Oh, how I miss you.*

As I sat in the audience, in the ambient glow of the stage lighting, I allowed myself to silently wonder about *her* life. What would she have done? Something wonderful, I knew. Biologically, she was perfect; every test told us so. Flawlessly developed, her body and her brain were ready to take on the world.

Joey, quickly approaching his second birthday, was so smart, amazing us every day. When I was carrying Julia, Joe and I had mused how she was genetically predisposed to have a healthy, competitive spirit coursing through her veins that would likely have pushed her to match, or even exceed, her big brother's accomplishments.

What would you have done, sweetheart? I smiled sadly, imagining her standing, surrounded by delighted family members, missing her two front teeth, embracing a giant spelling bee trophy. In my mind's eye, I saw a strong, athletic, teenage Julia, kicking the winning goal at the state soccer competition. My heart surged with pride as I watched my Dream Julia walk across the stage, graduating summa cum laude from the prestigious university of her choice.

Would she have been like us? A teacher like me? Or a technology guru like her daddy? Or would she have carved her own path? An artist? An advocate for social justice? Or maybe a research scientist, shattering the glass ceiling as she discovered the cure for SIDS, Alzheimer's, or even cancer, giving hope to families everywhere.

I closed my eyes as I imagined her as a doctor, delivering healthy babies to women who had long dreamed of holding a new life in their arms. I swallowed back a lump in my throat as I envisioned holding the hand of my grown-up baby girl, in a hospital bed, laboring to bring forth a daughter of her own to share with the world.

As the action onstage came to a close, spirited applause broke into my quiet reverie. A speaker stepped forward and thanked everyone for attending, and explicitly shared the message: *Every life matters.*

Your life mattered, Julia, I thought. *It still does.*

As brief as it was, as tragically cut short as it was, Julia's life mattered. Although she would never accomplish all of the dreams my mind conjured for her, her life had already made a difference. In the two months since her birth and death, there had already been so many stories about how she had brought people, families together. Mommies held their babies a bit closer, found patience they didn't know they had, because of Julia. Estranged family members found paths back to each other. Broken hearts found the strength to seek healing. We met, and experienced the generosity of people we never would have known without her life's influence. Although it would not take the space of an entire heartbeat for me to trade all of it for a life with her, I appreciated the light that came, inexplicably, from the darkness.

I recalled a conversation on my couch with Addie in those first few weeks, when she said, "Some people live entire lifetimes without making the difference Julia made in hers."

It was true.

Without having spoken a word, her little life spoke volumes. Even without taking a breath in this world, she, our precious baby girl, took our breath away by the lives she touched. While losing her brought us a sadness we never could have imagined possible, there was also joy—joy in having had her, even for such an inequitably short time.

My life, and the lives of so many others, had been blessed by hers. Her life did matter. It did make a difference. And it was *wonderful*.

Chapter 39

I stood in front of the mirror and smoothed down my close-fitting, black-and-white, graphic-print sheath dress and lightly touched the blown-out swoop of hair that had fallen into my face. It was probably the most dressed up I had been since Julia's funeral, I thought to myself with a humorless chuckle.

I touched my hair, still not used to my long dark layers now only barely reaching my shoulders. I had needed a change, I remembered. I had sat in the black leather swivel chair in the salon, staring at the foil packets that promised caramel highlights to my espresso natural color, wondering if I had made a mistake. I had not, I decided now, lifting my chin, then turning to the side to take a better look.

"Wow! You look great!" Joe declared enthusiastically as he joined me at the long white double vanity.

"You mean, wow, I made an effort," I replied dubiously.

"I mean, you look fantastic," he insisted, dipping his chin to look in my eyes.

Giving him a smile to acknowledge that I appreciated his comment, I turned away from him and back to the mirror.

"I have raccoon eyes," I observed aloud.

"You do not," he argued, sticking his toothbrush into his mouth. "You look beautiful."

I looked at him and smiled again. He knew it made me crazy when he tried to talk while brushing his teeth. I turned to him and tilted my head. His hair swooped, too, I realized. Up from the side part—just enough product to keep it in place, but not so much that it looked like a football helmet, he always said. It was also dark as a nighttime forest, like mine had been; like Julia's had been.

Instead of church today, we were going to a special memorial service hosted by our funeral home, honoring all of the families they had served over the past year. We'd been surprised to receive the invitation in the mail. Was this a thing other funeral homes did? The family-owned company did this every December, we learned. They would say Julia's name and we would light a candle for her, a way to honor her memory and thank us for choosing their services. We'd accepted gratefully, and made plans to attend with my parents. My brother and sister-in-law would watch Joey for us.

Joe spit into the sink and roused me out of my thoughts.

"You look nice, too," I offered, watching him rinse his sink and wipe his mouth with the towel hanging on the silver ring on his side of the vanity.

"Thanks, baby," he returned with a smile that I knew was going somewhere I did not want to follow.

"I need to go check on Joey," I announced, drawing in a breath and taking a quick step backward. The disappointment on his face sent the high tide of my anxiety into a crashing wave of guilt. He turned back to the sink and I started to apologize, but my mouth was dry, and my mind was blank. I closed my mouth, dropped my gaze to the linoleum floor. I squeezed my eyes shut, wishing I could take back my reaction. Joe deserved better, I realized again. He deserved a better partner. A better wife. A better mom. *A better mom who wouldn't have lost his baby at all.*

"Hey," he whispered, gently placing his hand on my arm and moving a tentative step toward me. "You're okay. What's wrong?"

"I'm sorry," I whispered, "You deserve better than me."

"Stop." He chuckled quietly, pulling me into a sweet embrace. "I love you. You know you're the best thing that ever happened to me," he murmured into my hair.

"I don't deserve you," I replied, looking up at him.

"Well, I *am* pretty great," he said with a playful grin that made us both laugh.

I reached for his hand and expelled a sigh of relief.

"Come on, let's go get Joey," he continued, lightly dropping a kiss on my forehead and nodding in the direction of Joey's bedroom just across the hall. "He's probably tearing his room apart by now."

Chapter 40

We pulled up to the busy intersection and the funeral home with its signature clock tower out front. The meticulously manicured landscape was now covered in a white blanket of shimmery fresh snow. My heart began to jackhammer, beginning in my chest and moving up into my throat, as my mind flashed back to the warmer October days when we had last been here. I clamped my eyes shut and squeezed my hands together, trying to quiet the anxiety roaring in my ears, but my knee started to bounce involuntarily, the energy determined to find an outlet.

Joe's warm hand reached over from the steering wheel and rested on my thigh. I looked at him in silent thanks, a self-deprecating smile and shrug conveying my embarrassment.

The light changed from red to green and we began moving forward again. Joe's hand returned to the steering wheel as we turned in and ascended the incline of the winding driveway. Memories flashed like a lightning storm in my mind. I felt my stomach twist and wondered, not for the first time, if we had made a mistake by coming.

"It's good," Joe affirmed, as if reading my thoughts. "It's gonna be good."

I watched as he slowly pulled into a parking space and shifted the engine into park. Looking back down to the floorboard, my vision started to glitch like a computer screen with a loose wire.

"I don't know if I can do this." I told him.

"You can. *We* can," he promised. "We don't really have to do anything. They are going to do it for us. All we have to do is light the candle. Today is all about her."

I turned to look out the window at the ice-laden tree branches. Unbuckling his seat belt, Joe reached his arm around me. I unbuckled mine and moved into his embrace.

"I know," he said soothingly. "It's going to be good."

A few minutes later, my parents pulled into the parking spot next to ours and we all walked together up the driveway and around the fountain to the main entrance. I held my breath as we walked through the familiar heavy oak doors, their cut-glass windows reflecting light from inside. I felt my breath quicken and Joe's hand squeezed mine, encouraging me.

The doors opened and a man in a dark suit whom I didn't recognize offered a kind and slightly somber smile. "Welcome," he greeted us warmly, holding the door open wide and ushering us in with a small sweeping gesture.

I took a deep breath and walked into what felt like a step back in time. The foyer was just as pristine as I'd remembered it, with its elegant chandelier, polished wood surfaces, and serene color palette. I looked past all of it to the doors that marked the entrance to the room where we had received guests for Julia's visitation. The doors were closed now, silently indicating that it would not be used today.

"Maria."

I heard a woman's voice behind me and turned to find Barbara, the woman who had answered my first phone call to the funeral home the day we'd come home from the hospital, smiling warmly. She wore a lovely emerald green suit over a silky cream blouse with ruffles and a bow at the high neckline. She enveloped my hands in hers with all the delicate softness of rumpled satin sheets.

"It's so good to see you all here," she continued, her crystal blue eyes sparkling with genuine hospitality as she moved to greet each of us.

"Thank you so much for the invitation," I said. I tried to force my voice to sound natural, but it came out a little high and strangled to my ears.

"We think of you and Julia often," she said, with such tenderness and sincerity that it brought tears to my eyes. It was so kind of her to remember us. So good of her to say Julia's name.

"Thank you," I whispered tremulously. "We are forever grateful to all of you for the way you took care of her, and us."

"We are still here for you," she replied. "Anytime." She smiled and squeezed my hands again before letting go and gesturing to her left. "Today's service will be in our chapel. I worked on Julia's candle myself. I'm so glad you came. It will be beautiful."

"Thank you so much," I whispered again.

"You're welcome, dear. Thanks to all of you." She shook Joe's and my parents' hands and ushered us into the chapel.

The vaulted wooden ceiling reminded me of our church, though on a smaller scale. The marbled stained glass windows along the wall brought

172

filtered bright light in from the snowy outdoors. A grand piano sat at the front of the room opposite a wooden lectern with a microphone, and a large circular stained-glass window of a peace dove created a focal point at the peak, above it all. I thought back to our choice to have Julia's funeral at our church, rather than in this sanctuary. While I didn't regret my decision, I did admire this chapel's simple, elegant beauty, its quiet reverence.

We sat shoulder to shoulder, watching as the people filled each row of long wooden pews. Soon the room was filled to capacity. *So many families,* I thought. So many mourners who had lost someone they'd loved in the last year. I wondered about their stories, the people they had lost. *How many of them had been children?*

A young woman in a black pantsuit made her way down the center aisle. She sat down at the piano and began to gently play a soothing hymn. When she finished, a young, middle-aged man in a dark suit and tie stepped to the podium. He was not a large man, but his presence was strong. His voice was gentle, yet commanding and confident as he welcomed us. He introduced himself as Pete, and he shared his family's appreciation for all of us who had chosen them to help commemorate our loved ones over the past year. "It has been our honor to serve you," he explained.

I tried to be consciously present, to relax and record each moment in my memory. But my mind skated. I was inundated by distracting memories and tangential thoughts about life, death, and loss. There was a poem and another song, then Pete stood quietly, turning his attention to the back of the room.

My breath caught as I watched our funeral director, Greg, and Steve, the director who had taken Julia from the hospital the night she was born, walk up the middle aisle with long, flaming candle lighters. They ceremonially lit large candles flanking the display table before standing sentry on each side, poised to assist mourners through the impending observance.

I took Joe's much larger hand in mine and squeezed it as hard as I could manage, attempting to release some of the nervous energy that was crushing me. He turned to me and smiled, with a "You can do this" narrowing of his eyes. My hands shook as I held the paper program in my hand, following the list of names with my eyes. Alphabetized by last name. We would be a little more than halfway down. I tried to breathe, to stay in the moment, as I watched each of the families walk up and light a candle as Pete called their loved ones' names. Some of the mourners were older adults, some went up carrying small children. Some groups were large, some were represented by only one person. Again, I wondered about their stories, those who had gone on, and the ones they had left behind.

When it was almost our turn. I elbowed Joe and pointed to Julia's name on the list, to give him time to get ready. I lined my hand with a few fresh tissues, straightened my shoulders, and waited to hear her name.

Julia Rachel Price.

As much as I had tried to prepare myself, hearing Pete read her name aloud stole my breath. Joe helped me to stand and we walked arm in arm up the long center aisle. We went to Greg's side of the table and smiled a silent *Hello, I'm so glad to see you* with our eyes before reaching for the long wooden stick and putting it in the flame. Together, we found the elegant cubed glass holder bearing Julia's picture and name and carefully transferred the light to that wick, watching it spark and dance to life. *We love you, Julia.*

We made our way back to our seats and sat down beside my parents. My mom rubbed her hand in circles on my back, and I felt some of the tension begin to release. Tears trickled down my face as I thought, *This is my life now.* Not birthday parties, or trips to see Santa. Memorial services at a funeral home. For my baby girl.

The soft piano music drew to a close and Pete led the congregation in a responsive reading. He shared some inspirational words and a prayer of blessing. And then it was over.

"That was beautiful." I heard the wobble in my mom's voice as she lifted a tissue to her eye behind her metal frames. I nodded in agreement at the mound of sodden tissues in my lap.

"Thank you for coming with us." I squeezed the words out of the top of my throat.

"Oh, thank you for inviting us," my dad said. He gestured with the handkerchief he always carried, folded into a neat white square, at the space around us. "Like your mom said, it was really beautiful. It's really special that they do this for people."

"We wouldn't have missed it," my mom said. Her tight smile rested below sad eyes, and I knew with certainty that she was speaking the truth. My parents' lives revolved around their family. They loved being grand-parents, doting on Joey and my nephews. I knew their hearts grieved for Julia, their only granddaughter. They had lost her, too.

I looked to Joe. His lower lip pressed up against his upper one, making a tight line, parallel to his furrowed eyebrows. He blinked and his expression softened slightly, and he nodded toward the memorial display at the front of the sanctuary.

"Do you want to go up and get her candle together?"

I looked back at my parents and we all shared simple, silent nods of agreement.

We walked together to the front of the hallowed space to retrieve Julia's candle. A base of dark cherry wood supported the graceful square holder that glowed from within, highlighting her photograph and the lovely pastel watercolor artwork from her memorial funeral brochure. It was still burning brightly, illuminating the space around it and creating dazzling reflections against its polished glass enclosure.

We stood watching that flame. I was thrilled by its mesmerizing beauty, unwilling to extinguish it. If the light represented Julia's precious life, wouldn't snuffing it out represent her untimely death?

I stood, paralyzed, recognizing that I was overthinking it, yet still reluctant to quench her little spark—again. I felt the eyes of the families behind us waiting, gently nudging us to move along. Joe's hand slid up my spine, and I know he felt it, too. My mom's cool hand reached out and surrounded mine, gently squeezing her love and support.

I knew I couldn't wait any longer. It wasn't symbolic, I told myself, it was just a candle. Her light would continue to shine eternally in my heart. I closed my eyes, making a silent wish for a different ending, but feeling the familiar burden of reality in my chest, I leaned over and blew it out. "I love you, Julia." I whispered. "I'm so sorry, baby."

From the office, we collected the extra candles we had ordered as Christmas presents. On our way, we saw Greg.

"Hi, guys," he said, cordially greeting us and shaking Joe's hand.

I was thrilled to see him. I would always be grateful for his unparalleled kindness, and for the living connection he was to Julia. We each extended our hands, but moved in for a hug instead. He shook my parents' hands, and smiled a warm but somber smile.

"I'm so glad you were able to make it here today," he said. "I know it could not have been easy."

"No," I admitted. "But we are grateful for the opportunity, for the beautiful service and tribute to her." My voice trilled up at the end, pinched by emotion that I couldn't quite suppress.

"It truly is our honor," he replied, closing his eyes and making a small bowing nod of sympathy. We talked for a bit longer before we thanked him again, wished each other a Merry Christmas, and parted ways.

We retrieved our coats and prepared to leave before we were stopped again by a couple, probably about our age. The man was taller than me, but shorter than Joe, with wavy, sand-colored hair. She was tall, her blonde hair long and straight, with bright blue eyes and a vivid smile.

"Hi," she said. Her tone was friendly, yet respectfully distant. "Are you Julia's parents?"

I blinked, trying to place her. She had an accent I couldn't quite place either; European, maybe? They seemed familiar somehow, though I wasn't sure how. Did they just put us together with Julia because of the service, the program?

"Yes," I replied warily, reaching out my hand for hers.

"Amelia," she said in introduction. "And this is my husband, Matthew."

"Maria," I returned, still not sure where this was going.

Joe introduced himself and we introduced my parents. Everyone shook hands and then stood, tensely awaiting an explanation.

"My friend told me about you and your Julia," Amelia began. "I'm so sorry for your loss."

My Julia. I liked that. But I couldn't keep my eyebrows from knitting together, still confused.

"Our daughter, Esme, passed away in June," Amelia said.

I felt my brows immediately unfurrow, my suspicion giving way to sympathy and a sense of connection with these fellow bereaved parents.

"We're so sorry for *your* loss," I responded.

We talked for a few minutes, sharing a few details. I could feel my anxiety rising as we exchanged contact information and vague promises to maybe connect sometime soon.

"Maybe after the holidays," Amelia suggested.

By the time we'd walked away, my face was flushed and I heard the blood rushing in my ears.

Other parents? Another baby—a girl, like mine? Like Julia.

"You okay?" Joe asked as we buttoned our coats and prepared to walk out into the December air.

I paused, unsure how to answer.

"I think so," I said. "I'm not really sure what to think."

"You think you'll call her?" he asked.

The thought of connecting, sharing, being vulnerable with another person, a stranger, was equal parts nerve-racking and exhilarating.

"I'm not sure yet. Maybe."

Chapter 41

We'd planned to go to the cemetery after the memorial service. Despite the several inches of newly fallen snow and bitterly cold air, I had to visit Julia.

"You don't have to go," I told my parents. "I know the weather is bad." Then with a sudden realization, "I guess I don't even know if they will have plowed there yet—"

"We'll go," my mom answered quickly, head nodding rapidly, not even giving me a chance to finish.

I looked into her eyes. They were large, bright with eagerness to be involved, but tired around the edges. "We want to."

"We'll come with you, and we'll just see," my dad responded, shrugging his shoulders, but the tension pinching his voice betrayed his casual tone. I knew this was hard for him. He was trying to be outwardly strong, but on the inside, I knew, his tender heart was hurting.

"Okay," I said slowly. "Let's go."

As we rounded the curves of the cemetery, I leaned back against the passenger seat and sighed in relief that the driveways had, in fact, been cleared of snow. As we got closer to Julia's plot, however, tension began to ratchet up again in my chest. I had no boots. I was wearing heels and a dress that only came just past my knees. I looked at Joe's suit pants and leather dress shoes.

I closed my eyes and laid my head back against the headrest. Was this crazy? The snow was at least eight inches deep, higher at the edges of the paths where the snowplow had pushed it into heavy banks. Clearly,

I had not come prepared. Yet, I knew, nothing was going to stop me from getting to her.

We pulled to a stop at the spot along the winding path where we always parked, and Joe turned to me. "You still want to do this?" he asked.

"Yeah." I answered, nodding. "You don't have to come. I'm sorry, I didn't prepare—"

"No," he stopped me, shifting into park. "I'm fine. I just wanted to make sure that you hadn't changed your mind. I'm with you."

I searched his face for any hint of sarcasm or trepidation, but found none. I looked past him to the little hill that had become so familiar to me, now covered in a shimmery winter blanket.

"Okay," I replied, returning my gaze to make eye contact again. "Let's go."

The snow was wet, cold, the best kind for building a snowman or having a snowball fight. It was up to my knees in spots as we trudged over the embankment and up the small incline to the spot where my grandparents' gravestone peeked out of the snow, marking the spot where they and Julia were buried. It was silent except for the sounds of our breathing and the crunch of shifting snow beneath our feet as we worked to keep our balance.

I stood entranced. We easily removed the snow from the top of my grandparents' large stone, but surrounding it, and rising up about halfway to the top, was a thick mound of dense, heavy snowpack.

It covered her. It covered *Julia*.

True to the estimation of the memorial stone company, her grave marker had not been completed before the ground froze. They had poured the foundation, but the stone itself would not be laid until spring, they told us. Now, she was not only lying in an unmarked grave, but she was covered by snow.

I used to love snow. Just a couple of months ago I'd been dreaming of a white Christmas, how I'd be snuggled up tight with my big boy and sweet baby girl—until our dream had turned into a nightmare, dashing my visions of sweet sugar plums. Now, standing in this spot, I wondered how I'd survive being separated from my precious daughter, not just by dirt and grass, but now, by cold, traitorous snow.

The winds began to pick up, and it sounded like a distant howling—or was it moaning, cruelly mocking my grief? I couldn't do it. How could I be expected to live here, aboveground, while my daughter, my baby, was a world away? I shivered, but not from the cold. I could not stand there and be separated by one more thing.

I dropped to my knees and began to dig, using my hands as shovels. I blinked as tears burned my eyes, then froze on my cheeks. Hot, fierce, rage warmed and propelled me onward as I thrust my hands into the icy mass at my feet. I felt the snow wedge up underneath my fingernails, and I wondered briefly if they might break off.

In my peripheral vision, I saw Joe squat down beside me. I felt his warmth next to me and expected him to protectively pull me back up to standing. But he didn't. He started to dig next to me. I gulped back my gratitude and kept going, digging until we reached grass. We dug until we had created a cavity the size and shape of our little girl's resting place.

I knelt, my hands resting on the ground in front of me, breathing hard from the urgent exertion. My mouth was hanging open, and I was staring, unblinking, as if in a trance.

We were so much closer to her, yet not any closer at all.

I flinched as I felt Joe's hand gently reach around me and come to rest on my arm, just above the elbow. It was as if the rest of my senses caught up to where I was. I felt the snow melting beneath my hands, heard my mom's quiet crying behind us, and noticed, with painful clarity, the absolute stillness of the moment.

I could not swallow the lump in my throat. I leaned into Joe and released a sob which turned into a moan, which turned into a wailing cry. He wrapped his arms around me and I felt his body convulse with silent tears.

Slowly our anguished cries began to melt away like the snow beneath our feet.

Joe moved his hands to my arms and rubbed up and down in a warming motion. Resting his forehead against mine, he whispered, "C'mon, baby, let's get you up."

We rose slowly, out of the little igloo we had made. I looked at my parents. My dad had his arm around my mom, his signature handkerchief in his hand. They were both crying now, and I knew it was for Julia, but also for Joe and me, and I felt guilt twist my stomach for what my outburst had done to them.

The quiet stillness of the moment was broken by the sound of a small SUV rounding the corner. I expected it to drive past us, on its way to another section of the cemetery, but it came to a stop, and I wondered who might be inside. In the two months that I had been making daily visits to Julia here, I had never seen anyone else stop here.

When the driver's side door opened, Kaitlyn, a young woman who was a dear friend of our family, stepped out. She was dressed in tall boots and a wool pea coat, holding what appeared to be a small blanket and a lantern in her hands. I watched her carefully tread over the snowy embankment up to where we were.

"Hey," I offered in greeting, a hint of a question mingling in my tone.

"Hey," she replied, with a smile that was friendly but layered in sadness. "So, I read your post last night, about the snow."

I closed my eyes, remembering the anxiety, the angst I had felt at leaving Julia alone in the cold and dark night, knowing that snow was forecast to fall by morning. I had shared my devastation on social media as an attempt to release, to express some of that pain.

"Yeah," I murmured, and a flush of self-consciousness began to creep up my neck, despite the winter chill.

"I . . . I didn't know you were going to be here," she continued slowly. "I didn't mean to interrupt."

"No, not at all," I said, trying to reassure her, searching her face, still wondering as to her purpose.

"I just . . ." she began again, her lower lip starting to tremble, "I just . . . wanted to bring something that might keep her a little warmer." She held out a buttery-soft plaid scarf and a decorative wrought-iron lantern, its frosted-glass panels enclosing a small battery-operated candle. "So now she can be warmer . . . and it won't be so dark."

I lunged at her, clasping my arms around her, squeezing her so intensely I was afraid that I might hurt her. Tears streamed hard and fast down my face. I had no words.

I had watched Kaitlyn grow up since her mother, a mentor of mine, had died suddenly and unexpectedly at a young age. She already knew too much of grief. Her mom was buried in the same cemetery, just a short distance from where we were standing.

I stepped back to look at her. Seeing my own sorrow reflected in her round honey-brown eyes, we moved back in for another embrace, like the expanding and contracting of a rubber band between two fingers. We stepped back again to see Joe, his eyes shining with gratitude.

"Thank you, Kaitlyn," he said as they moved in for a hug.

"That was so thoughtful of you, Kaitlyn," my mom chimed in affectionately, the next in line to embrace her.

"Real, real nice," added my dad, with a slight hitch in his voice as he lifted his chin and shook his head in grateful admiration.

When she came back around to me, we hugged again. The brushed wool of her coat stroked my cheek and her hair tickled my nose as I breathed my thanks into her ear.

"Thank you. So much. I have no words to thank you for this. It means more to me than you could ever know," I told her.

"I just . . ." she began, pulling back to look me in the eyes, "I just love you guys, and I love Julia. And I am so, so sorry this happened to you," she said, her voice and lower jaw quaking.

I nodded, unable to find either words or the strength to answer. We both looked down as she transferred the gifts she had brought from her hands to mine. I felt the weight of them, deeply.

Slowly, with vestiges of the ceremony we had attended earlier that day, I lovingly arranged the precious offerings in the grassy area we had just uncovered. As I switched on the tiny tea light in the lantern, I thought about how Julia's light had been extinguished, yet somehow remained within us. And I was incredibly grateful for the love that had created her, the love that surrounded us, and all the love for her that remained, *still.*

Chapter 42

At not yet two years old, Joey enjoyed Christmas, but was still a little young to have too many preconceived notions or expectations for the holiday. This was good for me as a newly bereaved mom.

I used to love Christmas. I played Christmas music as early in November as possible. I baked, crafted, decorated, and shopped till I dropped. For the finale to each season, I hosted an elaborate Christmas Eve and Christmas Day celebration with our family.

But not this year.

This year was different. I didn't even want to think about the holiday. We didn't put up the tree until a few days before Christmas. Outside our home, everything was twinkly lights and sugar plum fairies. Children sat on Santa's knee—little girls dressed in beautiful Christmas dresses and big glittery bows. Both on social media and in real life, happiness and joy were thrust in my face, but I felt none of it. I could not think of Christmas without missing the gift that had been given, then taken away from me.

I wanted to sleep through it. It was only because I wanted to give Joey as "normal" an experience as possible that I didn't just stay in bed.

Grief for Julia and guilt for Joey were constantly twisted, commingling in a strange, sad holiday jig. We took Joey to see Santa and to ride a holiday train one Saturday morning, and took a Christmas wreath to Julia's graveside later the same afternoon. A photographer friend, and fellow "loss mom," took pictures of him and the plush pink "Julia Bear" that had come with one of Julia's funeral floral arrangements, in a Christmas photo shoot. We hung her pink gingerbread girl stocking up next to his red gingerbread boy stocking, sadly noting how only one would be opened and enjoyed.

For Julia, we donated to charities in her honor and shopped for another perfect little dress she would never wear. We hung memorial ornaments, thoughtful gifts from friends and family members, on our tree.

For Joey, we bought more presents than he needed and treated him to more sweets than he was able to eat. I tried to pour as much love and attention on him as I could manage, hoping that these indulgences would compensate for the lack of energy and creativity that had made me more Scrooge than doting mom this year.

After all our presents had been opened on Christmas morning, Joey played happily with his toys, and Joe came over to sit beside me. He handed me a gift bag, covered in glittery pink and silver snowflakes, coordinating tissue paper artfully tufting out from its top. I looked at it and then back to him.

"Merry Christmas, Mia," he said, with a subdued smile that still made his eyes sparkle.

I returned his smile conspiratorially because we both knew I knew what was inside. I had chosen it.

I looked back down at the bag, taking it from him carefully. I removed the paper and pulled out a small black box, slightly larger than a deck of cards. I twisted the hinges to open it and found a delicate heart-shaped gold pendant laser engraved with Julia's picture resting against a shiny white satin lining. It was more beautiful than I could have imagined. Julia looked like any other sleeping baby, like a tiny cherub. I stared at it and felt my insides twist and wring out like wet rag.

I looked back up at Joe and saw tears in his eyes, too. I reached up to brush them away, feeling the dampness clinging to his long black eyelashes. We leaned back together into the couch and sat in a moment of silence, staring lovingly at the face that had changed everything.

Never one to be excluded, Joey hopped up onto Joe's lap and reclined against his chest.

"What dat, Mommy?" he asked, tilting his head curiously.

I cleared my throat and looked at Joe.

"It's my new necklace you and Daddy got me for Christmas."

His eyes widened as he looked from my face to Joe's and back again.

"Merry Christmas!" he shouted, pure joy dancing in his dark eyes. We all giggled at his enthusiasm and tickled him playfully.

After a moment, I held up the image and asked, "Joey, did you look at the picture? Who is this?"

"Dat Julia!" he cried, an incredulous grin covering his face.

"Good job, buddy. You're right. That's your sister, Julia," Joe replied.

"Ho ho ho! Merry Christmas!" Joey responded, in his best Santa Claus impression, before bouncing off the couch and returning to his new zoo play set.

Joe and I exhaled our relief simultaneously as we watched him play. We chuckled at the symmetry and exchanged bittersweet smiles. *He knew her.* He may not have understood everything—neither did we. But he recognized Julia, that she is part of our family. And that was a precious gift.

Rubbing the little heart between my fingers, I sat up and turned my back to Joe. He carefully moved my hair out of the way and clasped the chain behind my neck.

Once it was on, I couldn't stop touching it, feeling her close to me, in at least this one way.

"Thank you," I said, looking at Joe.

"Thank *you*," he sniffed with a sideways smile. "You picked it out."

I looked down, smiling sheepishly. When I returned my gaze to him, I narrowed my eyes, hoping to impart my sincerity. "Thank you for *everything*," I told him. "Thank you for loving me. I know I don't always make that easy."

His gaze never left me as he shook his head slowly.

"I do love you," he said, reaching out to take my chin in his hand and stare directly into my eyes. "Nothing you could do will ever change that."

I closed my eyes and leaned into him, resting my head against his heart.

"I love you, too," I whispered, and gave silent thanks for this man, this precious gift. His love was without limits. I did not deserve him. We had been through so much together, and I knew that I would spend the rest of my life loving him, the one who saw me at my worst, but still consistently gave me his best. *Still.*

My family joined us later that afternoon for Christmas Day traditions of dinner, presents, and family time. Joe carved the turkey, and Joey played with his cousins, but my arms were markedly empty. There was a somber tone to our celebration, like a rain cloud that hovered above us. Our family was painfully incomplete—just as it had been at Thanksgiving, and would always be, for every other subsequent holiday.

As we sat around our long dining room table passing the mashed potatoes and homemade stuffing, I couldn't help imagining an alternate Christmas—one where Julia wailed and wanted to be held just as we sat down to eat. My mom would rush through her food or eat one-handed, just to be able to indulge her littlest grandchild. At nearly eleven weeks old, she would be able to smile and coo by now, and everyone would want to take turns holding her, passing her around like the basket of warm rolls.

"Can I get you anything, babe?" my mom's concerned voice broke through my daydream, bringing me back to the moment.

I looked around the table. Some were trying to ignore and hide their concern, while others showed it with head tilts and knitted brows.

"No, thank you," I said, placing my napkin in my lap with a forced brightness that sounded false, even to me.

"You sure? There's so much here," my dad joined in the campaign, his hand gesturing at the full serving trays and casserole dishes that separated us.

"No, thank you," I repeated, shaking my head and lifting the fork to my mouth with another fake smile. "I'm fine," I lied.

We finished dinner, cleaned up, and read the Christmas story from the book of Luke, another family Christmas tradition. My nephews were old enough to read now, thank goodness. I smiled as I listened to them and stifled my emotions as they read about the celebrated miracle baby born in a manger.

Julia was remembered in the gifts we gave. Personalized ornaments for the tree came from my parents and my brother's family. The photograph memory books and candles from the memorial service we gave brought tears to all the faces in the room. Perhaps most meaningful of all was the handcrafted angel and note from my oldest nephew, Josiah, who was nine years old.

Gratitude mingled with grief, and I longed once again for a different outcome. As the cousins opened their presents, I imagined again a very different holiday, one where little dresses and baby dolls were mixed in among the action figures and remote-controlled cars. It was the Christmas we had never imagined or wanted, one much different than the one we had planned. I was grateful for a family who loved and celebrated Julia, but I also celebrated when the holiday was over.

Chapter 43

The next few days were a muddle of wearing pajamas all day, eating left-overs, and putting batteries in Joey's new toys. He loved animals and could name even the more obscure ones, like bison and okapis. He loved life and needed constant reminders to sit, not jump and land on his bottom before gliding down his new indoor plastic slide, giggling uncontrollably every time. Each time, I feared for his safety and reveled in his joy.

Slowly, as the week progressed, I began to feel a growing anxiety that I couldn't quite place. I found myself constantly stretching, or begging Joe to rub the tension out of my neck and shoulders. I was impatient and irritable—more than normal—and wasn't sure why.

At first, I thought it was the informal party invitation we had received, but not yet declined. I was not ready for even a low-key celebration. I just couldn't do it. It wasn't personal. I didn't want to go anywhere or do anything with anyone. Finally, I gathered my courage and made the call. The hostess was exceedingly gracious and respectful in accepting our regrets. I hung up thinking I would finally be able to relax.

But I couldn't relax. If anything, I was even *more* edgy than I had been before—forgetful, clumsy, and flustered. My anxiety seemed to grow each day, sending me into mild panic attacks for what seemed like no clear reason. I couldn't focus, and I wondered if it was a subconscious fear of figuring it out that kept me in the fog.

I settled into the couch with my phone and started scrolling through social media, coming upon an article from one of the online support groups I followed. *Why I Hate New Year's Eve*, it read. I felt my eyebrows rise in piqued interest.

I clicked on the link and read the article with tears streaming down my face. The author perfectly articulated the struggle that I could not identify. New Year's Eve and New Year's Day scared me—not because of the parties, or even the dreaded social interaction, but because I did not want to face turning the calendar to a new year without Julia.

These feelings were apparently common among many bereaved parents, perhaps heightened for those going through the first year without their child, but also commonly experienced every year thereafter. The holiday symbolizes the passage of time, a new beginning, neither of which I wanted to do without my baby. It felt like I was somehow leaving her behind.

Despite the anxiety that still lingered, I felt validated. I felt intense gratitude for this article, its author, and the community of other hurting parents, for not only helping me to make sense of what I was feeling, but also for dispelling the fear that I was just crazy. I had been pushing people away, not returning phone calls and texts, preferring isolation. Knowing that I was not alone felt powerful.

Maybe it *was* time to reach out.

I closed the link and opened my messaging app and reached out to Amelia, the mom I had met at the funeral home memorial a few weeks before. We conversed briefly and decided to set up a time to meet the following week. After thanking her and letting her know that I looked forward to our visit, I put the phone down and took in a deep breath. I lifted my chin.

It was a start, I thought. It might not be a path I would want to continue walking, but I could always turn around, I reasoned. It was a small start, but a start, nonetheless.

Chapter 44

About a year prior to Julia's birth and death, I had been named a women's ministry leader at our church. This role included hosting events to encourage, uplift, and strengthen women. I had instituted a prayer night on the first Thursday of each month, before. Despite how little I wanted to pray, or go out at all on a Thursday night in early January, I went, to fulfill this responsibility.

It became dark before five o'clock at that time of year, and was perpetually, bitterly cold outside. I turned on only one set of front lights in the church, giving the sanctuary an ethereal feel. I was alone. I sat, unsure what to say. The easy, trusting relationship I had had with God before we'd lost Julia seemed out of my grasp. Even if I wanted it back, and I wasn't sure that I did, I wasn't sure how to find it again.

Thankfully, one friend joined me several minutes later. We discussed the devotion I had planned, and prayed together. Afterward, I reached for my phone to turn the ringer back on. Three missed calls. A voice message. Text messages. All from Joe, who was home with Joey.

Panic instantly hammered hard inside my chest like the needle of a sewing machine. I looked at my friend, eyes wide.

"What is it?" she asked, concern wrinkling her smooth round face.

"I—I don't know. Joe called. He knows I'm here. He wouldn't call unless something was wrong."

She immediately bowed her head and began to quietly pray that all was well as I called Joe, fear wrapping its icy fingers around my throat.

"Hello," Joe said. Not a question, a statement. He knew why I was calling. He had been expecting it.

"I'm sorry. What's wrong?" The words tumbled out quickly, sounding strained as I pushed past the apprehension strangling my vocal cords.

"We're okay," he began, then trailed off. His voice was calm, and calming. He didn't want to worry me—but then why had he called? He wouldn't have called if it hadn't been an emergency.

"What happened?" I insisted.

"Joey was sick."

"What?!" It was all I needed to hear to set off an internal pyrotechnics show. Tears shot out of my eyes as I cried again, "What?"

"He's okay now."

"Now? What happened?"

"You need to calm down, Mia. I will tell you, but you need to try to calm down."

"Just tell me," I demanded, still breathing hard. The quiet inner voice that told me I was overreacting was drowned out by the cacophony of panic rising to a thunderous swell.

"He threw up. But he's fine now. He had been playing in the living room. I was in the dining room, working at the table, but I could see him. All of a sudden, he just got up and came to the doorway of the dining room, and he didn't look good. He just said, 'Daddy—' and he threw up a ton, all over himself and the floor."

I cried harder, gulping in breaths as I imagined my poor little boy in his dinosaur footy pajamas, vomit covering himself and the dark hardwood beneath him. He had never thrown up like that before. He must have been so scared. *Why hadn't I been there? Why was I here? Praying? What good was that doing?*

"Where is he now?"

"I have already given him a bath, and put new jammies on him."

"What about his temperature? Does he have a fever?"

"Just a low one, ninety-nine. I don't know if something he ate didn't agree with him, but he seemed like he felt much better after he got it out. After his bath, I put him on the couch with some toys so I could keep an eye on him while I cleaned the floor and he played. He's on the couch with me now, sleeping."

"I'm coming home." I gulped hard.

"Okay. Try to calm down first, Mia. Be careful. He's okay."

"How do you *know?*" I asked, the panic resurging.

"I know," he answered calmly. "I know it's scary, but we'll watch him. This is just one of those kid things that happen sometimes."

It just happens, I thought. *Just like with Julia.*

"I'm coming home," I repeated.

"Okay. Be careful. I'll see you when you get here," he replied, and his voice was a mixture of reassurance and worry, but about two different things. "I love you," he said.

"Love you, too," I replied, and ended the call.

I looked up at my friend who was watching me patiently, silently waiting for an explanation.

"Joey is sick," I told her, my voice breaking. "Or at least he *got* sick," I amended. I relayed to her what Joe had told me, snatching my coat and slinging my bag over my shoulder. "I should have been there. I knew this would happen."

"You knew he would get sick?" her voice was soft, but not patronizing. She was genuinely questioning, but not accusatorily so.

"I knew . . . I don't know. I don't know how to protect him." I felt like I was going to vomit, too. "I can't lose him, too!"

And this was it, the crux of my distress. The loss of one child had made me constantly fear the loss of the other. Julia's death had helped me to see the fragility of life, how uncertain our existence actually is, how little control we actually have. The trauma had accelerated me away from naiveté to the other extreme—paranoia and soul-gripping dread. Our children were with us one moment, and in the next, they could be gone. I had constant anxiety about Joey's safety. I was terrified to put him to bed each night, not knowing if he would wake up the next morning. I panicked putting him in his car seat for fear that it would not be enough to save him, and a car accident would take his life.

When I opened my eyes, she was watching me, her blue eyes searching mine, her lightly freckled face scrunched in concern. I wondered if she was thinking of her own toddlers at home. She reached out and gingerly touched my wrist.

"Oh, Maria. You have been through so much. I can't imagine losing a child, and what that does to your perspective. You are a good mama. You haven't done anything wrong. I know you're in a hurry. Do you want me to pray for you first?"

Holding my breath to suppress the sobs, I nodded, not daring to speak.

She prayed for Joey, for his healing and comfort. Then she prayed that God would also be *my* comfort and strength. That he would calm my anxieties and bring peace that surpasses human understanding.

"Thank you," I whispered when she had finished.

"Can I drive you home?"

I closed my eyes and shook my head, working to even out my tone.

"No. Thank you, but I'm fine. I just want to get home to him."

"Of course," she said. "Hugs to Joey and Joe from us. I'll call to check in on you in the morning. You'll call if you need anything before then?"

I nodded and we moved in for one last tight hug.

As I walked back down the long aisle and out to the dark parking lot, I considered her prayer, how quick I had been to accuse God instead of praying to Him, how fast my defenses shot up to keep Him out. Why should He listen to me? Why should He answer my prayer?

Bitter winds howled around me as I slammed my car door and jammed the key into the ignition. I was reexamining my thoughts about prayer and how it worked. But did it even matter what I believed? At what point would I exhaust even God's patience with me?

I used my open palms to clear the tears from my eyes, then shifted the car into drive and headed home to my son.

As soon as I walked through the back door I was hit with the lemony-fresh scent of floor cleaner. The house was dark as I walked through the dining room and into the living room, which was illuminated by the dancing blue glow of the television.

My breath caught in my throat when I saw Joey, sprawled out on his back on Joe's lap, sleeping peacefully. *Just sleeping, not still*, I told myself, blinking back tears.

Joe held his forefinger up to his lips as I rushed toward them. I shuffled out of my coat and let it drop to the floor. I sat on the couch beside them and Joe gently slipped Joey into my arms.

I exhaled a sigh of relief as I cradled him and he snuggled into me. I placed my hand gently on his chest, feeling for myself its rhythmic rise and fall.

"He's okay," I whispered to myself, *"My baby."*

At least for tonight, for now, he was safe. Grateful tears streaked down my cheeks as relief edged its way into my mind and heart. *My babies.*

Chapter 45

As weeks turned to months, we made it through our first Valentine's Day without our Sweetheart, our first Easter without our Jellybean, and Julia's half birthday in April. Each holiday, each Tuesday that marked another week was like a milestone in the journey of life without her. I grieved each one, and imagined how different our lives would be if she had lived.

As the bitter Iowa winter slowly melted into spring, my anxiety begin to build. In the back of my mind, I remembered the deal Joe and I had made to not talk about having another baby until summer. Yet I found I couldn't even entertain the thought in the privacy of my own mind. I still cried every day, multiple times a day. My heart ached for my daughter, and each day felt like it took me farther and farther away from her. My work was intensely stressful and only exacerbated the all-consuming grief. After teaching all day in a demanding classroom, I would come home to take online graduate classes to earn the endorsement I needed to keep the job. I was exhausted in every way imaginable.

Joe picked up my slack. He read to Joey and put him to bed each night while I worked and cried that I could not do the same for Julia. He cooked, and cleaned, and cared for me in every way I would allow him.

Finally, one day, on a walk through our quiet neighborhood, after Joey had been lulled to sleep by the fresh air and rhythmic movement of his stroller, I worked up the courage to broach the subject.

"I'm not ready," I said quickly, gripping Joey's stroller handle tightly as we made our way up a steep incline.

"Not ready for what?" Joe asked slowly, confused.

"I'm just not ready to talk about having another baby." I raced to get the words out, before I lost my nerve. "I know we said we would talk about it in the summertime, but I just can't. I can't even think about it. I'm sorry." I was breathing hard as we crested the hill. My heart was thrumming in my chest, more from anxiety than exertion.

Joe stopped walking and gently lifted my face so that my eyes would meet his tender expression. "It's okay." Then with both hands, he wiped the tears that were trickling down my cheeks. "Mia, it's okay. Really." He ducked his head to meet my gaze, a warm smile pulling at his lips. "We *don't* have to talk about this now."

I felt myself getting lost in the ocean of compassion in his deep blue eyes.

"I'm sorry," I breathed.

"It's okay," he repeated, folding me into his arms.

"I just don't want to disappoint you," I admitted.

"Listen," he began, pulling me out of his embrace to look me in the eyes again. "We already have two beautiful children. If we decide to have another one someday, great. If not, that's perfectly okay, too. I love our family and I love you."

Relief washed over me as he stroked my hair away from my wet cheeks.

"And you don't ever have to worry about disappointing me," he said, tiny tears gathering in the corners of his eyes and emotion gently twisting his mouth. "I love you so much."

As if on cue, a gentle spring breeze blew over us. Scents of newly mown grass mingled with our neighbors' dinners cooking on barbecue grills. I closed my eyes and rested my cheek against the smooth nylon of Joe's favorite athletic shirt, and he sheltered me again in the warmth of his embrace. In spite of everything we had endured, or perhaps because of it, I knew how blessed I was to love and be loved by him. We continued walking, together, on the path toward home.

Chapter 46

Joe and I quietly crept up the stairs to our bedroom. We were unsuccessful in our attempts to avoid each familiar creak and groan of the old house's winding steps. We silently winced and giggled at each other with each exaggerated movement, hoping that none of them would wake Joey, sleeping in his room, just down the hall. We closed the door gingerly, waiting for the tiny click that would tell us we had made it safely inside without hearing him stir through the baby monitor. We smiled at each other and sighed our relief. Tiptoeing to our respective sides of the bed, we silently climbed in, enjoying the feel of the crisp sheets and thick comforter.

We had been at the hospital earlier in the day—not the one where we had delivered our babies, but its sister site across the Mississippi River in Illinois, the one where Julia's autopsy had been performed. A colleague and fellow loss mom had told me about the Butterfly Blessings service, a memorial for bereaved families. I was nervous about attending, unsure what to expect, but I could not miss an opportunity to honor Julia and hear her name read aloud.

The staff had welcomed us warmly, and I had been able to connect with Shannon, one of the nurses from our hospital. She had recognized us immediately and called us by name, even before the service started. She told us that the thank-you note with Julia's picture was still displayed in the nurses' break lounge. I was touched by her sentiments, to know we were not forgotten when we left the hospital that day, that Julia was not forgotten.

My parents had come with us for support with Joey and to honor Julia. We sat down in a middle row of the small auditorium, and the service began with one of the same songs we had played at Julia's funeral. It was profoundly emotive. Everything, from the message from a fellow bereaved

Love You Still a memoir

mom to the prayer from the hospital's chaplain, from the candle-lighting ceremony to the tiny glass votives, felt like a rainstorm after a drought.

"You did a really great job today," Joe said, turning on his side to face me.

"Oh. Thanks," I replied, grateful for his kind words, though not necessarily believing them.

"Really," he insisted with a soft chuckle, "I'm proud of you. I know it wasn't easy to be around all of those people, all of the reminders of . . . everything. But you did it. I'm proud of you, and Joey and Julia are proud of you, too."

The mention of their names brought my gaze instantly to his. A tiny lump formed in the back of my throat, my tired eyes silently asking the question that my voice could not. *Really?*

He lifted his eyebrows and nodded tightly. His smile was so sweet, so genuine. Despite myself, I just wanted to keep looking at him, to stare wonderingly at the boyish twinkle in his eyes.

Slowly, cautiously, I felt myself moving closer to him. His eyes widened, and he looked as surprised as I felt. I paused briefly before gathering the courage to move forward and gently touch my lips to his. Electricity ran through us. His return was enthusiastic, but slow and tender, restrained, as if not wanting to spook a reticent animal.

My pulse began to quicken . . . with what? Anticipation? It had been such a long time since I had allowed him to get this close to me. *It's okay. I can do this*, I told myself. But with each passing moment the anticipation gave way to heightened anxiety. My heart was thudding in my chest. Air raid sirens began screaming in my head.

"Stop," but I only mouthed the word, unable to produce the sound, knowing the room was too dark. His eyes were closed. He couldn't see me.

"Stop," again, barely audible this time.

"Stop," a whisper, panic rising, arresting my movements.

"Stop, stop—*stop!*" I cried, extending my arms to push him away with more force than was necessary, breaking the physical connection between us before it had even really started.

I scrambled backward, drawing my legs up and hugging them into a defensive shield around myself. And then, crying in rickety breaths that matched my shaky hands, "I'm sorry. I'm sorry. I just . . . can't."

His face was a heartbreaking mixture of shock and bewilderment, giving way to sad understanding.

"It's okay," he whispered, a tiny sigh and nod revealing his acceptance that the moment was indeed over. "It's okay."

I closed my eyes and turned my face away, too ashamed to see what I had done to him.

How much longer could I expect him to put up with this? At what point would he stop accepting my brokenness and excuses? I buried my face into my knees and wept in earnest now. I was not only a failure as a *mother*, but also as a *wife*. Would this be our breaking point? How much longer could our marriage survive this?

As if reading my thoughts, he said, "Hey," softly. And then another "Hey," placing the gentlest touch on my upper arm.

I raised my head to look at him, dreading what I might find in his eyes. To my surprise, I didn't see anger, resentment, or disappointment, any of which would be a reasonable response. Instead, he was scanning my face, eyebrows drawn together, creating jagged lines that crisscrossed his forehead. He sighed, and I realized the unhappiness I was seeing was not born out of disappointment or anger, but rather from concern and compassion. I honestly wasn't sure if this made me feel better or worse.

Making direct eye contact, he said delicately, but convincingly, "Baby, it's okay. Really. Are you . . . all right?"

He was asking about *me?* Of course he was. He always thought of me, worried about me. I knew this man too well to expect him to be angry, although he would have been justified.

"I'm so sorry. I don't know what's wrong with me." I felt my face twist as new tears began to fall.

"No," he started, with a short, humorless laugh. "There is nothing wrong with you. You're just . . . not ready. And that really is okay. Come here."

Moving closer, tenderly, but with palpable caution, he drew me in. Wrapping his arms around me, he gently laid me down next to him. Deliberately, without any of the spontaneity of our previous interaction, we found a way back to each other, him holding me securely in his arms, me resting my head against his chest, listening to his steady heartbeat.

His heartbeat, strong, steady. Her heartbeat, gone.

I shook my head to push the thought away. I needed to focus.

"Shhh," he soothed, bringing his hand up to lightly move my hair away from my face.

"Are you mad?" I asked.

"No," he answered, sounding genuine. "I'm not mad."

"I'm not trying to . . ." I broke off, unable to continue.

"I know. I do."

"Really?" I asked, peering up at him, pleading for the truth.

"Yes. Really. Babe, you are hurting. And you're healing. I love you, and I'm not going to do anything that is going to hurt you more than you already are. We can take our time. We're getting closer." He grinned. "And I know we'll get there," he promised. "Now, you just need to relax. Breathe."

I took a shaky but deep breath. He squeezed me then, snuggling me tighter. He made me feel so safe, so loved. I did not deserve this man. Something was wrong with me. What? Was it normal to feel this way after child loss? Was anything *normal* anymore? Was I just being selfish?

It's not that I didn't love him. It's not that I didn't want to connect with him. So why? Why couldn't I do this? It was more than just the exhaustion. More than depression. More than sadness.

What had I been feeling? *Fear.*

Fear of him? *No.*

Then what? Fear of letting myself go? Fear of enjoying something? Like the guilt I felt when I would smile or laugh at something funny Joey said. I felt like a horrible mother for enjoying anything when my daughter's body was buried in the ground. How could I smile knowing my child was dead? How could I allow myself to feel anything good when all I deserved was punishment? Yes, punishment for allowing my child to die inside of me. That was what I deserved.

But what about Joe?

I broke away from my tumultuous thoughts to hear him breathing deeply, making quiet sounds that told me he had fallen asleep. My eyes felt impossibly heavy as I watched the gentle rise and fall of his chest. I closed them in a prayer of silent gratitude for him before kissing his forehead at the hairline.

He must have been exceptionally tired to fall asleep so quickly.

Tired of me?

I was tired, too.

Unable to consider these thoughts any longer, I allowed my weary body and mind to shut down and sleep.

Chapter 47

Joe loved Vegas. He had been there multiple times on business trips.

"I don't get it. You don't even gamble," I reasoned, handing him the last glass from the dishwasher.

"There's way more to do than just gamble. There are a million things to do and see. It's an experience," he insisted, returning the glass to a shelf I couldn't reach.

I closed the dishwasher door, leaned against it, and rolled my eyes dramatically, but couldn't resist returning his smile. "I don't know."

"You'll love it. And you *deserve* it. After the year we've had, and all you have been through with work, I *want* to do this for you. I want you to get away for a little bit."

"But Joey—" I began to protest.

"Joey will be fine! I'm sure your family would help watch him. He's been begging for sleepovers with the cousins. It would be a vacation for him, too!"

"I don't know." I exhaled again, but then felt the corner of my mouth turn upward involuntarily.

"I know that smile," he said pointing at my lips, a boyish, dimpled grin filling his face. "Yes! I know you will love it. Thank you, baby," he said, in an uncharacteristic rush.

"Why are you thanking me for letting you take me on a vacation?" I asked, narrowing my eyes at him.

"Because I love to see you smile," he replied tenderly. "And if anyone deserves this, it's you."

I closed my eyes and felt a blush redden my cheeks as I remembered again how lucky I was to have him. "I love you," I sighed.

"I love you, too. It's gonna be great," he replied, kissing me briefly before rushing off to presumably begin researching flights.

I shook my head and smiled, but then shivered as an inexplicable cold dread spread up my arms, chest, and back.

How can I go on vacation when my daughter is dead? How can I leave my son, my only living child, and go too far away to reach him if he needs me? What if something happens?

I tucked my chin into my chest and massaged deep circles into my neck and shoulders, attempting to displace the tension that seemed to live there now. I couldn't disappoint Joe, I thought. I had already done so much of that.

Weeks earlier I had been stunned to see tears welling up in Joe's eyes after Joey had done something silly to make us laugh.

"What's wrong?" I had asked him, alarmed.

"You smiled," he'd answered, lower lip trembling.

"What? What do you mean?"

He had stared down at the ground for a moment before returning my gaze.

"You might not realize it, but you don't do that anymore. It's been such a long time since I've seen you smile—since any of us have. Your family, all the people that love you—we talk about it. I was beginning to wonder if I would ever see it again—it's so beautiful."

Joe was so patient with me. He handled so much while I was busy with work, grad classes, and, of course, grief. When I broke down, he would hold me. He knew some of the things that triggered my emotions and would try to thwart them, or at least minimize the damage. He never complained, never pushed me to do anything that I wasn't ready to do.

His words and his uncharacteristic tears broke my heart. I hadn't realized I hadn't been smiling. Had it really been that long? Had I really worried everyone that much?

I closed my eyes and replayed Joe's words in my head. *You deserve it,* he had reasoned.

Maybe he was right. *He* certainly deserved it. Maybe we both did.

Everything would probably be fine. *Probably.*

Chapter 48

My family agreed to take care of Joey, so we bought airline tickets and reserved a room in Las Vegas for the week following the last day of school.

The stress at the end of any school year ramps up before summer vacation begins, and this had been, without question, the most challenging school year of my career. I was in the midst of proctoring assessments, writing reports cards, updating individualized education plan goals for each of my students, planning for transitions, and dealing with increasing behavioral problems related to those transitions. The pressure was intense. I just needed to get through one more week.

And I was *late*.

"It's probably just stress," I told myself. After losing Julia, the physical intimacy in our relationship had been infrequent, at best. I just couldn't stand to be touched, at least, not like that. *But, there was that one time . . .*

I couldn't even bring myself to consider the possibility that I might be pregnant. Just thinking about it robbed me of breath, like a herd of elephants stampeding across my chest.

After four more agonizing days of waiting, I knew I had to take a test. The memories of all the failed pregnancy tests I had taken while in the throes of infertility came hurtling back. I bought the same kind of test I'd bought then, the kind that shows a read-out in words—PREGNANT or NOT PREGNANT, not little lines, not pluses or minuses. I needed to know, without being able to talk myself into or out of anything.

"Please." I whispered a different kind of prayer today than the one I had constantly prayed back then.

Two minutes later, the result was clear.

PREGNANT.

I gaped at the tiny display as an incredulous mix of horror, wonder, and just the tiniest bit of delight wrapped itself like a python around my chest. My heart rocketed to a velocity that made the individual beats indistinguishable. My skin was on fire. Breaths came quick and hard; I was hyperventilating.

"How did this even happen?!" I closed my eyes as I realized, of course, that I knew *how* this had happened. The more pressing question was, how would I *survive* this? Then the tears came, hot like lava, flowing hard and fast. I sank into a fetal position, resting my burning forehead against the cool linoleum of our bathroom floor.

A *baby?* Another baby? What if this baby died, like Julia? Or what if this baby *lived?* How could I love this baby when I wasn't, and never would be, finished grieving Julia? It felt as if all of my heart space was taken up by Joey and Julia, with no room for anyone else.

"Shhh, shhh. Breathe. Breathe with me." I felt Joe before I saw him, kneeling beside me, pulling me into his arms, surrounding me like a favorite blanket.

"Joe . . ." I began,

"I know," he soothed. "It's okay. It's going to be okay," optimism lifting the end of each sentence.

"*Okay?*" I challenged. "No. How?! It's *not* okay!"

"It is," he insisted, bringing his strong hand to rest gently on my stomach, "It's our baby."

His gaze found mine and held it for a few, profound beats before I closed my eyes, pushing the pools of tears down my cheeks. We sat together, me crying against his chest, him gently stroking my hair, there on the bathroom floor.

Once again, it felt as if the world had been suddenly, irrevocably changed.

After several more minutes of vacillating between me crying hysterically and Joe convincing me that I would, indeed, survive another pregnancy, that we would get through it together, he helped me up.

I stared at my reflection in wonder.

Pregnant.

I shifted my eyes to Joe's reflection, standing next to mine.

"It's going to be okay," his reflection told mine. "You'll see. It's gonna be great."

I sighed heavily and brought my hands to my face, massaging large circles into my temples. I didn't have time to think about this anymore, not right now, or I was going to be late for work.

I quickly went about our morning routine and got everyone out of the house on time, barely. I arrived to work with puffy eyes and a worn expression. Lucky for me, this was not anything new and did not pique the curiosity of my colleagues.

I had worked out a plan on the drive there.

Despite the distraction looming heavily on my mind, I got through the morning's lessons and then, when my students went out to recess and lunch, I drove home and called the doctor's office. I had rehearsed what I would say on the short car ride home.

Knowing that the time I had before I needed to be back at school was limited, I took a deep breath and hit *send* on the saved number.

"Hello," tinkled the voice on the other end of the phone. "How may I help you?"

All my practice of maintaining my composure immediately felt like an utter waste of time. My mouth went dry and I could not will the words to come out.

"Hello?"

"I need to see a doctor." I forced the words out in a rush.

"Is this an emergency?" she asked cautiously.

Was it an emergency? It certainly felt like one, but I knew what she was asking.

"No," I clarified. "I took a pregnancy test this morning. It was positive."

"Okay," she proceeded slowly, cautiously. "Well, congratulations. The first thing we will want to do is schedule a blood draw to confirm the results at the lab, and then I can set you up to see the nurse, and a couple of weeks later, you will see one of the doctors."

"No," I persisted, perhaps a bit too forcefully. Between all of my visits during my pregnancies with Joey and Julia, I knew all of the front desk staff at the office. And, especially after our loss, they all knew me. I didn't recognize this one, though. Was she new? Was it possible that she didn't know my story?

"Please. This is Maria Price."

Silence.

"I'm already a patient. My baby. I—delivered a baby. My daughter. Julia Price."

I recognized that I must sound like a lunatic. How could I get through to this woman?

"She was stillborn. At term. She died, and Dr. Moshier delivered her. We have . . . we have a plan."

My tears were uncontrollable now. My hands were shaking, my chest on fire as I tried to convince this stranger to give me what I knew I needed.

"I can make you an appointment with the nurse."

"No. Please—I need to talk to Dr. Moshier."

"I'm sorry. That's not how this works."

"Fine." I huffed a heavy sigh, pushing my forehead into my open hand, then squeezing the bridge of my nose and attempting to quell the rage rising up inside me. I knew she was just doing her job. Through gritted teeth, I made the appointments, but had one final request.

"Would you *please* get a message to Dr. Moshier's nurse that I called, and ask her if she would please call me back?"

"Sure," she agreed, her tone betraying her hesitation. "I can do that."

I thanked her, and had barely hung up before the emotion that had been building up in my chest was released like water through a broken dam. I only had a few minutes before I had to be back at school.

I made my way to the bathroom to splash cold water on my burning face. I looked in the mirror, truth emblazoned across my swollen eyes and blotchy, red cheeks.

I need to get it together, I thought, looking at my watch. Lunch is almost over. *Lunch.* I hadn't eaten anything. How could I eat anything? *But, the baby . . .*

With a deeper breath than I thought I could manage, I threw some crackers and cheese in my purse and headed back out to my car.

I had barely walked through my classroom door before my phone rang.

"Hi, Maria. It's Ana." Dr. Moshier's nurse.

"Hi, Ana," I replied, a few octaves higher than normal. "Thank you for calling me back."

"Of course," she reassured me. "Doctor would like to see you whenever you are available. Do you want to come in today?"

Her kindness unleashed all of the feelings I had been trying so desperately to hold back. She didn't rush me or make me feel like I was wasting her time. We confirmed an appointment for the next afternoon, and at the end, she thanked *me* for calling.

Chapter 49

Joe and I walked hand in hand through the hospital's entrance. As the automated double doors parted, inviting us to walk through, my throat constricted. I gasped for air as I was flooded with memories of making this same walk, seven months earlier. Before.

Joe squeezed my hand and gave me his best smile. "You can do this."

I lifted my eyebrows in a silent question.

"Yes, you can. We've got this." His eyes twinkled with a strength and certainty that I envied.

I squared my shoulders, tucked my chin, and let out a slow, ragged breath. I nodded. "Let's go."

We walked through the frosted glass door to find the office staff standing together at the first desk closest to us. I am sure it was my pained expression, the redness of my eyes and nose that prompted them into action. Our favorite receptionist, Vanessa, with the crème caramel complexion and shiny obsidian hair that made me feel like she could be a cousin on my dad's side, greeted us and ushered us over to her station.

"Hi, Maria," she said, "I can get you guys checked in—go ahead and have a seat."

"Thank you," Joe replied, and I gave her the best smile I could manage as we moved to the left to find two chairs together in an inconspicuous part of the waiting room.

From the television mounted in the corner, a cooking show host brightly shared her best tips for incorporating fresh garlic into the recipe and the audience clapped in wild applause.

Seriously? I thought. I used to love cooking shows, but in that moment, I could only scoff at the insignificance of adding garlic to spaghetti sauce. Once again, it felt like the whole world was marching forward while my world stood still.

Joe sat next to me, sandwiching my hand between his on the armrest between us. I focused on breathing, in and out, remaining calm. But as with most things, telling myself to stop thinking about the fear that threatened to steal my breath meant that it was the only thing I could think about.

Don't cry, I told myself, biting so hard on my bottom lip that I thought I tasted blood.

I jumped when I heard the door to the nurses' hallway open, and I saw Ana, sunshine filtering in from the window behind her.

"Maria?" she called. Her voice lilted at the end, as if she were asking a question, although her steady eye contact and kind expression revealed that she already knew I was there.

"I can carry that," Joe said, taking my bag as he helped me to my feet.

I smiled in spite of myself, thinking how I wasn't at *that* stage of pregnancy yet.

A knot formed just under my collarbone as I acknowledged that my presence here meant I was, however, on that path.

"Hi, guys," Ana softly welcomed us, leading us over to the scale.

Great, I thought, slipping off my shoes and stepping on. I never liked standing on scales, but this time served as a reminder that I hadn't yet lost the last of the weight from Julia's pregnancy before beginning the cycle again.

So unprepared, I chided myself. *How did I let this happen?*

After Ana had written down the number on her clipboard, she smiled again and led us back to one of Dr. Moshier's exam rooms. She came in after us, closed the door, and sat down at the desk across from us. She drew her shoulders inward and her blonde hair fell in shiny waves around her face as she spoke.

"So, congratulations," she offered, lifting her eyebrows and smiling. "How are you doing?" she asked.

I hesitated for a second, glanced at Joe, then shrugged and shook my head.

"I'm not sure." I answered.

"Of course," she replied, nodding her understanding. "Do you mind if I start with a few questions? I'll get your vitals, and then we'll go from there."

I nodded my agreement. We updated my information and then made conversation as she worked. I knew she was trying to help me to relax.

When she'd finished, she gathered her supplies into a plastic tote and put them in her lap, then swiveled in her rolling seat so she was directly facing us.

"Doctor has a student with her today," she said, looking at us meaningfully. "It's up to you if she comes in with her. It's totally fine to say no."

Joe and I turned to each other. He tilted his head in my direction, indicating that he wanted the decision to be mine.

"Umm . . . well, yeah. I guess it would probably be a good learning experience for her, right?"

Ana nodded again and rotated back to the desk before standing up to go.

"Take care of yourself. You call for anything you need, okay?" Her voice was so earnest, I knew this was more than just a casual thing to say; she meant it.

"Thank you, Ana. You're the best," I told her.

"Thank you very much," Joe joined in.

"You're both so welcome," she replied, eyes soft. "We're here for you."

A few moments later there was a quick knock that made Joe and I sit up in unison. "Come in," he called.

Dr. Moshier, smiling, stepped into the room and closed the door behind her. No student. I breathed a sigh of relief, grateful that they had read my subtext. It would be difficult enough to have this conversation with my doctor. I honestly didn't want an audience for this.

"Hi, guys," she said, her eyes shifting from me to Joe and back again. "How are we feeling?" she asked.

"Okay," I said weakly, after a couple of nervous seconds. "Thank you so much for seeing us today," I told her.

"Of course." She tucked her chin to her chest and exhaled through her nose.

"Before we get started—" Abruptly, the tears that had been forming in the corners of my eyes began to trickle down my face. It might have been out of place, but I had to address the fear that had been pervading my thoughts since the previous morning. My breathing was hitched, my voice pinched, but I had to be strong; I had to keep going.

"We scheduled Julia's induction at thirty-nine weeks and it still—it wasn't soon enough. I know we talked about this before, at my six-week checkup—we have to know that we will be able to deliver this baby earlier than at thirty-nine weeks."

"Yes," she answered quickly, with a sharp, affirmative nod.

I blinked and sat back a bit, relieved. I had been prepared to make a case, to argue if needed with the people who make these decisions, whoever they were. The confident authority in her tone and body language, though, seemed to make it clear those measures would not be necessary.

"Yes?" I asked, just to be sure.

"Yes, we will make that happen. We can discuss this in more detail as we move forward, but we will make that happen."

I turned to Joe, releasing some of the air and tension from my body. Dr. Moshier must have already had these conversations on our behalf with her team after my six-week postpartum follow-up appointment.

"Okay," I said. I was grateful that she had taken these preemptive steps to care for us before we'd even walked into the room.

She grinned at us knowingly, and I closed my eyes and worked to calm my still-elevated pulse.

"We have the results from the lab work you had done yesterday," she continued, reaching for her tablet and swiping it open. "Everything looks really good."

Joe and I exhaled simultaneous sighs of relief. Our eyes met and we shared a soft chuckle at ourselves. We had been so nervous when he had met me at the hospital's lab after work the day before, knowing we wouldn't get the results that would confirm the pregnancy until today. My hands had been shaking, and the phlebotomist, not knowing our story, asked if I was afraid of needles.

When we looked back at her, Dr. Moshier was smiling broadly, too. She shared that my hCG hormone level was high, which suggested the potential for a healthy, viable pregnancy.

Julia's hCG levels were high, too, hissed the cynical voice inside my head. *This doesn't mean anything.*

I rolled my shoulders back, attempting to shake off the negativity and focus on what the doctor was saying.

"How are you feeling—physically?" she asked, tilting her head in apparent genuine interest.

"Tired, mostly," I admitted with a half-grin, glancing briefly at Joe to confirm this. "I have been exhausted, but I just kind of chalked it up to the end of a tough school year and chasing after a two-year-old, and, of course—everything else."

The grief was still exhausting. I felt like I was walking through a haze most of the time. I couldn't remember details—what I had already done, what still needed to be accomplished throughout the day, or even people's names. *Grief fog.* I had read about it in one of the online support groups. It was embarrassing and made me feel like I was losing my mind. Apparently, I wasn't alone in feeling it.

"Sure," she acknowledged, maintaining eye contact, but not in an invasive way.

"I have had some nausea, but it hasn't been terribly bad," I continued, thinking about the all-day sickness I'd often had with Julia. "But that's good, right? I mean, it means that the pregnancy hormone is strong, and the—baby is hopefully healthier?" I asked, anxiety strangling my tone.

She nodded. "Typically, those higher levels of hCG hormones can lead to increased nausea. And, yes, those higher levels of hCG do give us increased confidence about the viability of the pregnancy."

It struck me that her words were cautiously reassuring. Her tone was assertive but lacking the definitive authority I was hoping to hear. Nonetheless, I appreciated her honesty. She couldn't say that this baby, or any baby, would definitely be healthy, definitely be born alive, could she?

"We will want to continue to track those levels in regular blood draws. Is that okay with you?" she asked.

"Yes, of course," I replied quickly. "Anything we can do . . ." I let my voice trail off at the end, unsure how to finish.

"Good," she smiled and made some notes on her tablet.

"We just . . . we also wondered what else we could do, if anything."

She nodded, seeming to expect the question.

"So, we would like to do some additional tests in the beginning. We can do those when you get your hCG levels checked." She offered more guidance, including the now-standard addition of a baby aspirin with my daily prenatal vitamins, and I wondered if that change was a change in protocol, a precaution established in response to our family's tragedy. "We will keep a close eye on you, but many of the things we suggest will be some of the same things that we did before," she explained.

I knew what she meant. Julia shouldn't have died. She had had a strong healthy heartbeat, was moving well, and in position to be born at our appointment hours before we discovered she was gone. It should not have happened. This also meant there was not much we could do to prevent it from happening again.

"But I'm not necessarily more likely to lose this baby because of—"

I could not finish the question.

"No." She shook her head, compassion visibly softening her expression. It was one short word, but it helped to quell some of my panic.

"Okay," I replied, reaching for Joe's hand and squeezing it hard.

As we went on with the rest of the visit, we discussed more plans and precautions for moving forward. I asked questions about my fears, including seafood safety, caffeine intake, and sleeping positions. Finally, I asked about Vegas.

"Clearly, we did not plan to have a baby on the way when we made these plans," I told her, turning to Joe with a look of exasperation.

"It's fine. You are safe to fly—just obviously stay away from hot tubs, alcohol, any of the things you would already be avoiding if you were at home. You will be fine. I think it's good for you to get away. *Try* to relax," she said, smiling, "and we'll see you when you get back."

A brief laugh escaped me. "Okay," I replied.

We engaged in a bit of small talk, a couple of last-minute questions asked and answered, and then we said our good-byes.

She smiled once more before leaving. When she did, and the door closed behind her and we heard the latch click, I felt a sense of reality locking into place. I looked at Joe, new tears welling up.

This was happening. I was pregnant. Again.

Chapter 50

We still went to Vegas, but it was not necessarily the vacation we had planned. The morning sickness and fatigue set in hard, and walking through the desert in June caused my moods to swing like a metronome. In addition to the physical discomforts of early pregnancy, I was constantly distracted by the emotional ones.

The fears only amplified when we returned home.

How can I protect this baby when I couldn't protect Julia? How will I love him or her when my heart is still broken from the loss of Julia? Will that even be possible? Is there enough love left inside of me for Joey, Julia, and another child?

When I am holding the new baby, will I wish for Julia instead? Or will I love the new baby so much that I will forget about Julia? Will this little one take her place in my heart?

We did not announce our news until about a month later. Our friend, Kaitlyn, a talented budding photographer, took our family photo in a grassy park within walking distance of our home, on a bluff overlooking the Mississippi River. Joe held Joey and I held a pink helium balloon. We added the text, *"One miracle beside me. One miracle above me. One miracle inside me."*

Friends and family were ecstatic with the celebratory news, and new fears emerged.

What if everyone else forgets about Julia? What if they think that our plan was for this new baby to take her place? What if they expect me to stop grieving Julia because I have this baby instead?

I was hypervigilant about everything related to this pregnancy. I was careful about everything I ate and drank. I researched and purchased a Doppler heart rate monitor like the one at the doctor's office. Once the baby was big enough, I could place the wand against my belly and hear the baby's heartbeat whenever I needed reassurance—which was all the time.

Joe came with me to each doctor's appointment. Each time I climbed up on the table and lifted my shirt for the nurse to find the baby's heartbeat, we both held our breath until that tiny *buh-boom, buh-boom* came through the speaker. In the early weeks, when the baby was smaller, the heartbeat was sometimes harder to detect. The waiting was intense, making my blood pressure soar like a space missile.

"Oh, sometimes they're just naughty and like to run away," said one nurse. "Come here and stay still," she teased our baby.

I bristled at this. I didn't want this baby to stay *still*.

"Usually they have better luck finding him over here," I suggested, touching the right side of my abdomen.

"Oh, okay," she replied patronizingly. "Come on, ya little booger," she told my baby, promptly ignoring my advice.

After another minute of no heartbeat, tears gathered in my throat.

"Can you try over here?" I asked again.

"They found the heartbeat over there last time," Joe affirmed, leaving his chair to stand beside me and hold my hand.

She looked at me with an almost imperceptible impatient eye flutter and moved the monitor for a moment, then moved it back to my left, determined to be correct. Tears flowing, staring up at the ceiling, I didn't know what to do. I didn't want to be rude, but I knew my body, I knew my baby, and this nurse was not listening to either of us.

A couple of additional minutes passed and I couldn't take any more.

"Could you possibly ask Ana to help? She always seems to have good luck," I said.

It was bold to ask for a different nurse. I knew that sometimes they called on each other to help in these situations, so it wasn't necessarily outside of protocol. I didn't want to hurt this nurse's feelings, and I had never been this forward, but I couldn't lie there any longer and listen to her criticize my unborn child, even jokingly, while essentially ignoring me.

"Sure, we do help each other sometimes," she replied, a light layer of frostiness settling into her tone. "Let me just try one more time."

Another minute that felt like ten.

"Please," I insisted. "Would you please ask Ana? Please?"

"Sure," she said, setting down the gel-covered wand. "I'll be right back."

I felt awful, but I was also terrified. *My baby. No heartbeat. Not again.*

Joe stroked my hair back from my wet cheeks. "It's okay, Mia," he said, but I could see my fear mirrored in his face, hear the wobble in his voice.

When Ana came in it felt like windows opening in a tiny room. She got to work right away.

"Hey, Maria," she greeted me, her eyebrows knitted in concern. "Where is the baby today?"

"Here," I told her, touching my right side, gratefully.

"All right. I need you to breathe for me, okay?" she asked as she snapped the blue gloves on her hands. The other nurse stood behind her, arms folded.

I nodded, but couldn't get any air past the invisible cork in my throat. I watched the intensity of her eyes as she worked and remembered the nurses searching for Julia's heartbeat, finding none.

"Come on, babe, breathe with me," Joe coached, getting closer to make eye contact and modeling exaggerated inhalations and exhalations. "You can do it."

Suddenly the trapdoor to my trachea released and I felt oxygen rush into my chest.

"Good." Ana smiled. "And . . . there's our heartbeat."

A beautiful, rapid *bom, bom, bom, bom* filled the room and I felt my whole body shudder, shaking loose from the grip of fear. Joe's hand squeezed mine as he leaned his forehead against my temple in obvious relief.

Ana's bright grin spread all the way across her face. Even the other nurse was smiling down at us.

"Thank you," I whispered. "Thank you both."

They both smiled and nodded. Ana's eyes sparkled as she silently took off her glove and squeezed my hand firmly before leaving the room.

The other nurse quietly wiped the gel from my skin with a paper towel and packed up her tote. I didn't know what to say. The frustration I had felt for her earlier had melted away, replaced by overwhelming relief that our baby was safe. I hadn't meant to embarrass her; I wondered if she had any regrets. Should I apologize for being so direct? Should I tell her how afraid I had been that we were losing another baby?

"Thank you," I told her again, as she opened the door.

She paused at the door and smiled again. "You're welcome. The doctor will be in shortly."

Thankfully, it took a few minutes for the doctor to arrive, giving Joe and me a few extra moments to regain our composure. Joe rested his hand on my stomach and I rubbed gentle circles into the spot where Ana had found the little *bom-bom*.

"You gave us quite the scare, little one," I breathed.

"Yeah, no more of that, kiddo," Joe admonished.

A quiet knock at the door and Dr. Hannah peeked her head inside. The sun glinted off her medium-length amber hair, and bright, friendly eyes sparkled. She had been the first physician I had seen in this office, years earlier, to explore my infertility issues. Who could have predicted how much we would go through since that first visit?

She smiled at us in a way that made me sure she'd heard about what had just gone on in this room prior to her arrival.

"How are you feeling?" she asked.

Joe and I exchanged a look. "Better now," I told her.

"Good," she replied, taking and releasing a deep breath herself.

We discussed the progress we had made—various test results, questions and answers.

"Are you doing okay, otherwise?" she asked.

Heat climbed up my neck and face. How was I supposed to answer this question—politely, or honestly?

"Umm . . . I've been having a hard time."

I watched her turn to Joe. He nodded in agreement, and she turned back to me.

"Can you tell me about that?"

I told her about the panic attacks, about the everyday moments that stole my breath, about the fear I have of *it* happening again.

"I couldn't save her, and I can't be okay with that. She was my baby, and she died *inside of me*, and I *didn't even know it*." I cried in big, hiccupping gulps. I could hear my voice rising, feel my control slipping, but I didn't care. "She was my *baby*. She was there the night before, and then she was *gone*. How could I not have known? I was her *mama*! I should have saved her! I should have known."

Great, tumultuous sobs burst out of me, and I watched as Dr. Hannah suddenly rushed to embrace me. I had been watching her empathetic response, and for a fraction of a moment, I was surprised by her action, but in the same heartbeat I felt so validated, so heard, so known. I grasped onto her and wept into her shoulder. I treasured this woman, and her team of colleagues. I understood that they had also grieved the loss of Julia, and that they would do everything within their power to protect her little sibling.

Within a few minutes my hysteria had quieted to sniffling whimpers. Dr. Hannah offered the box of tissues to Joe and me before taking one for herself. I was panting, exhausted. I scanned the room, disoriented by the unexpectedness and intensity of this interaction, in a doctor's office.

"I'm sorry," I said, suddenly humiliated by my outburst.

We all took a few moments to recover. Then Dr. Hannah began speaking with a quiet insistence.

"Maria, there is nothing you could have done. You could not have known. We have been through your file over and over—all of us have." She leaned back and made a wide circle gesture with her hand that made me think she was talking about Dr. Moshier, the other two doctors in the practice, and herself. "You did everything right, everything we asked you to do." She squeezed her lips together. "Please don't blame yourself."

I felt my face contort again and I looked down at my hands shaking in my lap. I looked up again and nodded. I swallowed hard, but all I could manage was a whispered, "Thank you."

She observed me for a long moment before looking down and then back up again. She asked if I was still seeing a therapist. I told her that I had stopped seeing the counselor I had seen a few times because we just didn't seem compatible. She asked if I wanted to see anyone else.

"I . . . I don't know," I shrugged, trying to be honest. "I guess I would be willing to try if I thought it would be a good fit."

She gave me the name of a counselor she highly recommended. "We send a lot of our patients to her," she told me, handing me the small piece of paper on which she had written her name and contact information. "I hope that you'll call her. I think you'll like her a lot."

I glanced at the handwritten note and folded it neatly in half.

"Thank you," I told her again, smiling weakly.

We talked a bit more, then a light silence like a feather floated down to rest between us.

"Is there anything else we can do for you guys today?" she asked quietly.

I looked at Joe. He raised his eyebrows and dipped his head toward me, seeming to volley the question back in my direction.

"You've done so much for us. You all have. This," I said, gesturing my open hand between us, "this has meant more to me than you could know. More than I can say."

She crumpled slightly, then sat up straighter. "We are here for you. You are strong."

I exhaled an involuntary laugh of surprise.

"*You are strong*," she repeated. "You are doing this. Please don't hesitate if you have any questions, or if there is anything we can do to help."

"Thank you," I whispered.

With a final smile and a look back at us, she walked out the door and closed it behind her.

Joe stood and walked to where I was sitting on the exam table. He held me and I buried my face into his shirt. It felt so good to close my eyes, but I was at the doctor's office. I couldn't rest; we needed to leave.

I got dressed and considered all the events of the last hour. This is the road of loss, I thought. So much darkness and misunderstanding, but, miraculously, also enough glimmers of good to inspire strength to keep walking.

Chapter 51

I rubbed my palm into my chest and willed the internal fluttering to stop. I sat in my car and stared at the two-story building with its multicolored blond bricks, topped by wooden shaker shingles. I remembered the last time I had visited a counselor and wondered if I was making a mistake coming here.

I would be willing to try if I thought it would be a good fit, I had told Dr. Hannah. Now that I was here, though, all I could do was sit, staring at the building, afraid to get out of my car.

I combed my fingers through my hair and pushed out a long, slow breath.

You can do this, I told myself. *If it doesn't work out, you can just go home and never come back.*

I opened the door and stepped out into the warm summer sun. I preferred rainy days, as they made more sense to me. Sunshine always reminded me of Julia. She was gone; it didn't seem right to have it without her. However, the summer sun did afford me with an excuse to cover my eyes with dark sunglasses, which I appreciated.

I walked into the building and was hit by a refreshing blast of cool air-conditioning. It was a split-level foyer that reminded me of a house my cousins had lived in when we were children. The upstairs office appeared to be inhabited by a private investigation company. *Interesting,* I thought.

Noticing a welcoming seating area situated to my right, I perched on the edge of an overstuffed leather sofa beside a coffee machine. I exhaled slowly, feeling comforted by the homey surroundings.

"Maria?" called a voice over my shoulder.

I turned to see a woman standing in the entry to the lower level. She had close-cropped sandy hair and hooded eyes that crinkled into crescents when she smiled. Her smile and presence were as hospitable as her waiting area.

"Hi!" I greeted her, a bit too brightly, and made my way around the furniture grouping to shake her hand.

"Hi, I'm Beth," she said in a low, soothing tone.

"Maria. Nice to meet you."

As we descended to her lower-level office, I took note of her crisp linen pants, a bright poppy color, topped by a flowy blouse. I was comforted that she wasn't wearing a business suit with a tight bun. Did they teach therapists to dress in such a way as to comfort their clients? Was there a class for that?

We walked into her office and I was surprised that although we were at the garden level, the room was bright and airy. There were books on a shelf and some furniture, but it was not cluttered. I admired the unfinished mural painted on the wall. *A work in progress*, I noted. I sat back on the cream-colored love seat and released the breath I had been holding.

We chatted lightly about the weather, how warm it was getting, and how nice it was to see the sun today after the past few days of rain. I had learned to say this; it was what people wanted to hear. As our small talk trickled out, we both sat in silence for a moment, assessing the situation.

My pre-visit paperwork had included an electronic questionnaire where I could share information about myself and my reasons for seeking therapy. Beth built on this with a few general questions before asking me to tell her about Julia.

I took a deep breath and told her our story—how at first we weren't sure if we wanted to try to have another child, but when we did and discovered that she was a girl, it felt perfect. I shared how our pregnancy read like a textbook description of a normal, healthy pregnancy, and how we'd awaited her arrival with all of the joy and optimism expected of new parents. I told her of our devastation the day we lost her, how it felt to hold her, to kiss her, and to tell her good-bye.

It felt good to hear and say Julia's name, to share our love for her and our story with someone new. Beth listened attentively, nodding and verbally affirming throughout. As emotionally difficult as it was to relive those moments, I was surprised by how easy it was to talk to Beth. I felt her empathy. She never rushed me or made me feel like I was wrong for thinking or feeling anything. A therapist, not a friend, yet there was an unmistakable connection forming between us.

I shared how we had recently discovered that we were pregnant again, how this was not a part of our plan. I told her how terrified I was, how

I wondered if each day would be the day that we would lose this baby, too. I explained that all my research into baby loss and some connections with other bereaved parents had brought some comfort, but in the light of this new pregnancy, they also evoked an intense fear, knowing how fragile life really is.

I admitted that I was also afraid of what would happen if this baby lived. Would I be able to love another child the way I loved Joey and Julia? Would I miss her too much? Or forget her?

I felt the words pour out of me like lemonade from a pitcher, a little sour, a little sweet.

Beth did not recoil from my strong emotions. She leaned in and made me feel like I could tell her anything.

We talked about my previous therapy experience.

"It just wasn't—a good fit," I told her.

I sneaked a sideways glance at the graceful wrought-iron cross art that I'd noticed when we first walked into the room. We talked about faith. I wondered how she would respond to my strong feelings about God, my questions. Would they make her uncomfortable? Would she feel like *I* was not a good fit?

I shared how I struggled with my faith. I was apprehensive at first but picked up strength and momentum along the way. Since Julia's death, I had learned that my thoughts and feelings were offensive to some people. These people were uncomfortable with the kinds of questions I was asking. They wanted to comfort me with platitudes, or condemn me, both of which were hurtful.

I needed to be honest with her, I reasoned. Like in any relationship, we needed a foundation of trust. I needed to know that I could trust her to listen and provide the kind of help and answers I needed, even though I had no idea what they were.

"I hate it when people say 'Everything happens for a reason' or that it was 'God's will' that Julia died. I think it's just an easy thing to say to avoid digging deeper into the hard questions and feelings."

Beth watched me, her open hands resting on the arms of her chair, and it felt like she was waiting patiently for me to continue.

"I just—I don't think that God killed Julia. I don't think that He needs to let people—babies—die so that he can accomplish a 'bigger purpose.' I think He's God, and he has the power to accomplish His will without doing that."

Beth nodded slowly, and I looked out the window and kept talking.

"I don't believe that everything happens for a reason. I think some-times the 'reason' things happen is because we live in a fallen world, one completely different from the one God created and intended for us. But He also gave humanity the freedom to choose, and when we chose sin, it brought with it death, destruction, and injustice. That's why good things happen to bad people and bad things happen to good people. That's why babies die. It's not to accomplish a 'higher purpose'; it's because life isn't fair.

"I also believe that's why Jesus came to save the world, to overcome it, to save us from ourselves. I believe He can *redeem* our hurts. He can take this horrible tragedy of Julia's death and make something good come out of it. I just wish He had prevented it from happening in the first place. He *could* have done that, but He *didn't*. And I don't know how to be okay with that."

"I think it is only human to feel that way, Maria," Beth told me, shaking her head slowly after several moments of silence. "I think that is a beautiful explanation. I don't think having those questions or fears means that you *don't* have faith. In fact, I think it very much means that you *do*."

My shoulders shook with silent sobs of relief. I felt no judgment or condemnation, only validation, concern for my well-being, and love.

"Thank you," I said, forcing out the words in a whisper.

"Maria," she began, "I am honored to have heard about your Julia, and this new baby—everything you have shared with me today. You are a beautiful person, a beautiful mother to *all* of your children. I would feel privileged if you were to invite me to continue to walk with you along this path as you move forward. You don't have to decide right now. You can take your time."

I thought quietly for a moment, despite instinctively knowing my answer.

"I would like that," I managed, wiping away fresh tears.

She nodded. Her smile seemed to be a bittersweet combination of pleasure that we had come to this agreement and sadness that it was the death of my daughter that had brought us together.

We talked a bit more and she asked if she could end the session by praying with me. I nodded gratefully at the suggestion. In truth, she prayed and I bowed my head and listened to her inspirational words.

"Thank you," I whispered again, as we both opened our eyes and looked at each other.

"Thank you," she replied. "I will be praying for you, Maria."

"Thank you," I repeated.

A good fit, I thought. *I think it will be a good fit indeed.*

Chapter 52

A few more weeks passed quickly, and soon it was time for my twenty-week ultrasound. I felt nauseated, partly from the pregnancy, and partly from the anxiety of seeing this appointment creep up on the calendar.

Twenty weeks is a milestone in pregnancy, the halfway mark, the point at which a loss is no longer called a *miscarriage*, but a *stillbirth*.

So, if we lost him or her now, it would be called a stillbirth, I thought. I closed my eyes and grieved that this was something I even knew—that it would be a conscious thought.

This scan was the one where we would find out whether we were having a boy or a girl.

"Which one do you want?" people asked all the time, as if we were ordering an ice-cream cone—chocolate or vanilla. "Maybe you'll have a girl," they said excitedly, "one of each."

No. We already had one of each—Joey, our boy, and Julia, our girl.

I knew people were generally well-meaning, but these conversations always made my stomach clench. The cliché answer that we "just want a healthy baby" held new meaning for us, and I always wanted to insert "living" into the statement as well.

Even in my quiet moments, however, I was twisted with angst. With both Joey and Julia, I had a sense early on in my pregnancies about each of their genders, and I was right with both. With this new baby, I just didn't know.

Thinking about having another girl heightened my fears of replacing Julia with a new baby, of forgetting her. Would a new baby girl wear Julia's clothes? The ones we had received as gifts, the ones I had lovingly selected for her before *and after* her death? If we had a boy, I would not hesitate to put him in Joey's hand-me-downs, but what about hand-me-downs that had never been worn? Would we use the same nursery design, or start new? Would she be like Julia? *How would we know?*

Having a boy might un-complicate things a bit, I thought. But then I considered Joe and all the father-daughter dances he would never attend; Joey, my parents, and family never having a little sister, granddaughter, and niece to spoil. Joe's parents, who had been so excited to have a little granddaughter to love. I had already let them down once, I thought; would having a boy disappoint them further?

None of this was within my control, of course. The answer would be waiting for us in the doctor's office, along with more information as to the other anatomical structures of this little one. *Would he or she be healthy? Would he or she have a heartbeat?*

My head shook rapidly, uncontrollably, like an out-of-balance washing machine as I sat in the passenger seat on the way to our appointment.

"Mia, are you okay?" Joe asked from the driver's seat.

I swallowed hard and focused on slowing my breathing down to a normal pace.

"Hey," he said, shifting his gaze between the road and me. "You're all right." He took my hand and squeezed it, massaging it with his thumb.

I nodded and gulped again. I had shared my fears with Joe; he seemed to take them all in stride. *We will love this baby no matter what*, he had reasoned, *just like Joey and Julia.* I loved that he remembered to include Julia in our family, even though others forgot.

I leaned back on the headrest and tossed my head from side to side, willing the red light at the clinic's entrance to turn green so we could make our way up the steep incline to the parking lot.

It was the same extension office of the university hospital where we had had Julia's twenty-week scan, when she was safely inside my belly and the doctor had made only a casual reference to my advanced maternal age of thirty-six creating an increased risk for of stillbirth.

Breathe, I told myself as we crested the hill and drove around the curving entrance of the parking lot. My mouth was so dry, I couldn't swallow.

"I can't do this. I can't go back in there," I murmured.

"I know, baby," he said soothingly. "We'll do it together."

"It's too hard."

"I know," he concurred, dropping his head low. "I miss her, too."

I stared out the window at the wide building with its brick facade and dark windows contrasting against the bright late-summer day. How could I go in there again?

"Come on," he said, optimism injected into his tone. "Let's get you in there and you can see our baby."

I turned to face him and studied his expression. I knew this was hard for him, too. In addition to the stress of facing all of the post-traumatic stress and fear, he also felt he had to shelter me.

"Okay," I sighed, trying to sound more optimistic than I felt.

Walking through those dark glass doors felt like stepping through a time portal. Joe did all the talking as we checked in. I peered around nervously, remembering our last visit here sixteen months before.

By the time they called my name and took us back to the exam room, I felt dizzy and disoriented. Joe braced me, his hand gripping my hip, his arm taut around my back.

We walked into the room with the exam table surrounded by giant wall-mounted computer screens. I felt sweat on my face, despite the chilled, air-conditioned room. Flashes of Julia on the screen, our excitement upon hearing that we were going to have a baby girl—all of it played like a film in my mind. We had been so naive then, *before.*

The tall, slender nurse in black scrubs directed us to the chairs and sat down at a computer to get started. I gave her my name and date of birth. Then she asked the questions that we heard at every ultrasound appointment, the ones I dreaded.

"Okay, so how many pregnancies?"

"Two."

"How many live births?"

I paused. "One." Despite my preparation for the question, my voice always quavered with emotion in giving the answer.

I watched as she slightly bowed her head, her straight blonde hair obscuring her face like a curtain, before looking up at us again. "I'm sorry."

I closed my eyes and gave her a quick "You didn't know" smile, but I wondered who created this protocol of asking these questions at every ultrasound. Shouldn't there be a note in my chart, or at least a more merciful way to ask for this information?

After a few more preliminary procedures, we were ready to get started. Joe stood beside me as I lay back on the exam table. Our eyes were trained on the monitor in anxious anticipation. She put the warmed gel on my stomach and moved the transducer wand in a wide circle before landing in one spot.

Our eyes grew wide as we stared at the screen in front of us.

"Umm," she said, clearing her throat nervously, "did you want the gender to be a surprise?"

"Well," I replied with a voiceless chuckle, "no."

"That's probably a good thing." She giggled. "The cat's kinda out of that bag, huh?"

"Yep. I'd say so," Joe answered, smiling broadly at the sign that couldn't be missed, staring at us from the giant display.

"Congratulations! It's a boy!"

We all laughed together and Joe leaned over to kiss me on the forehead. "It's a boy," we told each other.

I closed my eyes and inhaled a slow, cleansing breath, then opened them to stare at the screen in wonder at this precious little boy inside of me.

The nurse went to get the doctor, giving me a moment to wipe up the remaining gel from my skin, sit up on the table, and process what we had just seen and heard before they reentered together.

"Hi there!" he boomed, shaking our hands and introducing himself. His big personality was evident, his round cheeks rosy at each end of his wide grin. "Well, I heard the little guy was pretty anxious to let you know he was a boy, eh?"

Joe and I nodded and we all shared a laugh together.

"Well, he looks good," the doctor continued. "All of his structures are in place, everything measures just as it should for a healthy baby at this stage of development."

"Great," we said, nodding. It was all good news. Our baby looked perfect. But I could feel the balloon expanding against my lungs. *But so did she.*

I don't know if the doctor read the anxiety on my face or if he'd already planned to move on to the next subject.

"So, I read from your file that you were referred here due to 'advanced maternal age'?"

I straightened my shoulders and answered, "Yes." Seriously? Couldn't they also come up with a better phrase than this one? It always made me feel ancient.

As if reading my thoughts, he smiled and shook his head. "I know. It just means that you're over thirty-five. They really should change the way they word that."

"They should," I agreed, smiling to show my gratitude for his perceptive kindness.

"I also see here that you have a history of loss," he said, making eye contact with each of us. The jovial tone in his voice was now gone. "I'm sorry," he said sincerely.

"Thank you," Joe said for both of us.

We discussed our current treatment, what tests we had done, and the results of each one. He recommended weekly ultrasounds to monitor the baby's growth and development and reaffirmed our plan to deliver earlier than the thirty-nine-week mark.

"Our daughter," I began working hard to make my voice sound normal, despite the tears that were already streaming down my face. "She was stillborn at term, thirty-eight weeks, seven days." Although I was sure all of this was in my chart, I told him what our doctors had told us about the clot in her umbilical cord, how there was nothing we could have done to fix or prevent it. "But, there's nothing that would necessarily make this baby more likely to . . . to have that same outcome, right?" I asked, my voice thick with concern.

"No," he assured me, just as my other doctors had done. "It's very rare, so if anything, because this happened you would probably be statistically less likely to experience it again. But we certainly want to keep an eye on you. I'm sure I don't need to tell you to keep all your appointments; I am guessing that you did that before."

I felt my face contort as I nodded and looked down.

"I am sure it must be terrifying," he continued. "Try to rest assured in the knowledge that he looks strong, and it sounds like you have a team who is doing everything right. All our very best to you."

I nodded, still unable to speak.

"Thank you," Joe replied for both of us again, shaking the doctor's hand appreciatively.

The nurse handed us printed images of the scan, and we thanked them both again before they left the room.

When the door closed behind them, Joe encircled me in an embrace. As we pulled apart, he rested his forehead against mine and found my eyes.

"We have another boy," he whispered, grinning at me happily.

In spite of myself, I couldn't restrain a giggle. "God help us."

He kissed my temple and we stared together at the little black-and-white pictures of our *third* baby. Our boy.

God help us.

Chapter 53

A few months after we lost Julia, our church had approached Joe and me with a proposal to build a playground on the south lawn of our campus and name it "Julia's Place." We envisioned Joey and his friends gliding down the slide and happily playing together on a structure named for Julia. We hoped that as he played in the sunshine, on the playground built in Julia's name, Joey would feel a sense of connection to his little sister. We felt that the exuberant laughter and joy of playing children would be the perfect way to honor Julia.

We went to work right away raising funds and choosing an industrial play structure that would stand as a lasting memorial. Finally, in September, the equipment and the recycled-tire playground mulch were delivered. A crew of volunteers from our church showed up, and for two days, men and women of all ages and backgrounds came together to build and install Julia's Place.

That Sunday, we hosted a ribbon-cutting ceremony with a glossy hot-pink satin ribbon in honor of the little girl for whom it was named. The sky was a bright cerulean, the grass emerald green. The buttery yellow slides were dappled with golden sunlight piercing through the mature shade trees that lined the lawn. Delicious aromas began wafting over from the parking lot, where food trucks began prepping to serve guests after the dedication.

After all of the final touches had been made, for a few quiet moments I stood mesmerized by the poster-sized, framed photograph of Julia we'd placed on an easel next to the structure, in preparation for the ceremony. Her presence was captivating, breathtaking.

"I miss you, baby," I told her. "This is all for you; I wish you were here to enjoy it."

I felt Joe's hands move around my hips, coming to rest on my emerging baby bump. We stood there together for a few minutes, saying nothing, simply appreciating the angelic face of our little girl. I leaned my head back against his shoulder.

"I miss her," I told him.

He turned his head to plant a kiss in my hair. "I know, baby. Me too."

"She's the only one not here," I said quietly.

He paused for a couple of beats. "Hmm. You think?" he asked.

I turned toward him, warily.

"Maybe she is," he suggested, lifting his eyebrows. "I'd like to think maybe she is here."

I couldn't suppress a smile at the optimism twinkling in his eyes. I turned back to Julia's Place and leaned back into him. "Maybe."

Soon people started filing out of the building and walking over to surround Julia's Place. We were delighted when friends and colleagues greeted us, eager to remember Julia in a new, special way. Joe's best friend since childhood, Dan, even made the hours-long trip with his two young girls to be with us for this bittersweet day. I was so grateful to him for coming. Dan and his wife, Meghan, got married the same year we did, and they lost a little boy shortly afterward. Joe occasionally talked to Dan on the phone, but they were only able to visit in person like this rarely, due to the physical distance between them. It was good for Joe to have someone who would ask about how he was doing today.

Joe and I climbed up to the highest platform, at the top of the double slides, and welcomed our guests. I cleared my throat and lifted my chin, working to keep the warble out of my voice as we thanked the church and all those who had given generously of their time, talent, and treasure to make this vision a reality.

"We are thrilled to know that this playground will be a backdrop for exuberant laughter, imaginative play, and unbridled joy for the children of our church and our community. We can think of no better way to honor the memory of our baby girl. We hope that as her brothers and her peers run and slide and pretend at Julia's Place, it will be a bit like playing with the sister, cousin, and friend for whom it was named."

We bowed our heads and prayed, and then, hands trembling, cut the bright pink ribbon to the boisterous applause of the crowd. Joey giggled jubilantly as he and my great-uncle, a senior member of our church, made the inaugural glide down the double slides together. Children rushed the structure, whooping and cheering as we welcomed them to play.

We carefully climbed down and greeted our guests. For over an hour, we visited with friends and family members. We hugged and talked about how beautiful the day was. They shared kind words of condolences and congratulations. It was important to Joe and me to thank each of them for coming to share in the day with us.

Eventually, the crowd filtered away, and Joe and I were left standing alone. The sun shone warm and bright above us.

"You want to go get something to eat?" he asked me.

I nodded yes, but my heart pulled against itself, as if being dragged by locomotives headed in opposite directions. I turned back to Julia's photo, in the foreground of her poignant memorial. I kissed my fingers and brought them to rest on her precious lips. I was inexpressibly grateful for this perfect tribute to my daughter's life, but equally devastated by the fact that we needed one at all.

Chapter 54

It was early October, days before Julia's first birthday, and I was sitting on the love seat in Beth's office.

"I just—I mean, I knew that I should expect it to be hard as we approached this milestone, but I just never imagined that it could be *this* hard," I told her.

She nodded slowly, giving me time to continue.

"I guess I have just been surprised at how much even the weather has impacted me. I'll walk out the door and the sun is shining and it's warm but not hot, cool, but not chilly, perfect—just like it was then—and I feel like I'm transported back in time to the last weeks of my pregnancy with her, and I can't breathe or even move. It's like I know what's coming, but I can't stop it from happening. Then my brain remembers that it's not *then*, it's *now*. It's over, and she's gone, and there's still nothing I can do to change it."

"I'm sorry," she said with empathy. "We have talked before about that lack of control and how hard it is to accept."

I nodded and drew in a shuddering breath.

"I mean, I would expect to be affected by seeing babies or driving by the hospital, but the temperature and the breeze? It just feels like the triggers are coming in from every direction right now."

"The mind is a funny thing in how it remembers," she began. "The senses are so powerful in evoking memories. It makes sense to me that the physical sensations of that day and the days afterward, when you experienced such unbelievable trauma, would become closely associated in your mind. Now that those sensations are coming up again, so are those memories."

I nodded again and turned to stare out the window at the fire station across the street. The firefighters were washing their truck. Cars zoomed in opposite directions on the street between us. *Average, everyday life. Like nothing had ever happened.*

"My dreams are intensifying," I told her, still watching the firefighters.

"Do you want to tell me about them?"

"I've always had dreams about traveling. I know they're anxiety dreams. They're never about the enjoyment of exploring a new place, always about the anxiety of getting there. There are always these crises that present themselves at the worst possible moments. Like, I'll be at the airport and suddenly realize that I don't have my boarding pass, or I neglected to purchase tickets altogether. I didn't pack any luggage. I don't have a camera. I can't find my family to say good-bye. I don't want to go. I never know the language; sometimes I don't even know the destination. I'm just getting on a plane to go somewhere, always completely unprepared for the trip."

Beth sat quietly, listening attentively. "What do you think?" she asked after a moment.

"I don't know," I confessed, shaking my head. "I know they must mean something. I've had them for years. They always seem to come up when I am experiencing some kind of change or anxiety. But I have had them consistently over the last year. I'll go through peaks when I have them every night, sometimes even more than once a night. Other times, I won't have them for a week or so, but then they start up again, both in frequency and intensity. I'd love to have your thoughts."

Beth nodded, still listening. She shifted in her chair and raised her brow.

"Well," she replied, her tone light and speculative, "I know you've talked a lot about grief being a journey, one that you never planned, or ever wanted to take. It seems to me that these dreams might be a reflection of those waking thoughts and feelings. You feel unprepared. You are going somewhere new. You don't know what it's going to look like, or be like. And although you have supportive family and friends, your grief journey is deeply personal and potentially lonely, one that you have to travel alone."

I sat staring at her with my mouth hanging open. It was like someone had pulled back a heavy drape in a dark room. This explanation made so much sense, provided so much clarity, that I couldn't believe I hadn't realized it sooner.

I *was* on a journey, a trip that no parent would ever choose to take. I would never feel prepared or ready for the experience of losing Julia, of living a lifetime without her here. And even with all of the support and empathy I'd received from others, this journey was one that I had to walk alone.

I felt focus return to my eyes and realized they must have been glazed over, staring at nothing. I was breathing audibly, apparently from the exertion of my mental processing. I closed my mouth and nodded my head briefly, then looked up at Beth.

"Yes," I said finally. "That's it. That's it exactly. Thank you."

She let silence hang in the air for a while before speaking again.

"What are you thinking about?" she probed gently.

I took a deep breath.

"Just thinking about the journey metaphor," I answered. "I miss her. I don't want to spend the rest of my life without her here." I heard my voice break and it was like a dam opened, releasing a river of tears. "I just don't know how to do that."

Beth waited patiently, but with palpable concern radiating from her like heat from an engine. "I know your pain is unbearable. I am so sorry that you have to walk this road that, you're right, no parent should ever have to walk." She paused, then continued. "I wonder if you have given any more thought to the idea of healing."

"No," I said flatly, straightening my back against the cushion behind me. "No, I don't want that. I can't . . . I'm sorry. I just don't want . . . I can't think about it. Healing feels . . . like letting go, and I just can't. I feel like I have already lost so much of her. I just can't lose any more."

"That is absolutely understandable, Maria. You have been handed a tragedy, an unimaginable one. And I don't want you to think that I am in any way suggesting that you need to 'move on' or forget Julia or minimize the place that she will *always* have in your family and in your heart."

"No, I know." And I did. I recalled a couple of recent comments on social media from friends and family telling me it was time to "move on," time to "let go." In my heart, I knew most of them wanted to help, but in my ears, their words sounded like callous, hurtful disregard for my daughter and my grief.

I did not feel any of that indifference or insensitivity from Beth.

"I'm glad. Because that is not anywhere near my intention. You love Julia, and you will love her for the rest of your life, Maria—nothing will ever change that. The love you have for your daughter is so evident, so pure; it will always be a part of you, just like she is a part of you. I know that you have the hope of Heaven, and that you will see her someday, and that you will find healing then. My hope for you is that, in time, when you are ready, you will also find some degree of healing in *this* life—a healing that does not include leaving Julia behind, but rather, taking her with you into a place of peace. Peace in knowing that you love her, and that she loves you, her mom. And Maria, I acknowledge that this is your path, but I count it a privilege to come alongside you in your journey and to help you in any way that I can."

I could not breathe, I could not sit upright. I bent at the waist and covered my face with my hands and moaned. I wanted to lie down. I felt like I was disintegrating, like the pain was too much to survive and that I would break into tiny pieces of the person I had once been, falling and being absorbed into the ground.

I thought back to the early days of my grief, when the pain was so palpable, so raw, that even a kind word would send shock waves through me. There was a constant heaviness closing in on me. I cried oceans of tears. Every. Single. Day.

But now there were some nights when I wouldn't cry myself to sleep, and there were times that I could say Julia's name without dissolving into tears . . . and it scared me. It felt like I was dishonoring her memory. It felt like if I didn't hold on to the anger and fear, that it would remind me of how empty my arms truly were. And that was terrifying.

I didn't know how to survive this pain. I didn't know if I had enough strength to try.

Chapter 55

Unlike the day she was born, the sun was hidden behind the clouds one year later on Julia's first birthday. This made sense to me; my Sunshine had gone away. Rain fell intermittently, and it felt like even Heaven was crying with us.

Joe took Joey to daycare, and I took the day off work, knowing that I would be useless there. I'd wanted to plan a walk, a memorial, something special to mark the day, but I just couldn't do it. I felt like Sisyphus, endlessly pushing my giant grief boulder up a hill, only to watch it fall back down again.

It was a day full of *should-have-beens.* We should have been busy with parties, balloons, and presents. Instead, we planned to meet my family at the cemetery in the late afternoon to visit her grave. I should have been picking up sprinkle-laden cupcakes for a giant celebration. Instead, I spent the morning delivering cookies and fruit to the doctors, nurses, and staff that had taken care of us in the aftermath of her death.

When I went up the stairs to Labor and Delivery, I was bombarded by the memories of 365 days before. I turned my face away from the glass wall that overlooked the garden and gazebo where we had called our families to share the heartbreaking news that Julia was already gone.

As I approached the looming double doors of the secured unit, my hands began to tremble, and I feared I would drop the tray I was holding, along with my resolve.

What was I thinking, coming here today?

In flashes, I saw myself walking through this door, Julia still in my belly, then leaving through the back door, the next day, without her. I wiped my sweaty palm on my black cardigan and reached over to push the intercom button. I gave my name and asked to be admitted to share a gift with the nurses.

"Hi," I managed as I approached the wide circular nurses' station. "I brought these—I, umm . . . today is my daughter's birthday," I began, but immediately regretted it when I saw their happy expressions. "She, umm—she died, though. She was stillborn—at term—at thirty-eight weeks, seven days," I told them, not able to look at their faces, feeling guilty for not rehearsing this, for taking them through this gamut of emotions. I felt like an idiot.

But they were gracious, offering their condolences and thanking me warmly for the gift.

"Umm . . ." I continued, fighting the urge to run away, "sorry, one more thing. Dr. Moshier told me I could—if there's no one in our room—the one we delivered in—that we could visit . . . I could visit, if that's okay?"

"Of course," they agreed together. I told them the room number and one nurse led me to the room at the end of the hall, all the way around the edge of the nurses' station.

"Thank you," I whispered tightly.

"Absolutely," she nodded. "Take all the time you need."

When she shut the door behind her, I felt all of the ropes holding me together burst apart, and all of the pent-up emotions poured out of me in the safety of those walls. The bed where I had labored, delivered, and held Julia, the scale where they had weighed her, the sink where they had bathed her, the chair where my parents had sat to hold her for the first time, the nurses standing over me when I lost consciousness, Kelcy taking pictures . . . the door they walked through when they took her away.

It was like reliving each distinct memory from that night in a single moment.

I reached out for the bed with its crisp, white sheets and balanced myself against it. I wanted to lie down, to sob into the pillow and remember the feel of the mattress, hoping that it would inspire the memory of how Julia felt in my arms. But if I disturbed it, that would create more work for the nurses to prepare for another laboring mother. A mother waiting to hold her baby—her living baby.

Feeling dizzy and nauseated, I carefully traced my hand along the footboard, then sat on the couch where Joe had slept after they took Julia away. I buried my head in my hands and sobbed, consciously working to stay quiet, so as not to alarm any nearby families enjoying their first moments with their long-awaited newborn babies.

Twisting sideways on the couch, I brought my arms and knees up around my new baby belly as best I could in a modified semi-fetal position, a physical reminder that I was grieving one child while carrying another. I leaned my head against the back of the couch and took in a staggered breath, my sinuses feeling like an overfilled water balloon.

"I miss you, baby," I whispered to Julia. "I miss you. I have missed you every second of every day of the last year. I wish our story could have ended differently. I wish instead of missing you in a hospital today, I was holding you at home, watching you take your first wobbly steps, listening to you say your first word. Maybe it would have been *Mama*?"

I closed my eyes, felt hot new tears rush down my cheeks.

"I'm so sorry I couldn't save you, sweetheart. I'm so, so sorry, Julia. I love you. I loved you then, and I love you still. I always, always will, no matter where you are. Happy birthday, baby."

I looked up to the sound of tiny drops of rain beginning to patter against the window. I stared up at the overcast sky, full of angry gray clouds. *Angry at the injustice*, I thought.

The clouds suddenly broke open and tiny droplets fell, steady and strong, mirroring my tears.

My Sunshine has gone away.

Chapter 56

I took note of the leaves, how they were changing to their autumnal hues, falling from the trees and gathering in heaps on the pavement below. As I ascended the steep hill in my SUV on my way to work one early November morning, my anxiety also began to climb. Panic widened my eyes. My breaths were quick and short.

When did I last feel movement? Had I felt him this morning? I couldn't remember. Why can't I remember? Do I have the Doppler? Did I put it in my bag? No. It's still at home.

I attempted deep breaths as I pulled into a parking space.

No. This can't be happening again.

I forced a smile as I walked past all the familiar faces that greeted me every morning.

"Good morning, Mrs. Price! How are you?"

"I'm good, thanks. How are you?"

Am I good? Is my baby good? Is he still alive?

I swallowed hard as I sat down at my teacher's station in my classroom. I breathed a sigh of relief that my students were still safely in the cafeteria for breakfast. I needed time to figure this out. I took long gulps of water that froze in transit inside my chest. *This has happened before.*

Thinking back to that morning just over a year earlier, I remembered the advice from the doctor's office: *Eat something, and if that doesn't work, come in to get checked out.* An anonymous friend had been leaving little chocolates at my desk every day, a thoughtful token of kindness and support. I tore open the package ferociously. I swallowed hard after only a few bites. Nothing. I jerked my pencil drawer open to find more candy I had saved from previous days, and ate them, too.

My hands shook as I reached across my desk to pick up the phone and call Joe's office in the school district's administration building across town.

"Hello, Mia," he answered casually, not yet having a reason to be concerned. I called him every day, usually more than once.

"I can't feel him," I whispered.

"What?"

"I don't feel the baby moving. I think something's wrong. I tried to drink water and I ate some chocolate, but nothing seems to be working. I think I need to go to the hospital," I choked, panic rising with each word.

"Okay," he began. His voice was calm, but I could hear the rustling of his movements as he was already preparing to leave. "You're doing all the right things. He's probably just sleeping. I'm coming to pick you up. Try to stay calm. I'm going to have to hang up, but you can call me on my cell. I'm on my way."

"Okay, thank you."

"You don't have to thank me. Just try to breathe. Put your feet up. I love you. I'll be there soon."

"Okay, I love you too," I told him.

"I'm coming, baby. Be strong and breathe." I nodded even though I knew he couldn't see me, and hung up the phone.

"C'mon, buddy. Please. Wake up." Emotion formed a blockade at the back of my throat. Tears shot out of the corners of my eyes. In that moment, every step I felt I had made back to a relationship with God felt like it instantly fell away, crumbling into a sinkhole of doubt and fear. I closed my eyes, and tried to leap past it. *No. Please, God. Not again.*

The door opened, and one of the classroom para-educators stopped suddenly in visible alarm, upon seeing my face. "Are you okay?"

"No. I can't feel the baby," I heard myself say.

I watched the color drain from her face before she turned and ran from the room.

Seconds later, I was surrounded by our school secretary, Steph, Nurse Erin, and health para, Gwen—all friends who had been a part of our story.

"What's going on?" Steph asked.

"I don't know. I can't get him to move."

"Let's put your feet up."

"I already called Joe, and he's on his way," I said.

"When did you last feel him?"

"I can't remember. I listened to him on the Doppler last night."

"Is your Doppler here?" asked Erin.

"No, I left it at home. Oh, God."

"Drink this," Gwen insisted, rubbing my back and lifting a carton of juice from the cafeteria to my lips.

"It's okay. Deep breaths," urged Nurse Erin as she gently but firmly positioned her hands on my belly. "What did you eat today?"

"An egg-white omelet on flatbread? I ate some candy I had in my desk a few minutes ago. I thought the sugar might wake him up," I cried, holding the wrappers up as evidence. "Please," I begged, hot tears rolling down my cheeks. "I can't do this again."

Desperately, I searched each of their faces. In each one, I found compassion, but also fear.

"Is this all your stuff? Let's take you to the office; Joe should be here soon," Steph said, picking up my teacher bag and purse.

Through the large windows I watched as Joe careened into the bus circle, the car barely in park before he jumped out and flew through the office entrance. His face was a mix of stifled concern and forced optimism. He had always been the strong one. *How could I break his heart again?*

"It's okay. We're going to be okay," he insisted in gentle, reassuring tones as he walked me out to the car. I looked into the blue of his eyes and wondered if he was trying to convince me or himself. Both, I realized.

The scenery in the window whizzed by and we reached the hospital in record time. We had been here so many times in the past year—OB-GYN appointments, ultrasounds, blood tests. Yet, my heart could only remember walking in, fully pregnant with Julia, just before discovering that she had died inside of me. *God, I cannot do this again. Please.*

"Ready?" Joe asked.

He'd opened my door and was holding his hand out for mine. Our eyes met as we contemplated his question, also pregnant with meaning.

"Ready."

We walked into the emergency department, my hand in his, his arm supporting my back. We explained our situation to the attendant on duty. It seemed to take hours for them to get us upstairs. Why couldn't they understand the urgency of our situation? Even if our words failed, didn't our heartbroken and terrified expressions convey the crisis we were experiencing?

Finally, we were sent to the second floor, the very same place where our world had fallen apart thirteen months earlier.

"I can't do this," I whispered past the emotion choking my breath.

"You can," Joe promised. "We're doing this together."

We walked through the double doors to a brightly lit nurses' station. Bright with hope, bright with expectation. Lightheaded, I felt like I was floating as we were led to a triage room and I was instructed to lie down on the neatly-made hospital bed.

The nurse was kind and professional, not revealing any opinions about our situation as she wrapped two heart monitors around my baby belly, one for me, one for my child.

I began to feel dizzy, a swirling sensation overtaking my vision. My hands started to tingle, then went numb, and my head and limbs felt impossibly heavy. Tears flowed as I lay back on the bed, in a hazy jumble of déjà vu. I was reliving the moments before we learned we had lost our daughter while simultaneously dreading the same future for my son.

Then, miraculously . . . *lub, lub, lub, lub.*

My eyes flew to the nurse's face. She smiled broadly, with visible relief. "That's your baby!"

A yelp of joy escaped from beneath a deeply held breath, rushing out of my mouth. I turned to Joe, relief washing over him like a spring rain.

He enveloped me and we clung to one another, reveling in the beautiful sound of our baby's healthy heartbeat. *Thank God.* We were confronted by the contradiction of our two experiences: one of utter devastation, one of pure joy. The memory of our loss intensified our elation, turning it bittersweet.

Our nurse attended to our needs, making us comfortable for the three hours of monitoring and assessments that would follow. I thought I saw a tear glitter in the corner of her eye as she squeezed my hand and left the room.

We contacted our families. This time, we had not let them know we were going to the hospital, as we'd had neither the time nor the strength to do so.

We had a biological physical, a series of tests to assess our baby's health and viability. He passed all eight of eight criteria. We watched him wriggle and squirm on the ultrasound screen and were reassured by Dr. Hannah, who was the doctor on the Labor and Delivery floor that day: Our son was healthy and alive.

"He was deep in a sleep cycle," she explained with a slight smile tugging at the side of her mouth as she held the ultrasound transducer to my belly, sending his moving image up to the screen.

"Are you serious?!" I asked incredulously. "I tried to wake him up with water, sugar, poking him, everything I could think to do. I was so scared."

"I know," she sympathized, everything we had been through showing in her face. "Sometimes they just get really sleepy and don't want to wake up until they are ready."

I closed my eyes and rubbed my belly with a deep sigh. "Stinker."

After the three hours of testing were over, they released us to leave. I wanted to go home, but I was also intensely afraid. What if this was like the night before Julia died, a perfect examination one day, gone the next? How would we ever be sure?

We couldn't be *sure*, I realized. We could only do everything we knew to do, and hope that would be enough. And that was horrifying.

Chapter 57

"A Christmas baby?" Joe and I nervously laughed together with Dr. Moshier at our appointment. "That's exciting," I noted apprehensively.

"It is," she agreed. "It would be three weeks before your due date, at thirty-seven weeks gestation."

Although we were all smiling, there was an unmistakable tension in all of our voices.

I thought back to the beginning of this pregnancy, when Joe and I had come in prepared to demand to be permitted to deliver sooner than the thirty-nine-week limitation set by the state of Iowa for normal pregnancies without extenuating circumstances. We had met with no resistance from our team of doctors. They agreed that our request was reasonable, and petitioned the decision-makers for this allowance. Thankfully, my "advanced maternal age" of thirty-seven, and the previous loss of Julia, at term, had been extenuating enough to justify our cause to those making the decision to allow an early induction.

I was absently alternating between twisting a strand of my hair tightly around my finger and letting it loose. Joe and I looked at each other, communicating wordlessly.

"Yes, let's do that," we agreed.

"Okay," Dr. Moshier said, smiling, sitting up a little straighter. "So, sometimes at thirty-seven weeks, the baby's lungs are not yet fully mature for birth. We would want to do an amniocentesis to verify that before we go ahead with the delivery."

"His lungs?" I asked, suddenly conscious of the air moving in and out of my own chest.

"Yes. If we deliver too early and his lungs are not developed, he could have some serious complications, so we definitely just want to be sure."

Joe and I met eyes again. *Complications? Would this be the way we would lose this baby, too?*

As if reading my mind, Dr. Moshier leaned forward to emphasize her point.

"We are committed, like you, to delivering a healthy, living baby. We just need to carefully weigh the risks and benefits, and not put him at any unnecessary risk."

Any unnecessary risk.

Was my insistence on delivering early foolish? Was I putting my baby in danger because of what happened to his sister? All of the doctors we had seen had been confident that it was highly unlikely what had happened to Julia would happen again. But could we be certain?

I squeezed Joe's hand and whispered, "Okay."

Dr. Moshier explained the details of the amniocentesis—what it would be like, the risks and benefits of the procedure itself, and how they would use it determine fetal lung maturity.

"So what if his lungs aren't mature?" I asked slowly, not wanting to consider this scenario. "What happens then?"

"Well," her words were slow, her tone cautious, "then we wouldn't deliver yet. We would reevaluate and come up with a new plan."

Joe crooked his head to look at me, making eye contact. He raised his eyebrows, and asked, "What do you think? Are we good?"

I looked into his face, more confident than concerned. Finding the strength I needed, I lifted my chin and looked back at the doctor. "Yes, let's do it."

The snow was flying at us at downward angles, like so many tiny white arrows as we drove along the highway to the University of Iowa Hospital. I adjusted the warmer on my seat and shifted on the leather, trying to get comfortable. It was the week before Christmas, our plan to have the amniocentesis done at thirty-six weeks, seven days foiled by the hospital's holiday closure schedule.

It was only a few days earlier, thirty-six weeks, two days, but in a gestational period, when babies are developing rapidly within the womb, a few days can make a significant difference. I sighed into the window, making a large, cloudy circle of condensation on the glass.

"You okay, babe?" asked my mom from the backseat. She had offered to come with us, eager to help, to provide whatever support she could give throughout this process. "Are you feeling all right? Do you need anything?"

I twisted in my seat to look back at her. "I'm fine, Mom. Just trying to get comfortable."

"Do you want my pillow? You could put it behind your back. Do you want me to massage your shoulders? Do you want a cereal bar? Are you drinking enough water?" she asked the questions in rapid fire, her words tumbling on top of each other.

I shook my head and smiled. "I'm okay. Really. Thank you, though."

She returned a sheepish grin, recognizing that she was being overly helpful. She shrugged one shoulder and added, "I'm just saying, if you need anything, I'm here to help."

I couldn't suppress a voiceless chuckle. I looked back at her and knew it was true. Her crystal blue eyes were enthusiastic, yet there was also a tiredness in them, and an anxiety that mirrored my own. Like us, she had been devastated to lose Julia. I knew that she bore the additional pain of watching me, *her* daughter, suffer with the grief of losing *my* daughter. I knew she really would do anything to make things better.

"Thanks, Mom," I told her. "I love you too."

Chapter 58

The only sound I could hear in the room was the abnormally loud noise of my own breathing. I tried to lick my lips, but my mouth was completely dry. I sat bolt upright in the reclining examination chair, waiting for the doctor to return.

"You okay, Mia?" Joe asked, breaking my concentration.

I turned my wide-eyed stare to him, blinking rapidly. "I'm fine," I replied.

"Do you need to use the bathroom again?" my mom asked. "She said your bladder needs to be completely empty, right?"

"Yeah, but I'm fine," I told her, a thread of worry hanging from my tone, threatening to unravel everything.

"It's gonna be fine, Mia," Joe said lightly rubbing his hand up and down my back. "They're going to have an ultrasound on to watch him every second. They do these all the time."

"I know," I murmured.

But I *didn't* know. How could anyone *know* that everything would be all right? They were sticking a giant needle through my skin, into my womb, right next to my baby. The risks for injury or complications were low. *But so were Julia's.*

The door opened and the high-risk obstetrician, Dr. Wilson, walked in, followed by the nurse and sonographer. She also had three students with her; we had agreed to allow them to watch the procedure, but now I was wondering if that was the right choice. What if they asked a question and distracted the doctor while she was inserting the needle? What if one of them sneezed? What if I sneezed?

"How are you feeling?" the doctor asked. Her hair was a mass of dark corkscrew curls restrained by a thin tortoise-shell band. She carried herself with a confidence that felt comforting.

"Okay," I said, trying to sound stronger than I felt.

"Good," she smiled. "I think we're ready to get started." She reiterated the details of the procedure. I lay back and the nurse spread the cold, yellow antiseptic soap into a circle on my side. The sonographer got into place, bringing up my baby's black-and-white image on the screen.

"It's going to be very important that you do not move at all during the procedure. We'll keep an eye on your baby through the ultrasound," the doctor told me again.

I looked at the screen and whispered, "Stay still, buddy." *Still.* The word caught in my throat. *That was not what I meant!* I looked to Joe, horror filling my face.

"It's okay, babe," he soothed. "I'm right here."

I squeezed my eyes shut, trying to ignore the fear that was pinching my throat, squeezing my lungs.

A moment later there was a sharp jab in my side. I gasped, surprised by the pain despite my preparation for the moment.

"Stay still," the doctor repeated, sounding slightly exasperated.

Tears sprang to my eyes. I didn't think I moved, but I couldn't be sure. They said I would feel a slight sting, but it felt like so much more than that. I was used to needles, but this was different. Was it the pressure or the fear that made it so much harder to endure? Was my baby okay?

Another moment and the needle was out. Dr. Wilson held up the slightly murky liquid and grimaced lightly.

"We'll take it back and test it," she told us. "I'm going to be honest with you—I see a lot of these and I can pretty much tell when they are going to come back with mature lungs or not. Usually, when they are mature, the liquid is cloudier because of the oxygen, but we'll see. In the meantime, let's get you over to Recovery where they will put you on a monitor so we can keep an eye on you and your baby."

My heart sank. *My baby. Not cloudy enough? Too clear? Not mature?*

I looked at Joe, the fear in my face mingling with disappointment and defeat.

I saw only a flash of disappointment in his eyes before he turned to me, lifted his chin, and drew in a deep breath. "It's okay, Mia," he soothed, gently squeezing my hand. "Let's just wait and see what the results tell us."

I lay reclined on my back in the recovery room, staring up at the ceiling above me, tears gently trickling down across my temples and into my hairline. The room was a large rectangle, curtains dividing the room into four separate bays. Joe and my mom sat with me in the last bay against the wall. Heart rate monitors were strapped around my belly, and I listened intently to each movement, each heartbeat, with mounting anxiety that they might suddenly stop.

"Do you need some more water?" Joe asked.

"I'll go get you some," my mom offered.

I closed my eyes and shook my head back and forth on the pillow under my head.

"No, I'm fine," I whispered.

But we all knew I wasn't fine. We were waiting for the doctor to come back and give us the verdict: Were the baby's lungs healthy enough to deliver, or not? And if not, what did that mean?

We heard footsteps on the other side of the curtain and a voice that sounded like Dr. Wilson. I sat up and swiped the tears away from my eyes. The metal curtain rings screeched against the rod hanging from the ceiling, and then she stood before us.

"Hi, guys."

I searched for clues in her face, her tone, as to what the test results might indicate about my baby's lungs, but she didn't make me wait.

"So, we did not get the level we were looking for on the test. It doesn't look like your baby's lungs are ready for him to be delivered yet."

I felt a lump rise in my throat, tears involuntarily rushing to my eyes as she gave us numbers, the risks of delivering a baby with immature lungs, respiratory distress.

"Thank you, Doctor," Joe responded when he saw that I was too upset to speak. "Can you advise us as to our next steps?"

She seemed to soften at his question.

"Well, I would advise that you not deliver yet, but his lungs are developing quickly at this stage, so a few days can make a big difference. I know you weren't planning to induce until—next week?" She checked the clipboard in her hands. "So, I'll call Dr. Moshier and give her my recommendation. I think she'll probably be in touch with you to discuss your team's thoughts and, potentially, devise a new plan."

"But that plan won't include another amniocentesis." I was asking a question, but phrased it as a statement.

"I wouldn't think so, no," she replied, shaking her head slowly.

I nodded my understanding and we thanked her for her time. She wished us luck and left the room, closing the curtain behind her.

My body shook with tiny, inaudible sobs.

"Mia, I know it's disappointing that his lungs aren't strong enough yet. It doesn't mean that they won't be soon. Look at how much he's grown and developed in eight months. He's just not ready; that's why we did the test, so we'd know. It's good data that will help us to make a solid, healthy decision moving forward."

"I know you're right," I told him, "But—how will we know? How will we know when they *are* developed enough? I know what they say about it being unlikely to lose this baby like we did Julia—" My voice was cut off by the resurging lump in my throat, "But, what if—what if we don't have enough time to wait?"

The next day, we received a call from Dr. Moshier. She had met with the team of other physicians and reviewed the findings from the amnio-centesis and concurred with the advice from Dr. Wilson at the University. We would wait until after the following holiday week, continuing to monitor the baby through our weekly non-stress test and ultrasound. Then, if the baby did not come on his own, we would induce on January 3.

Chapter 59

"Mommy, I feel really upset." Joey sat down next to me on the couch, hunched his shoulders, and poked out his lower lip dramatically.

I stifled a small giggle, sensing that this was a ploy.

"Oh no, Joey. Why do you feel upset?"

"I just do. I feel very sad." He shook his head miserably. Joey had always been a very empathetic child, even before Julia's death. Since then, although we tried not to traumatize him, he had been exposed to our grief, and we talked a lot about feelings. At almost three, he was increasingly proficient at sharing his emotions.

"Oh, I'm so sorry to hear that, buddy. Is there anything I can do to help?"

"Yeah, sure!" He perked up immediately, sitting up straight with a smile that brightened his whole face.

"Great!" I smiled at him. "What can I do to help you feel better?"

"Cake!"

Joe and I erupted in laughter, and I pulled Joey in for a deep cuddle. I kissed him on his head, his thick, wild hair prickling my nose. I thanked him for sharing his feelings, said that maybe we could have cake after dinner, and tried to offer some healthier ways to feel better. He wasn't interested, though. He gave up and went back to playing with his toy animals. *Sweet boy.*

I watched him play and wished to be a better mother to him. I missed the mom I had been *before*. I had been happier, of course. Less fearful, more spontaneous. More naive, less cynical.

I did, however, also love him more fiercely, more protectively than before. I was more appreciative of each hug, each sweet moment like the one we had just shared, each breath that he took, because I never knew if it would be his last. I closed my eyes in gratitude for my children, that I was chosen to be their mom, and for all the ways they made me better.

It was Christmas break, so schools were closed and I was home with Joey. We read books, watched classic children's Christmas movies, ate too many Christmas cookies, and tried to ignore the anxiety that was burning a hole in my stomach.

Joe and I had narrowed our name choices for Baby Brother, as we had come to call him at home, down to two, but hesitated to make a decision. I counted kicks and regularly used the Doppler to listen to the baby's heartbeat. Joey enjoyed playing doctor and listening to Baby Brother, too. His eyes and mouth would widen to large circles each time he held the probe to my belly and heard the miraculous *ba-bom, ba-bom, ba-bom* through the handheld speaker.

We had donated Joey and Julia's bassinet to the church nursery earlier in the year, before we knew that a new baby would be joining our family. A new, swiveling bassinet stood sentinel in our room, waiting, *praying* with us for Baby Brother to come home.

For a second year, I wished that I could hide and sleep through the holiday. Like Scrooge, I felt haunted by the grief of Christmas Past, and the guilt of Christmas Present. I knew I was cheating two-year-old Joey out of the Christmas I would have given him if his sister were there. But I just couldn't do it. I could only think of how Christmas *should* be, how different that was from reality, and how, now, Christmas would always be this way for our family.

And, of course, I now faced the persistent fear of Christmas Future—what would happen with Joey and Julia's little brother? Could we protect him? How?

On Christmas Eve, a large box was delivered to our door. I cataloged in my mind all of the different online shopping orders I had placed and received. I could not recall what was missing. As I turned the box around to read the return label, my airway squeezed shut. "Molly Bears."

Molly Bears is a nonprofit organization that creates plush bears for bereaved families. Volunteers lovingly sew and then weigh bears to the precise weight of babies at their time of passing. Because all of their work is done by volunteers and because of the heartbreakingly high demand for these precious keepsakes, Molly Bears only accepts a limited number of orders per month. It takes a few more months for bears to be created and shipped to their families.

I had ordered our Julia Bear in July, on my Grandma Julia's birthday. She was the one who had inspired Julia's name, the one with whom she now rested in the cemetery. It seemed somehow appropriate that we would request our Julia Bear on her special day.

My hands shook as Joe, Joey, and I tore back the tape and opened the package together. For Joey, it was an exciting pre-Christmas gift opening. He squealed with excitement as we carefully lifted back the flaps and reached in to see what was inside.

"She's heavy," Joe observed, pulling her out of the box and setting her gently in my lap.

"Seven pounds, fifteen ounces," I whispered.

She was stunning. She was covered in ballet slipper pink fur that curled slightly at the ends, creating a light, cloud-like texture. Her shiny beaded eyes were black in the middle and brown around the rims. I didn't know what color Julia's eyes were. Brown like mine and Joey's? Or blue like Joe's? We would never know.

"It's a bear!" Joey exclaimed. "Thank you! Can I play with it, Mommy?"

Joe and I looked at each other apprehensively.

"This is a special bear, Joey," explained Joe. "It's for our whole family."

"This is Julia Bear," I told him, a tear trickling down my cheek. As beautiful as the bear was, I realized, she was only a substitute for the sister he should be playing with tonight.

Joey looked from the bear to me, to Joe, and back to the bear.

"It's Julia Bear," he repeated, gently stroking her silky fur with his tiny toddler hand.

"Yes, buddy, Julia Bear. We need to be gentle with her," Joe's voice was gentle, yet firm.

Joey nodded with an understanding I didn't expect from him. Bending over, he kissed Julia Bear's embroidered pink nose, then leaned into me for a hug before running back to his zoo animal set on the other side of the living room.

I closed my eyes and leaned back against the couch with Julia Bear against me and attempted to transport myself back to that evening 439 nights before. I tried desperately to remember what it felt like to have the pressure of her body skin to skin, seven pounds, fifteen ounces, on my chest, silent and still. She had never come home, never been inside our house.

In the ambient light of the Christmas tree, I imagined a different Christmas, one with Christmas music playing in the background and cookies for Santa on the dining room table. Joey and Julia would be in matching Christmas jammies, playing happily on the floor, together. Joe and I would be smiling from the couch, softly rubbing circles on my belly as we anxiously awaited the birth of their little brother.

But that was not this Christmas. That would never be our Christmas story.

I cradled Julia Bear and gave thanks for the kindness and generosity that had inspired the organization that brought her to us. I prayed a blessing on Molly's family, who would certainly also be missing their baby girl this Christmas Eve, too. Grateful that she had come to us on this special night, just in time to get us through another Christmas Day without her, I squeezed that sweet bear tightly to my body, even as I also held tight to my unrequited Christmas wish—that we had *Julia* here instead.

Chapter 60

The days that followed Christmas were spent on high alert. Every movement, or lack thereof, created a spike of anxiety. Tension pulled hard on my neck and shoulders. I questioned everything. Was that twinge the start of labor, or just gas? When was the last time I felt movement? Is my baby safe, or slipping away? How will I know?

Christmas was on a Monday. We had more than a week to wait and see if our baby would come on his own before our rescheduled induction the following Wednesday. By Friday morning, I had developed a persistent headache. It wasn't strong, but the over-the-counter medication suggested by my physicians was not eliminating it. This was one of the warning signs of complications. *Was it dehydration? Tension? Or something more serious—preeclampsia?*

There was also a massive snowstorm on the way—*Snowmageddon,* the meteorologists had called it. *And* it was New Year's weekend. Wasn't there some old wives' tale about maternity wards filling up during snowstorms and holidays?

I called my doctor's office and left a message as I had done many times before. As I hung up the phone, I attempted to calm myself.

Deep breaths. It's not a bad headache. I don't have any vision changes. Kick counts are good. I heard a strong, steady heartbeat on the Doppler.

Yet, how could I be sure? What if I thought he was fine, but he was in danger? What if my baby died—again?

The nurse called me back and relayed the message from my doctor: Please come in, just as a precaution.

We dropped Joey off at my parents' house on the way to the hospital. By the time we arrived, snow was already beginning to fall in large, heavy flakes.

Joe and I held hands as we entered the familiar double doors and walked up the stairs to the second floor.

"We're going to need a urine sample," the nurse with a freckled face and long red ponytail said, smiling apologetically as she handed me the clear cup with the dark blue lid.

"No problem," I told her. "I know the drill."

The bathroom had a poster about preeclampsia's risk factors, symptoms, and potential effects. *Maternal and infant death.* I blinked hard, screwed the lid shut tight, and delivered it to the hospital courier waiting outside to take it for protein level analysis in the lab.

Our nurse showed us to a triage room where she took my blood pressure. *Normal.* The nurse, Joe, and I all shared a collective sigh of relief. One symptom down.

"That's great. Now we'll just put you on the monitors while we wait for your lab results to come back," she said with a bright smile. She stretched the pink and blue belts in place around my stomach and patted them gently. "I'll watch from out there," she told us, still smiling. "Let us know if you need anything."

She closed the door behind her, and Joe and I shared a look.

"It's gonna be fine," he said, but I wasn't sure if he was reassuring me or himself.

The nurse came back in to check periodically.

"You're definitely having contractions," she said. "Are you feeling them yet?"

"No, not yet," I replied, apprehensively.

"That's okay. Everybody has contractions in the weeks before going into true labor. It's just your body preparing for what it needs to do," she explained.

I knew this, but it only reinforced my fears that changes were happening inside my body without my knowledge, without my power to control them.

"Your protein test results came back normal," she said. "We'll just continue to keep an eye on you for a while longer, and Doctor will look everything over, too."

I nodded, trying to feel comforted but unable to ignore the weight settling in my chest.

She brought us some water and left again, promising to come back soon.

Joe and I watched the peaks and valleys on the screen that tracked our baby's heartbeats, and began to talk about what we would do when we left, picked up Joey from my parents' house, and went home, hopefully before the storm outside became too dangerous.

The door opened and the nurse walked over to the monitor. I watched her face. She was calm, did not appear flustered or concerned, yet something about her body language told me that something was not quite right.

"What is it?" I asked, working to keep the panic out of my voice.

Her tone was neutral, professional.

"The baby's heart decelerated when you had your last contraction—"

"*What?*" I whispered. Joe reached for my hand.

"It went right back up, though," she continued quickly. "Doctor is on her way."

"Good, thank you" Joe replied evenly. We looked at each other, trying to breathe, trying to understand what we were hearing. *What did this mean?*

"She'll check things out, and she'll probably keep you here to induce today."

"What?" I repeated, audibly this time, my eyes bulging at her.

"She might not," she quickly amended, "but with your history, and all of the other factors involved—she might." There was a hint of a smile in her tone.

She left again and I rested my head back against the pillow. Thinking about it, I wasn't sure why I was so surprised by this news. Hadn't I been expecting it? Expecting something and having it actually happen, though, were two different things. I closed my eyes in an attempt to focus, but it felt like I was spinning in circles on ice, unable to regain traction.

"Mia, it's okay." Joe's voice felt far away. "Hey, look at me."

I felt tiny dots of sweat begin to form on my forehead as I blinked my eyes back open. His face was inches away from mine.

"You can do this. We're here at the hospital and they are taking care of us. This is the best place we can be right now, but I need you to stay with me, okay?"

I closed my mouth and inhaled through my nose. I nodded at him. We had known this was a possibility. It would put a stop to the endless kick counts, Doppler checks, and worrying at home. So why was I so shocked to hear it?

Dr. Pauli entered and we both turned to her abruptly.

"Hi, guys," she began.

Dr. Pauli was the newest doctor in the OB-GYN office. She was young, fresh-faced, and from our few prenatal visits with her, she seemed very sharp. I wondered how long she had been out of medical school, how many cases like ours she might have encountered.

"Hi," we replied nervously.

She went over the summary of our visit, test results, and the recent heart rate deceleration.

"I'd like to keep you here," she said finally, her dark chocolate brown hair bouncing with each nod as if to emphasize her statement. "Your test results are good, but with your history, the concerns that brought you in today, and now the deceleration in baby's heart rate, I'd feel most comfortable if we kept you here and just delivered your baby today."

Today? A sharp exhalation rushed out of me. Weren't we expecting this? Hadn't we expected to deliver earlier this week if his lungs had been ready?

"His lungs—" I began, my brow tightly knitted. "Do we think that his lungs have been able to mature by now?"

"We definitely want to keep an eye on him," she said, nodding, "but your amnio was over a week ago, and looking at the levels he was at then, we can be reasonably confident his lungs are mature enough to deliver. It's definitely a consideration. We need to weigh the risks and benefits of all the factors involved." She sat down in the chair next to my bed and carefully outlined our options, and how we might proceed.

Joe and I looked to each other and wordlessly agreed that delivering today was the best option for our family. *Today.*

I looked down at my belly, full of baby and covered in monitors and medical gel, and felt a small, stupefied grin spread across my face. I turned to Joe. He pressed his lips together and gave me a tight nod. I lifted my chin and turned back to the doctor.

"Okay, let's do it today."

"Good." She smiled warmly. She went over a few logistics and left with a pledge to return to check on us later.

"Thank you, Doctor," we told her, shaking her hand firmly before she walked out the door. We stared at each other with dazed expression. This was actually happening. Today. We were going to meet our baby today.

Chapter 61

We called our families quickly and relayed the plan. We had barely hung up when there was a slight rap on the door and a familiar face peeked around the corner. It was Natalie, the sweet, bubbly nurse who had done the non-stress tests the night before and the day we lost Julia, the one who had first discovered that Julia's heart was still.

I stared at her, breathless. She smiled at us, and we shared a moment of unspoken wonder at the symmetry of the moment.

"Hi, you guys," she said, with a head tilt that exaggerated her inverted bob.

We exchanged small talk as Natalie led us down the hall to the delivery rooms. I wondered as we walked if she would take us to "our room," number 214. But she stopped halfway around the hall and showed us into the corner room. Our eyes widened at the view of the city from the large picture windows that lined half of the large room. Cars maneuvered along the streets that were already lined with thick mounds of snow.

"It's really coming down out there, isn't it? Gonna be a busy night around here, probably," she said raising her eyebrows dramatically.

We moved past the monitors and the warming table where they keep babies warm during exams after birth—live births. We sat on the bed and she wrapped the identification bracelet with my name and date of birth printed on the outside.

"We'll have a matching one for baby, too, for security," she told us, holding up a miniature version of the one around my wrist, and I couldn't remember if Julia had worn one. But then, she wouldn't have needed one, I realized.

We signed paperwork and she asked if I wanted an epidural.

"Yes," I told her. "I didn't have one with Joey, but then I did—with Julia," I felt the familiar tingling in my nose that meant tears were coming. I paused and cleared my throat before continuing shakily, "I want one."

"Yep, sure. We can do that," she nodded, tucking her hair behind her ear. She explained the timeline. I would get dressed in the gown, they would start an intravenous line that would increase my contractions, I would labor for a while until contractions started becoming uncomfortable, then we would call for the anesthesiologist to administer the epidural. Dr. Pauli would monitor us throughout, and be the one to perform the amniotomy—rupturing the amniotic sac.

I closed my eyes and turned toward the window. I blinked hard and my eyes were wet with memories of doing all of these things 444 days earlier. *But this is not then*, I reminded myself. *This will be a different experience.*

I turned back toward Natalie and forced a smile. "Sounds good."

She nodded, but her face had fallen a bit. There was a sadness in her eyes that told me she was thinking about Julia, too.

"I'll give you some time and then I'll be back," she said quietly, resting her hand on top of mine for a few seconds before walking away and closing the door behind her.

"They really gave you the luxury suite," Joe smiled.

We both surveyed our surroundings. The room seemed more spacious than all the others, with an amazing aerial view from the wall of windows. The floors, furnishings, and wall art had been a part of the hospital's update project. It felt fresh and inviting.

I turned to Joe and we shared an unhappy smile, considering *why* they had given us the best room on the floor. Was it because they felt sympathy for us because our other baby had died? A sad consolation prize?

He sat down next to me on the bed and settled his arm around me.

I leaned my head against his cheek. "I miss her," I sniffed.

His lips grazed my temple as he murmured, "I know. I miss her, too."

Chapter 62

Shortly after I had changed into my hospital gown and Natalie got my IV line started, my mom arrived at the hospital in as much of a flurry as the snowstorm outside.

"I'm so excited," she squealed. "How are you feeling? Are you doing all right? How is our little Peanut?" She had started calling the baby Peanut since we still had not decided on his name. "Have your contractions started yet? Do you need anything? What can I do?"

"Mom." I breathed out a laugh. "I'm fine. Try to relax. Breathe like this, *hee, hee, hoo,*" I told her, mimicking the patterned breathing technique for active labor. We all chuckled, enjoying the break in tension we all felt.

"All right," she grinned, jutting her chin and shaking her head at me. "Fine. I'm just really excited!"

I knew she was ecstatic. She was the one who had taught me to be a mother. I studied my mom's face, fair and soft. Her smile was full of joy and eager anticipation to meet her newest grandson. Yet, behind her stylish glasses, her eyes held something else—concern for me? Grief for her only granddaughter? Certainly both.

My dad had stayed home to take care of Joey. I knew that if Julia had been alive and healthy when we had induced, he probably would have stayed home with Joey then, too. Like Joe, he was a family man. He was a strong protector, who also felt and loved deeply. He hated to see me cry, and I knew how hard it had been for him to come to the hospital that day. It was out of grief and a solemn show of his love and support that he had endured the devastation of watching me labor for and lose my daughter.

Both of my parents had taught by example how to love, relentlessly and unconditionally. From childhood to teenage years, college to my wedding day, and even in my journey toward becoming a parent myself, never in my life had I ever questioned their devotion and willingness to step in to help when I needed it. Even in my failures and disappointments, I knew I could depend on them to be there to love me through it.

"Thank you," I replied, watching my mom's face through bleary eyes.

"What do you mean? What for?" she asked, her voice rising in concern.

"Just—for everything," I told her, biting the inside of my cheek, attempting to still the tremble in my jaw. "Thank you for loving me so much, for teaching me how to be a mom."

"Oh, honey." She stepped toward the bed and leaned over me, carefully maneuvering around the cords and IVs to pull me into a gentle embrace. "I love you so much. And I love Julia. And Joey. And this little Peanut that I can't wait to meet." She moved her hand from my belly to my hand and turned her attention to look into my eyes. "You're a great mama, and I am so proud of you. You love *all* of your babies, and I love them, too."

My face twisted with emotion, I nodded, unable to speak.

We held each other gently, and I gave thanks for her, and for the unbreakable bond that exists between mothers and children. It is a connection, I realized, that withstands even the most impossible odds—even death.

Chapter 63

It was not until a couple of hours later, as the sun was just beginning to set on the snowy cityscape outside our window, that my contractions became uncomfortable enough to call in the anesthesiologist. I wondered if it would be the same gentle man who had delivered the epidural with Julia. Would he remember us?

It was a different doctor who came, but he was just as kind and patient.

"I'll wait," he told me. "For one contraction to stop before we inject the needle. You will want to stay very still."

Still, I thought, and I wondered if a doctor who knew our history would choose that word.

Anthony and Car, my brother and sister-in-law, joined us shortly after the doctor left.

"How are you feeling?" Car asked, shaking off her winter coat. I remembered how they had left their vacation last year to drive for hours to join us the night Julia died. I was so grateful that they had been able to hold Julia that night. I smiled, thinking how they'd driven through a blizzard this time, to hold her little brother.

A couple of hours later it was completely dark, only city lights illuminating the persistent deluge of snow. The meteorologist on the early evening news projected pictures of Godzilla on the radar screen as he talked about how "Snowmageddon" was continuing to wreak havoc on the region.

Dr. Pauli returned, and after her examination, determined it was time to perform the amniotomy, to break my waters.

I lay back and turned my head into the pillow while she performed the procedure. As the warm amniotic fluid rushed out of me, so did hot rivers of tears. My body was in fight or flight, consumed by memories, and I wanted to run, but the medication had paralyzed my lower body. I lay there, on the hospital bed, trapped, helpless, and thought of what my therapist, Beth, had said about how physical sensations are so closely tied to memories. It's no wonder they can create such an effective assault of post-traumatic stress.

"I can't—" I told Joe. "I cannot do this."

"You can," he told me, eyebrows raised. "You are!"

"No. I can't. I don't know how."

"I know, Mia, but you're doing it. Your body knows. It's okay; your body is doing the work."

I considered his words.

My body may have been doing the work, but what about my heart? How was I going to love this baby like he deserved to be loved? How could my heart hold another child when my arms still ached for another? What kind of mother was I for even having these thoughts while actively laboring to bring life into the world? And what—*what if he didn't live after all?*

The contractions were coming faster and harder, keeping pace with my anxiety.

"Let's breathe through it," coached Joe.

"You're doing great! It won't be long now," Car said, clapping excitedly. She was a nursing student, and I was so grateful to have her there for her support and medical knowledge.

"Good job, baby! Peanut will be here soon!" my mom cheered.

The pain was intense, even with the epidural. I had expected more relief, remembering the minimal physical pain I had experienced with Julia's labor. But then, I realized, they had probably been able to be liberal in their use of painkillers since they did not have to consider harm to the baby. Or maybe it was also because the emotional anguish had been so penetrating that it had overshadowed the physical sensations.

As we approached the time to push, medical personnel began to file into the room. Neonatal and respiratory specialists and assistants, and nurses who had introduced themselves to us earlier, came in and took their respective spots, ready to provide instantaneous support to my baby, if he needed it.

After finishing a particularly brutal contraction, I leaned back against my pillow, panting from the exertion, and saw the door open and a scrubbed figure rush inside. A thrill ran through me as I recognized Lauren, our nurse, Julia's nurse, from the night Julia was born. She flashed past all of the professionals and equipment to my bedside. Like magnets attracted by force, we connected in an instant, powerful embrace.

I did not know her well, but I loved Lauren. She cared for us in the darkest, most difficult night of our lives. The way she held, bathed, and took precious hand- and footprints of our baby girl with such love, such gentle compassion, had made an indelible impression on my heart. I cried tears that were equal parts joy and gratitude to have her there with us as we labored to bring Julia's baby brother into the world.

"How are you?" she asked breathlessly, when we finally released each other.

"I'm okay," I replied shakily; then, "I'm scared."

She pulled me back in and I felt her nod her understanding. She pulled back and fixed me with her gaze.

"I know you're scared. But you are strong. You *can* do this—you *will*. I'm gonna be right here to help you."

Just then, a powerful surge of sharp, stabbing pain hit my abdomen. I leaned forward into it, twisting the white sheets into my fists.

"Don't forget to breathe; that will help," Lauren soothed, rubbing figure-eights into my back with the palm of her hand. Finally the moment passed, and Lauren bent her head to make eye contact, holding my gaze. She reached for Joe's hand and squeezed it, too. Her tight smile and narrowed eyes wordlessly communicated her compassion and commitment to take care of us. I returned a nod of sincere gratitude.

Contractions continued to come in shorter intervals and with increased intensity.

Soon, Dr. Pauli came in, performed an examination, and let us know it was time to start pushing.

Anxiety flooded up from my stomach into my chest and down through my arms. Heat flashed up my neck and face. *I wasn't ready. How was I going to do this?*

"Okay, Maria," Dr. Pauli told me, as a nurse covered her in a long blue gown, gloves, and face shield; she looked like she was preparing for battle. "It's time. I'll let you know when it's time to push, and we're going to bring this little boy to you."

My head felt heavy and woozy. I looked over at the monitors, tracking my baby's heartbeat in peaks and valleys.

"Okay, time to push!"

I followed the doctor's instructions in a series of push and rest cycles, and felt like fire was spreading up my body with each exertion. After a big thrust, panic started to boil out of me.

He was almost here. My new baby was almost here and I didn't even know his name! I didn't know if I would be able to love him. I didn't know if I would look into his little face and wish for his sister.

"I can't. I can't. I can't do this," I gasped, shaking my head violently from side to side. The adrenaline forced the words out in one rapid stream, like they were a single word. I looked at Joe who was now standing with the doctor, waiting to see our baby boy and cut his umbilical cord. *His umbilical cord.* I was sobbing, pleading with him, "I can't."

His face was a mix of pity and admiration that I didn't understand.

"You're doing it, Mia. You *are* doing it. He's almost here. It's going to be great."

"Maria, look at me," Lauren called, forcing my eyes to stay locked with hers. "I need you to breathe. You are doing this. You are an amazing mom, and right now your baby needs you. You need to breathe, so that he can breathe."

"Okay." And it was like the lights came back on in the room. Lauren's words focused me on my baby. *He needs me. I can help him. I am his mama.*

I breathed and I pushed.

"There he is!" "He's beautiful!" "Almost there!" "One more push!"

And then, it was done. Our baby boy, Joey and Julia's baby brother, was born.

Panting, I sat up to see Joe cut the umbilical cord. I closed my eyes and fought off the memories, desperate to stay present in the moment. Finally, they handed him to me, and I pulled him in. I watched the exquisite rise and fall of his chest, his arms and legs moving in stiff, jerky thrusts.

But he was silent.

Panic-stricken, I looked from Joe to Lauren, to Dr. Pauli.

"Wh—why? Why isn't he crying?" my voice was barely a whisper as I struggled to get the words past the tightness in my throat.

"It's okay," they reassured me. "Sometimes they do that."

"Come on, baby, please cry," I whispered to him. "Please let me know you're okay. I love you."

And as if he had been waiting for permission, Baby Brother let out a wail that reverberated in my soul. Tears of immense, inexplicable joy rolled down my cheeks.

I loved him. Not because he was Julia's brother. Not out of some maternal obligation to do so. I just *loved* him.

I missed Julia just as much as I did before, but my love for her did not, in any way, minimize my immeasurable love for this precious boy. I did not resent him. *I loved him.*

I clutched him to my chest and rocked him, letting my tears fall like a cleansing rain over both of us. "Thank you, God. I love him."

"Hey," Joe breathed as he planted an affectionate kiss in my damp hairline. "You did it. He's perfect."

I hadn't noticed him coming around to the side of the bed, but looking up at him, his eyes glossy and bright, his dimpled cheeks flushed a rosy pink, I could stifle neither the stream of tears nor a joyful, shaky laugh.

"He is," I agreed, turning to gaze again at the precious boy in my arms. "He is. I love him, Joe. I really do." I looked back up at Joe, my tone a mixture of insistence and relief.

"I know, Mia. Of course you do. You always have. I never had any doubt." He kissed me again.

"He is beautiful," I stated again, staring wonderingly at this tiny miracle.

"He looks just like her," Joe observed.

I smiled and nodded slowly. He was right. We marveled at how Baby Brother had Julia's button nose, but Joey's little rounded chin, and a deep hairline of his very own. At just over eight pounds, he was the biggest of them all. He was the only one we hadn't planned to have, yet one we needed just as much.

Later that evening, we named him Benjamin. Not a family name like the others, Benjamin was a biblical name. Benjamin was the youngest son of Jacob, a patriarch of the Jewish faith. Benjamin's older brother was Joseph, and his mother was Rachel, like Julia's middle name. When Rachel knew she was dying in childbirth, with her second son, she declared that he would be named *Ben-Oni* son of my pain or distress. Jacob, however, despite his grief at the tragic loss of his beloved wife, renamed their child *Benjamin*, son of my right hand, or power.

For us, the choice to name this child Benjamin was steeped in meaning. After the loss of Julia Rachel, I could not imagine that birthing another child would bring anything but more pain and distress. I had spent the nine months of his pregnancy in constant fear and anxiety that he would either replace Julia in my heart or that I would not be able to love him at all. Yet, in the miracle of motherhood, I learned that neither of those scenarios was plausible. I loved this child just as much as I loved his older brother *and* sister—I always had, always would. He was mine. He was the perfect, final addition to our family.

We named him Benjamin because, in him, I was empowered with this truth about the love of motherhood: It does not divide the heart; it multiplies it. It is instantaneous, it is all-encompassing, it is impenetrable, it is forever. It is the enduring, unbreakable bond that connects a mother and child in the womb, in life, and beyond.

I love them. All of them. *Still.*

Chapter 64

"Mommy! Daddy!" Joey ran through the door to our hospital room and over to the bed where we were waiting for him. Joe picked him up and tossed him into the air, eliciting Joey's exuberant giggle. There were hugs and kisses as my parents and nephews followed him into the room, our newest visitors.

"Hey, buddy!" Joe greeted him, giving him a big squeeze.

"Hi, Jojo! I missed you!" I told him.

"Mommy! I missed you, too!" His smile and his eyes widened when he looked into my arms and saw Benjamin there. "Who's that?"

"This is Benjamin," I told him.

"Benjamin?" His eyes were wide and sparkly as he looked from the baby to me, and then to Joe.

"That's right, Jojo. Benjamin is your baby brother," Joe told him.

"Baby Brother!" Joey exclaimed, moving in for a closer look.

"Careful," I warned. "Be gentle."

He looked at me and nodded slowly. "Baby Brother," he repeated, closing his eyes and placing a gentle kiss on the top of Benjamin's head. "And Julia!" he added.

All movement in the room stopped as everyone followed Joey's eyes and tiny outstretched index finger to Julia Bear, sitting on the nightstand beside us. Joe and I looked at each other breathlessly. Joe picked up Julia Bear and placed her in the middle of our circle on the hospital sheets.

"That's right, Joey. Baby Brother *and* Baby Sister, and *you're* the *big brother*."

"Yeah." Joey snuggled in, hugging both Benjamin and Julia Bear, before looking back up at me. "Mama, we're the *best* brothers."

I looked at Joe, then around to the rest of the room of happy, loving faces, before looking back at Joey and placing a kiss on his little forehead. "Yes, buddy. You are."

Chapter 65

Several months later, on an early-summer evening, we'd gone out for dinner as a family. Nothing fancy—burgers and fries, and frozen custard for dessert. We'd left the restaurant and Joe was strapping Benjamin in his infant car seat. I'd taken Joey by the hand to walk him around the car and get him strapped into his big boy car seat.

Abruptly, he stopped walking. I looked over to find him gazing up at the sky.

We talked a lot about the sky. We still sang about our Sunshine and the special star twinkling above us. Sunsets with their ribbons of pink and coral always made me think of Julia, though she was never far from my thoughts.

I followed his gaze upward. Twilight was settling into beautiful pinks, lavenders, and blues. A jet stream mingled with the clouds, and there was an ethereal glow in the fading sunlight. A single twinkly star seemed to sparkle and dance just for us.

I closed my eyes and then looked back at Joey. He was tall for a three-year-old, off the charts according to his latest pediatric well-check. He brought his hand up to his hair, thick and dark as a nighttime forest, and began to twist it in circles around his index finger, like he always did when he was concentrating on something.

His chocolate brown eyes never left the sky as he asked me, "Can she jump down? Can our sister jump down?"

Astonished by his question, I swallowed back my emotion, trying to keep my voice even.

"No, honey. She can't."

He paused, his furrowed brow indicating he was deep in thought.

"Can you catch her?"

"No, baby, I can't," I breathed.

He turned to look at me and pulled his little hand away from mine. His thick, curly lashes swept over his eyes as he blinked in confusion.

"But . . . why?"

"It just doesn't work that way, sweetheart. I wish it did. But Julia is with Jesus now, remember?"

"But I want to see her," he reasoned, his little face crinkling with disappointment. "I want her to be here."

"Me too, baby. Mommy wants that, too," I assured him, my voice unable to withstand the combined burden of my grief and his. My heart hurt for him. "We will see her, someday."

He paused at this. His eyes pulled away from mine, becoming contemplative as he tilted his head back again to the sky. "When we see her, will she stay for a long time with us?"

"Sweetie," I began, silently praying for strength and wisdom that would both satisfy and honor his curiosity. "When we see her, we'll all be in Heaven, and we'll be together forever, and we won't ever have to say good-bye again."

I watched him as he looked down at the pavement at his feet, apparently taking in my words. Returning his gaze to mine, he reached again for my hand, leaned into my leg, and said, "Yeah."

And that was the end of our conversation.

We walked hand in hand the rest of the way around our SUV and he climbed up into his seat. I kissed him on the forehead before buckling him in and closing the door.

As Joe drove us home, I sat in the passenger seat, replaying Joey's words, and his heartbreaking innocence, in my mind. We had talked to Joey about Julia consistently since returning home without her from the hospital, but we had tried to let him lead the conversations, crafting our responses to his developmental level.

How could we explain to a three-year-old what we could not understand ourselves?

I turned my head to look out the window and wept for my sweet girl, and for her sweet brothers, who would spend a lifetime without her.

Chapter 66

"I just don't understand it. Or maybe I just don't want to accept it? I just can't."

Months had passed since that summer evening spent staring up at the sky and answering Joey's questions about Heaven. I was driving home from running some errands after school, asking God some questions of my own. I often prayed while driving, with my eyes open, of course. It was a quiet, semi-private place where I could be honest with God and myself about how I was feeling.

My relationship with God had improved significantly since the early days and weeks after Julia's birth and death. I had read the words of nineteenth-century theologian, C. H. Spurgeon: "To trust God in the light is nothing, but trust him in the dark—that is faith." I felt like I was trusting God in the dark.

There were biblical truths that I understood, and I had a relationship with God, but there were also questions. I'd begun to realize that I'd likely not receive answers to these questions until I reached Heaven. I didn't know if God would explain everything for me when I got there, or if it would just be like opening my eyes and really *seeing* for the first time. Either way, it seemed like this was the crux of faith: knowing that God is who He says He is, and that if that is true, I can trust Him for the rest.

Understanding this, however, did not take away my longing for my baby. I wanted to see her, to hold her. Yes, she was God's, but she was also mine. I could not stand knowing that she and I would be separated for a lifetime.

I had learned, through my earlier struggles with infertility, and, more recently, in my grief, how important it was to be honest with God. To tell Him the truth about what I was thinking and feeling. This, after all, was important to building any relationship based on trust.

I believed that God gave us human relationships as a gift, not only to make life on Earth more enjoyable and fulfilling, but to teach us about Him. My relationship with Joe, my parents, my friends, my children— all relationships demonstrated aspects of my relationship with God and helped me to develop a deeper understanding of His love for me.

"I just miss her, God," I told Him as I sat at a red light in the middle of the city. "I miss her every minute of every day, and I don't know how to live without having her here with me. It's not right. And it's too much for a mother's heart to bear."

I know. That's why. It was not an audible voice, but I heard it with piercing clarity in my heart.

"God? What does that mean?" I asked, sitting up in the driver's seat, instantly alert.

That's why I came for you. You are my child, and I love you more than you will ever know, and I couldn't stand to be separated from you either.

Clarity, like the brilliant sun emerging from a dark horizon, flooded me. I was breathless, stunned, speechless. That was the essence of the Gospel. God became a man, Jesus, and died a horrible, humiliating death on the cross so that He could be reunited with His lost children. This unconditional, parental love was why, even when I rejected him, He kept pursuing me.

You are my daughter, and I love you that much.

Just like I loved Julia, except somehow infinitely more, God loved *me. He* desired connection with *me*, the way *I* desired connection with *Julia*. He loved me that much. He loved all of us that much. That's what it was all about.

I sat at another red light, a small gas station on my right and cars whizzing past in the oncoming lanes to my right. I bowed my head and let deep, cleansing tears wash over my face and my heart. I felt no condemnation, no reprimand in His words, only deep, relentless love.

It was profound in its simplicity.

A mother's love, a Father's love—enduring, reaching, pursuing—*still.*

Chapter 67

As I packed the boys' suitcase, I missed the dresses and bows that should be taking up some of the space there. I sadly noted how we would be able to put the third row down to accommodate more luggage, since we didn't need the space for a third car seat.

When we'd decided to plan a summer trip to Minnesota, we knew that while we would have fun and make memories together, it would be another bittersweet experience—a family vacation without our whole family. It had been two and a half years since we had lost her. It was like learning to live with an amputated limb: We moved forward, coping the best we could, but never forgetting what was missing.

The morning of our departure, Joey was running around the house in a flurry of excitement and Benjamin was busy toddling after him. I tried to keep busy folding clothes, packing snacks and activities for the car, and trying to hold myself together, so as not to upset the boys. I went about all of the final tasks necessary to prepare the house to remain empty while we were gone. Before locking the front door, I checked the mailbox. As I did so, I noticed how beautifully our "Julia" plant, a gift purchased and planted by thoughtful friends, was growing, its large, fiery red-orange coneflowers beginning to bloom. As I observed its progress, I was delighted to see a beautiful monarch butterfly fluttering around it, sharing in my admiration. I watched with tears stinging my eyes as she landed squarely on top of one of the newly grown blossoms.

Many bereaved parents feel a special connection to butterflies and their metamorphic symbolism. Some believe that they are messengers from loved ones in Heaven. Whether or not I believed this in the literal sense, I absolutely saw this winged creature as exquisitely symbolic. I was a caterpillar. Joe was a caterpillar. We wanted Julia to stay our perfect little caterpillar baby . . . but this was not to be. Even as we held her tiny body, she had already gained her wings to fly. Transformed, high above us, her perspective was beyond what we could even imagine. I knew and took comfort in the truth that she was safe in the arms of Jesus. Still, I lived every moment wishing she were here.

Tears trickled down my cheeks that morning as I spoke to the butterfly, telling her all the things my heart had been holding for my Julia.

"I love you so much, sweetheart. I wish you could have stayed. I'm sure Heaven is beautiful, even more so because you are there. I can't wait to hold you forever.

"I know you probably know we are leaving today for a short trip. Your brothers are so excited. They are getting so big. Joey is four and Ben is already one and a half; but I guess you know that, too. We talk about you all the time. I wish you were here to go with us, Julia. I miss you. I'll take you with me in my heart. We all will."

I kept expecting her to fly away, but she stayed, listening attentively to all I had to say. I am not sure how long we stayed there, watching each other. It was time to go, but how could I leave her there?

"I'm so sorry, baby, I have to go," I told her, my voice becoming higher and tighter at the end. "Daddy and the boys are waiting for me in the car. I don't want to leave you, Julia."

An older couple walked by our house with their golden retriever. I realized that to everyone in the neighborhood, it probably looked like I was having a very emotional conversation with our mailbox.

I closed my eyes, and with a final "I love you," blew Julia a tender kiss. As I did so, I watched with a mixture of relief, regret, and astonishment as she took flight once again. She fluttered past me, an inch from my face, around the house toward the backyard and the garage.

I exhaled a long, slow breath as I marveled at the interaction we had just shared. I locked the door and walked around the side of the house to the back.

"Thank you," I whispered to the brilliant blue sky and puffy white clouds, convinced that, at least this once, God *had* sent that tiny messenger to visit me.

Closing the gate behind me, I noted Joe and the boys each in their respective seats. I took my place in the front passenger seat and smiled at the silly kids' song pouring through the speakers. As I shifted to reach back for my seat belt, however, I noticed a beautiful monarch hanging just below the rearview mirror. Catching my breath, I realized it was a realistic-looking craft butterfly, attached by a barely visible wire to look as if it were in mid-flight.

My lips parted in surprise, I turned to Joe, a silent question in my eyes. He was already returning my gaze, a sad smile tugging at one side of his mouth.

"I just thought she needed to come with us," he explained.

I told him about the experience that I'd just had moments before on the other side of the house. I watched as bittersweet wonder swept over his face. We shared a brief humorless laugh, and our foreheads came together in a moment of gratitude for the blessings we had and longing for those we never would.

"Are we going now, Mommy?" came Joey's exuberant voice from behind me, anxious to get started on the vacation we had promised.

Joe and I turned together to look at him, then smiled meaningfully again at each other. Joe turned and put on his sunglasses and adjusted the rearview mirror. I turned to Joey and Benjamin.

"Yes, buddy. We're going."

And we were. I thought of the hours-long trip ahead, and the lifelong journey we had begun two and a half years earlier. We were going, together.

As Joe shifted the engine into reverse, pulling us out of the driveway and onto the road, I reached up to lightly graze the little butterfly hanging from the mirror, grateful for this sweet reminder of the other precious life traveling with us the entire way.

The next morning, we prepared for the adventure of exploring the Mall of America with two young children. We navigated the parking ramps, busy entrances, maps, and elevators with a stroller for Ben, lots of snacks, drinks, a diaper bag, and two very excited little boys. We had detailed plans and high expectations, but we were not prepared for the surprise that awaited us there.

It took our breath away.

A giant, multistory, interactive monarch butterfly art installation seemed like it was created and placed there especially for our family. Suspended from the atrium's skylight was a single, massive monarch butterfly with a thirty-foot wingspan, surrounded by hundreds of smaller monarchs fluttering in several flocks around it. Every detail, from the fur on its legs, to the brilliant orange color and black and white patterns of its wings, made it feel like we were looking at a real butterfly under the world's largest microscope. It was absolutely majestic.

A thick rope descended from the central butterfly down to a vine-covered arbor. Joey and Benjamin squealed with delight when they pulled on the rope and made the enormous wings take flight.

It was the reminder we needed that, although we can't see her, our girl is always with us in our hearts. This doesn't mean that we do not still ache for her. We do. We miss her because she is missing from us. Forever in this life, our family is incomplete.

As we travel our lifelong grief journey, we will always long for Julia. We will miss seeing her, holding her, kissing her, and watching her grow. We wish for her presence even in the mundane. Our hearts will always grieve the lifetime of beautiful milestone moments we should have had together.

The butterfly is a reminder that she is always with us, though not in the form we would have chosen. Despite our empty arms, we hold tight to her memory, the love we have for her, and the lessons she has taught us. From her, we learn that nothing, not even death, can destroy love. The love of a marriage that, even in the face of unimaginable loss and grief, only grows stronger. The love of a Father that remains and deepens even within a crisis of faith. The love of a mother for her child that will last as long as her grief: forever.

Both hope and grief remain, intertwined in a lifelong, slow dance. We will always long for her, until we are reunited, transformed together one sweet day. We will continue on this grief journey, always holding her close. We miss her, and we love her.

Still.

Image courtesy of Now I Lay Me Down to Sleep,
Photographer: Kelcy Hanson

Julia Rachel Price
October 11, 2016

A Note from the Author
What Helped Me
For Grievers

If you are reading this book because you are grieving the loss of a child, let me begin by offering my heartfelt condolences to you and your family. Whether your loss was due to miscarriage, stillbirth, infant loss, or a loss anytime later in life, I am so sorry that you are going through it. Parents should never have to outlive their children. It is heartbreakingly tragic, and I'm profoundly sorry that it happened to your family, too.

I hope that our story has provided you with some solidarity, some comfort, and some strength for the lifelong journey. I am no expert in the psychology of grief, only a fellow traveler on what can be a long, lonely road of child loss. In the next couple of pages I will share with you some of the things that have helped me along the way, in hopes that they will help you, too. Everyone is different, every loss is unique; if these things don't help you now, perhaps they will at some point in the future.

Give yourself grace and permission to grieve: It took me awhile to learn what it meant to give myself grace. Maybe you, too, hold yourself to a high standard when it comes to "getting things done." Our culture puts tremendous value in a person's ability to "grin and bear it." But you don't have to do that. It's okay to be sad when your baby dies. It is okay to step away from commitments or expectations, even when they are your own. It's okay—and *necessary*—to grieve, in whatever way is meaningful to you. You must give yourself the time and energy to do so without feeling guilty about it. Be as gentle with yourself as you would be with others. I give you permission; I hope that you will give yourself permission, too.

Just say *No*: Related to the first point, it's okay to decline invitations to baby showers, social gatherings, or interactions that make you uncomfortable at whatever stage of grief you are currently enduring. The intensity of the discomfort you feel at first will likely not last forever. When you are ready, you can rejoin and reconnect at a pace that is comfortable for you. You don't have to make excuses, apologize profusely, or feel guilty for taking care of you. Good friends should and will understand and respect that.

Take a break from social media: I unfriended some people. I had to snooze and unfollow a few others. And you know what? I don't regret it. Especially early in my grief, I felt like I was inundated by posts about beautiful little girls with their beautiful little bows and their beautiful little lives. So many pregnancy announcements or birth announcements of healthy, living children lit up my screen, and I felt each one, viscerally. I was happy for my friends, but it hurt to have my what-ifs illustrated as I scrolled down my newsfeed. I still wanted to be able to connect on social media because early on in my grief, it was some of the only socialization I could manage. I didn't have to have an uncomfortable conversation with the person, I just did it. Again, it didn't last forever, but it was so freeing. And again, I don't regret it.

Share on social media/blog: It may seem strange, after reading this book, to learn that I am typically a private, introverted person. But, in the midst of my grief and the loss of my daughter, I *needed* to share my thoughts, feelings, and experiences. So strong was that urge that my therapist compared it to the urge to push in childbirth. She was right. I needed to get it out. It surprised me how much relief this sharing brought to me. In large part, people were supportive and kind. I pray this is your experience. There were also some who told me it was "time to move on" or who told me that my "sin" was the reason why Julia died. I pray that this is not your experience. If it is, shame on them. Most people want to help, even if they don't know how. If your story is too difficult for them to handle, or triggers a deep hurt from their own past, try to extend grace to them, too, and then keep going. You keep doing what you need to do to heal and say your child's name.

Visit her grave: It helped me to be able to visit Julia's grave, to have a quiet, tranquil place to talk to her and tend to her. If your child is not buried in a cemetery, perhaps try to find a physical location that is meaningful to you. It might be a park bench, a hiking trail, a spot near a body of water, a garden, or a cozy chair in your home. Wherever it is, I hope that you can find privacy to connect with your child.

Buy her clothes: I recognize that this one is not for everyone. I get great joy out of buying clothes and accessories for my children. I dress all of us in coordinating outfits for holidays, and enjoy selecting just the right ensemble for each occasion. I had really looked forward to doing this for Julia, so when she died this secondary loss seemed like another shattered dream. I worried that others would consider it a waste of time, energy, and finances to purchase clothes that would never be worn. But Joe was predictably supportive, and a dear friend gave me the good advice to do whatever I needed to do to honor and remember Julia in meaningful ways. So I did. Whatever meaningful traditions you would have instituted—or hoped to institute—with your child do not necessarily have to die with them. If you can still do them, even if others don't approve or understand, and if it is safe, healthy, and brings you healing, do it.

Go to therapy: As you've read in the book, I went to therapy. I still go to therapy. For me, it is an integral part of my grief process. I love my therapist and literally thank God for her. You will also recall that I went to a different therapist first. I am grateful for what the first counselor did for me; it just didn't work out. I am convinced that the therapist–client connection is not unlike a romantic relationship. Keep going until you find the right one for you.

Go to support groups: It is hard to be vulnerable enough to share with strangers, but we do it because we need to give and receive support from others who are enduring similar experiences. I have ugly-cried my way through several support group meetings, and I am so grateful for the women I met there. They listened and they cried with me. I cried with them and gained strength in their stories about their much-loved children. I have also found great encouragement, inspiration, and cama-raderie in online support groups and social media pages. I encourage you to explore groups that meet your needs, even if it requires an expansion of your comfort levels. This road is too lonely to walk alone.

Reading: Thank you for reading this book. Reading other people's stories and experiences with grief have also helped me to feel less alone. It has helped to validate some of the feelings and fears that I was too afraid to admit, even to myself. There have been some books I have had to put down, because I was not ready for them yet. That's okay. If you need to set a book aside, you know that, like a good friend, it will still be there for you when you are ready.

Push past guilt: This one is so hard, but necessary. It has taken many, many conversations with my doctors over more than three years' time, lots of therapy, and support from my own tribe, and I still struggle with feeling like I could have, should have done something to prevent or predict Julia's death. So many of my bereaved mom friends have expressed these same paralyzing feelings of guilt and shame. It is scary to admit the guilt to others, and even to ourselves. I hope you will talk about it, especially to doctors, therapists, or a trusted network of supporters, who can understand, empathize, and hopefully alleviate your fears. Grief is onerous enough; guilt is too heavy a burden to bear.

Asking for help: When a loved one dies, friends and family members are quick to tell the griever to "let me know if there is any way I can help!" Sometimes, this is just something people say. But other times, people really do want to help. Let them. This goes back to the concept of giving yourself grace. If friends are willing to pick up groceries for you, let them. If family members are willing to mow your lawn, let them. It will likely also allow them to feel helpful in an otherwise helpless situation. You don't have to do everything yourself. Grieving is enough. If your tribe wants to support you, let them.

Let go of hurtful people: Not everyone will be able to walk with you on this journey. Some people have had their own hurtful experiences in life, or have personalities that make them ill-suited to support you during this time in your life. Maybe they think their advice is helpful, or maybe they made the decision to walk away, leaving you feeling abandoned. These are all difficult secondary losses to bear. Ideally, you will have an open, honest conversation with these friends, and understanding will mend the hurts between you. But if that doesn't work, it is okay to grieve the relationships that will end when your child dies. It is also okay to take a break from these friendships. Maybe you will be able to pick back up where you left off later, or maybe it will be a permanent end to that part of your life. Either is okay, albeit hard. Give them the grace to go, and give yourself the grace to step away from someone who is hurting you.

Be honest with God: This one might be a little controversial for some, but it is absolutely pivotal in my life. I encourage every bereaved parent to tell God how you feel, really. We even have models for this in scripture. Consider David, the great king and hero of both Jewish and Christian faiths. He wrote many of the Psalms. Read them and be encouraged that God is big enough to take your biggest feelings.

I grew up knowing and loving God from childhood. In my college years and into adulthood, my relationship with Him deepened. I trusted Him through the difficulties I experienced. Nothing prepared me, though, for the loss of my daughter. Even then, I had zero doubt that God could have prevented or healed Julia, but He didn't. I could neither understand nor accept this. So, we were at an impasse. I was angry with Him—too angry to talk to Him, or to listen to what He might have to say to me.

Well-meaning friends told me "God had a better plan" or "God has something better in store." I disagree with these platitudes even now. They wanted to help, but didn't know what to say. Especially in the early stages of grief when I was still trying to sort out how I felt and what I believed, it only hurt more to hear those words.

The healing in our fractured relationship came when I was completely honest with God and myself about how I felt. I did not hide my questions, my doubt, or my anger, and He didn't "strike me down" or condemn me for a lack of faith. Rather, I only felt love and acceptance, empathy from the God of all creation. I would submit that His compassion for me was there the whole time, waiting for me to be willing to see and accept it. I hope that the book has reflected this truth: God loved me *through* my pain—He didn't make me choose. He accepted me with all my big feelings and frustrations—more than some Christians did.

I still don't understand all of it. I still have questions, I think I will feel that way until I reach the other side. Yet, it seems like God and I can both live with that. His love and compassion give me the grace to move deeper into a relationship built on trust and honesty. He didn't condemn me for my feelings; He loved me, *still*.

Find your tribe: As you have read, I have been surrounded by an incredible network of supportive family, friends, and professionals. I am eternally grateful for them and the influence they have had on my life and grief journey. I hope that your experience is the same. If not, I hope that you will seek out those people in your life who have loved you and accepted you as you are. They are the ones who will sit and listen, cry with you, or do things to honor and remember your child. They will put aside their own opinions or urge to "fix" you. They will accept the frustration of helplessness that comes from watching someone you love suffer. They will do this because they recognize that supporting you means standing alongside you in empathy as you process heartbreaking grief—something only you can do for yourself. They will not be upset if you cancel plans at the last minute. They will accept your refusal, and still ask next time.

Find these people and tell them what you need. Be honest with them about what is hurtful and helpful, in as kind and loving a way as possible. If they want to help you, they will be grateful and try hard to honor your requests.

Say your child's name: In whatever way feels right, in whatever timing is best for you, in whatever way helps you grieve, say your child's name. If you never were able to name your child, I would encourage you to do so. In addition to the power of a name, I would encourage you to embrace your child's existence. Perhaps you only want to say it to yourself; perhaps you want to shout it from the rooftops. Honor him or her in the way that is right for you. The love we have for our children exists before they are born, and lasts long after their deaths. We loved them then; we love them *still*.

A Note from the Author
What I Have Learned
For Supporters

If you are reading this book because someone you love has experienced the loss of a child, thank you. Your bereaved spouse, partner, sibling, child, friend, or family member needs you. I hope that reading our story has helped you to develop a deeper understanding of the thoughts, emotions, and experiences that your loved one may be enduring in the aftermath of child loss.

You may be feeling lost when it comes to knowing how you can help. But the fact that you are asking these questions and reading this book in an effort to understand is a testament to the invaluable support person you are, and will continue to be, to your loved one.

It is important to recognize that everyone is different. Every griever is different. And what a person needs in the early days and weeks of the grief journey might look very different from what s/he will need later. The following suggestions are based on my own experiences and those of other bereaved parents who have generously shared with me. I hope that they will be a helpful starting point for you.

(Note: I have used the masculine and feminine pronouns interchangeably in the next few pages to apply to both girl and boy babies, and bereaved mothers and fathers.)

THINGS TO DO:

DO give space and grace: Grief, especially early grief, is all-consuming. It takes all the attention and energy that we have to give. For some, it is difficult to cry in front of others, to be vulnerable. For some, it may be difficult to do anything *except* cry. It may be especially difficult to attend baby showers, birthday parties, or anything else that reminds them of all the milestones they will miss with their own children. Post-traumatic stress is real and applies to many parents after the deaths of their children in a variety of situations. Please extend grace to them. Please let them know that you accept that they need to say no sometimes; it may be a matter of self-preservation. Give them space and grace enough to grieve in the way that makes sense to them.

DO just listen: One of the best things you can do is to just sit quietly and listen. So few people in a griever's life are able to do this. Nod your head and actively *listen* to what the griever is trying to tell you. Don't interrupt. Don't judge. Just listen. And if it means just sitting quietly together, or letting him get it out, please do that.

DO offer practical help: Many people will tell a bereaved parent to let them know how they can be of help. This is kind, and many people who say this truly mean it, but some don't. In the fog of grief, it is hard to tell the difference. Additionally, for many bereaved families, it is hard to know *what* they need, apart from having their child back. Asking *how* you can help is a great start. It is great to follow up with suggestions of things you are willing to do: pick up groceries, mow the lawn, shovel the walk, do some laundry, send a cleaning service, or deliver a meal. Or, if it is not too invasive, just do it.

DO pray: People often say they are "sending thoughts and prayers," but then neglect to actually do it. If you are a praying friend, pray for your friend. Pray hard. If your friend is open to it, you can pray for him while you are together, letting him hear the words from your heart. Pray for his strength, comfort, and peace. Pray that God will lead you to be the kind of friend that he needs.

DO say the child's name: Make yourself comfortable enough to say the child's name, especially in conversation with the parent. It might feel hard or awkward, but it is one of the most precious gifts you can give a bereaved parent, to hear her child's name coming from another person's lips. It might feel like you will be bringing up painful memories, but rest assured, our children's names are never far from our thoughts. It shows that you remember the child, you validate her existence, and you honor her place in the bereaved family and in your life.

DO honor the child: This can be on as large a scale as you choose to do it, but know that even the smallest acts of kindness done in their child's name will be meaningful. Take a picture of a sunset and send it to your friend, with the caption "Thinking of [baby's name] today." Give a donation to a charity that is special to the family in the child's name. Bring flowers or spend time at a grave or special place of remembrance. Plant a tree or flowers in the family's yard or in a pot that you can bring to them. Do a random act of kindness and dedicate it to the child. Take a picture or send a card or text to let the family know that you did these things—not so they will recognize your kindness (though they will do so), but to show that you recognize their child's impact on the world.

THINGS TO NOT DO:

DO NOT rush them: The platitude "Time heals all wounds" is wrong and hurtful. Please do not say this. The love of a parent begins before birth and continues after death into forever. Your friend will never "get over" the loss of a child. Please don't give this advice. Yes, the grief will change over time, but it will never go away.

DO NOT ignore them: It is uncomfortable to think about a child dying. It is heartbreaking and terrifying for anyone who has ever loved a child to consider the fragility of life and the injustice of child loss. Bereaved parents feel all of these things, too. If you change the subject when a parent tries to talk to you about her deceased child, or ignore her cries for help, she may feel that you don't care about her or her grief. If you want to help, but aren't sure how to do so, please refer back to the "DO" list above.

DO NOT use platitudes: *Everything happens for a reason. God has a (better) plan. God is in control. You'll see her again someday. Look on the bright side. There is always a silver lining. Maybe this experience will help you help someone else someday. God just needed another angel. There is a higher purpose. Keep the faith. He's in a better place.*

Platitudes are cliché statements that are meant to soothe and comfort, but they are often hurtful. Sometimes they are used in a veiled effort to change the subject, to alleviate the discomfort created by discussing the death of a child. Sometimes they do come from a loving, well-intentioned place, but they still hurt. God does not "need another angel." There is no "bright side" to child loss. The hope of seeing a child "someday" does not take away the pain that comes from being unable to spend a lifetime on Earth with him now.

Platitudes hurt, they don't help. One of the best sympathy cards I ever received was from a dear friend who had tragically lost her husband a few years earlier. I don't remember what the actual greeting card said, but she wrote a simple message inside: "I'm sorry this happened to you. It is so unfair." These words were so refreshingly honest they caused me to sit back and read them again. She didn't try to make me feel better; she simply sat with me in the injustice. That brought more comfort than "Everything happens for a reason" ever could.

DO NOT shame: Do not shame your friend by asking her to think about her other living children, to consider how her grief might be affecting others, or insinuate that the loss was her fault. Grief is enough of a burden to bear.

2 9 1

DO NOT ask personal questions: Even when doctors or other professionals reassure a parent that there was nothing that could have been done to predict or prevent the loss, the guilt parents put on themselves can be overwhelming. Doctors may not have a clear answer to this question, so when you ask for an explanation of "why" a child died, it can be confusing or difficult to discuss. Be sensitive in letting the parent lead the conversation here. The key is not *how* the baby died; it is *that* the baby died.

Please do not ask if your friends are going to "try for another baby." This can make conception sound like a fishing expedition, and devalues the life of the baby they just lost and of any subsequent children. Sometimes families suffer recurrent losses or secondary infertility, without talking about it. Again, if your friend wants to provide those details, let him lead in that.

DO NOT assume that a "rainbow baby" will heal the hurt: A "rainbow baby" is a term sometimes used to refer to a baby born after the death of an older sibling. The assumption is that the baby is the rainbow of hope after a storm. *Warning:* Some people are deeply offended by the use of this term because it associates the deceased child with the negative "storm," and the next child with the positive "rainbow."

The decision to expand a family is a personal one. Pregnancy after loss can be stressful and may end in another loss. Every baby is special; one cannot replace another. If your friend is having a baby after a loss, ask how you can support the family during this new pregnancy. Listen to fears and concerns. Continue to acknowledge their deceased baby's existence and meaningful place in their family.

DO NOT compare: Just as every baby is special, every loss is unique. There are so many factors that go into a person's life and death, it is impossible to compare them. We are all shaped by our experiences, our upbringings, and our personalities. Even two parents who lose the same child will have at least subtle nuances in the way that they process their grief. The same person will likely deal with grief differently in year ten than they did in year one. Please do not assume that because you know someone who lost a baby, or because you have experienced a loss yourself, that you know *exactly* how that person is feeling, or that you should give them advice on how to act or feel. Do not assume that an early miscarriage will be easier or harder than the loss of a toddler or adult child. All losses are hard. All losses are heartbreaking. Respect that the griever is doing the best she can and meet her there.

DO NOT forget about the dad: It is easy to focus on the bereaved mom who carried and birthed the child. It is easier to forget that fathers have lost their children, too. Involved dads are often the labor coaches, the caretakers, the ones who sleep on the pullout couch in the hospital room while hospital staff focuses on the laboring mom. Everyone handles grief differently. In our case, I was the one who was always a mess. Joe felt that he needed to protect me and support me, even though he often felt helpless in this role, but he was grieving Julia, too. Please don't forget to check in with the bereaved dad—ask how he is doing and support him, too.

DO NOT give up: If you ask your friend to lunch this week and she declines, ask next week if you can bring her coffee. You don't have to inundate her with calls, but don't stop calling. Your friend might not be ready to visit now, but someday she will be ready, and she will need you. She may have been hurt before and hesitant to let people in. Be patient. Be kind. Try to be the friend that she needs at the time she needs it. She will thank you for that.

Resources

(not an exhaustive list)

Now I Lay Me Down to Sleep
https://www.nowilaymedowntosleep.org/

Molly Bears
https://www.mollybears.org/

Saying Goodbye
https://www.sayinggoodbye.org/

The Brink of Being: Talking About Miscarriage
Book by Julia Bueno

Still Standing Magazine

A Beautifully Burdened Life
https://abeautifullyburdenedlife.com/

I Will Carry You: The Sacred Dance of Grief and Joy
Book by Angie Smith

Acknowledgments

It is overwhelming to think about how to properly thank everyone who made *Love You Still* possible. I could fill page after page with stories of kindnesses shown to me, and expressions of gratitude for the people who have loved and supported our family through the love and loss of Julia. Some of them are included in the pages of *Love You Still*, but many are not. To the family members and friends who encouraged and uplifted us in countless ways, Joe and I are eternally grateful. Thank you for showing the world how to love a family through tragic loss.

To the medical and mental health professionals, funeral home staff, nonprofit groups and volunteers who worked to provide us with care and compassionate support as you walked us through some of the most painful moments that we never expected to encounter. Thank you for being a model of how to serve with excellence for so many professionals in your fields.

In my darkest, loneliest moments of grief, I was inspired by the stories and friendship of brave men and women who choose to break the silence that surrounds infertility and loss in support groups, books, blogs, websites and one-on-one conversations. Thank you for sharing your stories and for encouraging me to share mine. None of us would choose to be a part of this community, but I am so grateful for its existence. I know that our children will be waiting to introduce us to their friends some sweet day.

Thank you to Jane VanVooren Rogers. You saw me as an author long before I was willing to accept that title. I will never forget the day we met and discovered the connections within our stories and our Julias. Thank you for inviting me to go with you to Vermont and for traveling with me on the unexpected adventure of *Love You Still*. Thank you for your professional expertise and constant encouragement. You are a gifted author and editor and a treasured friend.

Steve Eisner and your entire team at When Words Count. When I went to Vermont, I thought I was going for a vacation and an idyllic place to write for my own healing. Steve, you believed in this project before it was a project. Thank you for believing in and advocating for *Love You Still* and its power to reach and bring awareness and healing to hurting hearts. Your coaching with Sally taught me, pushed me, and shaped me into a better writer and ambassador for the cause. Thank you for *seeing* Julia and me. I hope to make you proud of us.

Thank you, Sally Newhart for your coaching and your kindness. I will not forget the stories you shared of how Julia's story touched your heart.

Steve Rohr and Marilyn Atlas, I am honored to have had your insights on *Love You Still*. To have had your eyes on my work and to have had discussions about it was a privilege. Thank you for sharing your kindness, creativity, and professional expertise in the creation of a stronger memoir and author.

Amber Griffith, is there anything you can't do well? I knew that you were an amazing chef, but that is only the beginning of your many talents! Your organization, creativity, and incredible kindness have blessed me in countless ways. I will always be grateful for your heartfelt words of encouragement and reminders to practice power poses.

Asha Hossain, your creative genius is matched only by your beautiful heart. When you and Steve presented the cover design for *Love You Still*, I saw Julia. I am confident that other families will see their babies as well. That is an incredible gift. I am so grateful for the time and talent you poured into this project and honoring my Julia. I know that those little feet will continue to make an indelible impact on the world thanks to you.

Peg Moran, where do I begin? I was so nervous to send in the first manuscript for editing! I had no idea what to expect, but your impeccable talent and your unending kindness were beyond my imaginings. I do not have the words to tell you how much our collaboration has meant to me. You have made me better. You consistently showed how much you cared and I knew I could trust you with Julia. In helping us to better tell her story, you became a part of it. Thank you!

Ben Tanzer, I never imagined that I would be able to say that I have a publicist. From our first conversation, I knew that there was a special connection. Thank you for your willingness to teach me all the things in such a patient and respectful way. I am so grateful for your experience and your commitment to telling our story well.

David LeGere, Colin Hosten and your team at Woodhall Press, thank you for taking a chance on a novice writer and for your belief in the power of people's stories! Thank you for your patience and your guidance through the realization of a dream. I respect and appreciate the heart and hard work you have already put into *Love You Still*, and am so grateful to be on this journey with you.

Melissa Hayes, thank you so much for your editing genius. Your eye is incredible. Your thoughtfulness and sensitivity is more than I could have expected. Thank you so much for the extra time and energy you put into our story. I am forever grateful.

Addie, you have been there through it all. You know all the things. I could never say in a single paragraph how much your friendship means to me. You have been there from the day we discovered we'd lost Julia, to hold her the night we said our first good-bye, to the night we were found out *Love You Still* was going to be published, through all the writing and editing, and every day before and after. Thank you for all of the pep talks, for not letting me give up, for making me laugh and for letting me cry. Everyone should be blessed with a friend as amazing as you—the world would be a better place. I love you.

To the many special friends who read and provided feedback and much-needed prayers and encouragement during the creation of *Love You Still,* thank you so very much. You will never know how much I needed you and your encouragement to stay true to the story and open to the plan that is bigger than all of us.

Ron and Kathy, we love you so much and are so grateful for your love and support of us and of *Love You Still.* I will never forget how it felt to hug you as we grieved together and the love and grace you showed me in my brokenness. Thank you for loving all three of our babies well.

Anthony, Car, Josiah, Xavier, and Mason, we love you so much. Thank you for always remembering Julia and honoring her place in our family. I wish she were here with us now, but I am grateful to have a family that loves her well even as she waits for us in Heaven.

Mom and Dad, you taught me how to parent. You showed me how to love my child more than I love myself. I know that you love Julia that much, too. Thank you for your endless support of *Love You Still,* my family and me. Thank you for taking care of the boys and being willing to walk through an Iowa snowstorm for your family. I love you!

To my boys, Joey and Benjamin, I love you more than words can say. Thank you for being (mostly) patient with me and giving me time to write our story. You are little now, but I hope one day you will come to appreciate how this story is not just mine or Julia's; it's all of ours. I am so grateful to have been chosen to be your mama. You inspire me and give me courage to do hard things. I am so proud of both of you and your hearts for God and other people. I can't wait to see what He will do in you and through you. You already make the world a better place. Thank you for making me better.

Joe, my whole heart. I never could have imagined when I looked into your face on our wedding day, how much more my love for you would grow. I never dreamed we would experience the heartache that could have destroyed us, or how it instead made us stronger. There is no one in this world with whom I would rather share this road. Thank you for loving me when I was unloving. Thank you for constantly believing in me when I did not believe in myself. Thank you for all of the loads of laundry, dishes, and domestic duties you took on without a single complaint. I am so grateful for the way you took the boys on all the "Daddy Day Adventures" so that I would have time to write, edit, and freak out over this book. Thank you for not letting me quit. Thank you for believing in the message and in the calling to share it. I love you; thank you for loving me still.

To my Heavenly Father, without You, none of this would be possible. Thank You for gifting me with all three of my precious children and for teaching me how to love them by Your perfect example. You are close to the brokenhearted and Your love is relentless and unfailing. Thank you for seeing past my anger and pain down into my heart and loving me there. I am honored to tell the story of Your unconditional love. May *Love You Still* be a tool in Your hands to reach the brokenhearted and bring them back to You.

About the Author

Maria Price makes her home in Iowa. While she makes a living as a teacher of the deaf and hard of hearing, Maria makes a life as a wife, and a mom to three beautiful children: Joey and Benjamin on Earth, and Julia in Heaven. Maria is passionately involved in supporting bereaved parents on social media, in support groups, and in quiet local coffee shops.

Made in the USA
Monee, IL
30 September 2021

79030208R00177